"*Encountering God through Expository Preaching* ~~accomplishes~~ what few books on preaching even attempt—it touches heart *and* head, worship *and* instruction, sermon *and* delivery. Dismissing any false dichotomy between skillful, well-planned preaching on the one hand and Spirit-anointed preaching on the other, the authors present an expansive vision for preaching that is as pastoral and practical as it is worshipful and theological. Expository preaching is an invitation to meet with God in the Word he has given, and this marvelous book warmly invites the preacher to prepare himself well for this glorious task."

—**Hershael W. York, Victor and Louise Lester Professor of Christian Preaching, The Southern Baptist Theological Seminary, and senior pastor, Buck Run Baptist Church, Frankfort, KY**

"I know all three authors of this book well. Two of them I know very well. One I know extremely well. One of the authors of this book was my pastor years ago in a different city and another has been my pastor for several years in the city where I now live. I know each of the three to be men of God, men who love their families, men who love the church, and men who love pastoral ministry, especially the preaching role in pastoral ministry. I have heard each of them preach, and can attest that all three men are excellent, effective expositors of the Word of God.

Thus far I have told you what I think of the men who wrote this book, but nothing about the book itself. Good men do not always write good books. But in this case, three very good men have written a very good book on preaching. I can't imagine a pastor who wouldn't profit from reading this book, especially those who are hungry to grow in their ability to preach effective, expository sermons. Just the chapter on 'Reading the Scriptures Well,' if applied, would transform the pulpit ministries of most churches. And is there any other book on preaching that devotes three chapters to the role of the Holy Spirit in the sermon? Preacher, read this book!"

—**Donald S. Whitney, professor of biblical spirituality and associate dean of the School of Theology, The Southern Baptist Theological Seminary**

"This captivating and thorough work on preaching is profoundly spiritual and immensely practical. The book won my heart in the very first chapter, and each subsequent page only increased my appreciation. This is not just 'another' treatise on the mechanics of exegesis and exposition. It is equally an exhortation to holiness, prayer, and absolute dependence upon the Holy Spirit. This is what makes this book unique and necessary for this generation of preachers. It is a 'must read' for every man who stands behind a pulpit!"

—**Paul David Washer, founder and missions director, Heartcry Missionary Society**

"Pastor, think of this book as a gift to your church. *Encountering God through Expository Preaching* will make a discernible difference in your preaching. Your church will take note and be grateful."

—**C.J. Mahaney, senior pastor, Sovereign Grace Church of Louisville, KY**

"This book attempts to capture a mystery. It's an exegesis of unction. For the green preacher or the seasoned, this book will spur on their expectancy of what God can do in glorifying himself through the Word preached."

—**Clint Humfrey, lead pastor, Calvary Grace Church, Calgary, Alberta, Canada. He also serves on the council for the Gospel Coalition, Canada**

"Offsetting a half century of fad-chasing tendencies in some corners of the evangelical world has been a heartening and welcome promoting of the bread-and-butter of Protestant ministry: devout, prayerful, expository preaching. Orrick, Payne, and Fullerton contribute to this heartening tendency with their sane and insightful *Encountering God through Expository Preaching*, which includes expected instruction on the personal preparation of the minister and his sermon, and some unexpected insights about meeting/encountering God and about the literary sensibilities needed for sound exposition. Those who have encountered God through competent expository preaching will cherish this contribution to the encounter."

—**T. David Gordon, professor of religion and Greek, Grove City College**

"For those of us trained in expository preaching, it may seem axiomatic that the task of opening the Word of God to people in the local church is best achieved by systematic expository preaching. And yet, even among many evangelicals, the case still needs to be made. I was excited to read this book by Orrick, Payne, and Fullerton because the case is definitely made comprehensively, with clarity and conviction. The authors show that expository preaching is more than choosing a book of the Bible to work through. It involves care in how we preach, how we read the Bible in public, how we depend on God's Holy Spirit to speak through the Word, and in the use of language as well as in delivery. I say to preachers who think they know it all: read this if you dare!"

—**Graeme Goldsworthy, former lecturer in biblical theology, hermeneutics, and Old Testament, Moore Theological College, Sydney, Australia, and retired minister, Anglican Church of Australia**

"I listen to sermons just as much as I listen to music and have noted that not all 'expository' sermons are created equal. This book discusses how expository preaching is not merely a consecutive verse-by-verse exercise, but rather exposing the text in its fullness. This is a must read for pastors, both young and experienced, who desire spiritual growth for themselves and their congregations. It is a valuable resource that is easy to read and leaves you with the necessary tools to become an excellent expository preacher."

—**FLAME, Grammy-Nominated Christian Hip-Hop Recording Artist**

ENCOUNTERING GOD

THROUGH

EXPOSITORY PREACHING

JIM SCOTT ORRICK, BRIAN PAYNE, RYAN FULLERTON

ENCOUNTERING GOD

THROUGH

EXPOSITORY
PREACHING

CONNECTING GOD'S PEOPLE TO GOD'S PRESENCE
THROUGH GOD'S WORD

ACADEMIC
NASHVILLE, TENNESSEE

Dedications

To my father, Jim B. Orrick, who has been a faithful
preacher for more than sixty years. Every day of
my life you have shown me what an honor and
responsibility it is to be a preacher of God's Word.

—JIM SCOTT ORRICK

To Dr. Al Jackson. You have demonstrated to me and
to countless other pastors in training what it means
to toil and strive as an expositor and as a shepherd
because you have your hope set on the living God,
the Savior. For five decades you have commanded
and taught these things faithfully to us.

—BRIAN PAYNE

To my beloved co-elders, past and present, and
to the pastors, church planters, and international
missionaries of the Immanuel Network. May God
allow more and more of His people to encounter
more and more of His presence through your
faithful expository preaching.

—RYAN FULLERTON

CONTENTS

PART THREE: "COME AND EXPERIENCE GOD WITH ME
IN THIS TEXT": FINAL PREPARATION

FOREWORD

by R. Albert Mohler Jr.

Evangelical Christians have been especially attentive to worship in recent years, sparking a renaissance of thought and conversation on what worship really is and how it should be done. Even if this renewed interest has unfortunately resulted in what some have called the "worship wars" in some churches, it seems that what A. W. Tozer once called the "missing jewel" of evangelical worship is being recovered.

Nevertheless, if most evangelicals would quickly agree that worship is central to the life of the church, there would be no consensus to an unavoidable question: What is central to Christian worship? Historically, the more liturgical churches have argued that the sacraments form the heart of Christian worship. These churches argue that the elements of the Lord's Supper and the water of baptism most powerfully present the gospel. Among evangelicals, some call for evangelism as the heart of worship, planning every facet of the service—songs, prayers, the sermon—with the evangelistic invitation in mind.

Though most evangelicals mention the preaching of the Word as a necessary or customary part of worship, the prevailing model of worship in evangelical churches is increasingly defined by music, along with innovations such as drama and video presentations. When preaching the Word retreats, a host of entertaining innovations will take its place.

Traditional norms of worship are now subordinated to a demand for relevance and creativity. A media-driven culture of images has replaced the Word-centered culture that gave birth to the Reformation churches. In some sense, the image-driven culture of modern evangelicalism is an embrace of the very practices rejected by the Reformers in their quest for true biblical worship.

Music fills the space of most evangelical worship, and much of this music comes in the form of contemporary choruses marked by precious little theological content. Beyond the popularity of the chorus as a musical form, many evangelical churches seem intensely concerned to replicate studio-quality musical presentations.

In terms of musical style, the more traditional churches feature large choirs—often with orchestras—and may even sing the established hymns of the faith. Choral contributions are often massive in scale and professional in quality. In any event, music fills the space and drives the energy of the worship service. Intense planning, financial investment, and priority of preparation are focused on the musical dimensions of worship. Professional staff and an army of volunteers spend much of the week in rehearsals and practice sessions.

All this is not lost on the congregation. Some Christians shop for churches that offer the worship style and experience that fits their expectation. In most communities, churches are known for their worship styles and musical programs. Those dissatisfied with what they find at one church can quickly move to another, sometimes using the language of self-expression to explain that the new church "meets our needs" or "allows us to worship."

A concern for true biblical worship was at the very heart of the Reformation. But even Martin Luther, who wrote hymns and required his preachers to be trained in song, would not recognize this modern preoccupation with music as legitimate or healthy. Why? Because the Reformers were convinced that the heart of true biblical worship was the preaching of the Word of God.

Thanks be to God, evangelism does take place in Christian worship. Confronted by the presentation of the gospel and the preaching of the Word, sinners are drawn to faith in Jesus Christ and the offer of salvation is presented to all. Likewise, the Lord's Supper and baptism are honored as ordinances by the Lord's own command, and each finds its place in true worship.

Furthermore, music is one of God's most precious gifts to his people, and it is a language by which we may worship God in spirit and in truth. The hymns of the faith convey rich confessional and theological content, and many modern choruses recover a sense of doxology formerly lost in many evangelical churches. But music is not the central act of Christian worship, and neither is evangelism nor even the ordinances. The heart of Christian worship is the authentic preaching of the Word of God.

Expository preaching is central, irreducible, and nonnegotiable to the Bible's mission of authentic worship that pleases God. John Stott's simple declaration states the issue boldly: "Preaching is indispensable to Christianity."[1] More specifically, preaching is indispensable to Christian worship—and not only indispensable, but central.

The centrality of preaching is the theme of both testaments of Scripture. In Nehemiah 8 we find the people demanding that Ezra the scribe bring the book of the law to the assembly. Ezra and his colleagues stand on a raised platform and read from the book. When he opens the book to read, the assembly rises to its feet in honor of the Word of God and responds, "Amen, Amen!"

Interestingly, the text explains that Ezra and those assisting him "read from the book, from the law of God, translating to give the sense so that they understood the reading" (Neh 8:8 NASB). This remarkable text presents a portrait of expository preaching. Once the text was read, it was carefully explained to the congregation. Ezra did not stage an event or orchestrate a spectacle—he simply and carefully proclaimed the Word of God.

---

1. John Stott, *The Challenge of Preaching*, ed. Greg Scharf, abr. and upd. ed. (Grand Rapids: Eerdmans, 2015), 1.

This text is a sobering indictment of much contemporary Christianity. According to the text, a demand for biblical preaching erupted within the hearts of the people. They gathered as a congregation and summoned the preacher. This reflects an intense hunger and thirst for the preaching of the Word of God. Where is this desire evident among today's evangelicals?

In far too many churches, the Bible is nearly silent. The public reading of Scripture has been dropped from many services, and the sermon has been sidelined, reduced to a brief devotional appended to the music. Many preachers accept this as a necessary concession to the age of entertainment. Some hope to put in a brief message of encouragement or exhortation before the conclusion of the service.

As Michael Green so pointedly put it: "This is the age of the sermonette, and sermonettes make Christianettes."[2]

This book represents a welcome departure from the paltry preaching that characterizes so many churches. Orrick, Payne, and Fullerton's *Encountering God through Expository Preaching* is a compelling presentation of the role preaching plays in the life of a local church. As they explain throughout the book, preaching is not a dry, lifeless activity. Instead, "preaching occurs when a holy man of God opens the Word of God and says to the people of God, 'Come and experience God with me in this text.'" That notion of preaching needs to be recaptured in our day and reinvigorated in the lives of many preachers.

The anemia of evangelical worship—all the music and energy aside—is directly attributable to the absence of genuine expository preaching. Such preaching would confront the congregation with nothing less than the living and active Word of God. That confrontation will shape the congregation as the Holy Spirit accompanies the Word, opens eyes, and applies that Word to human hearts.

---

2. From the editor's preface to John R. W. Stott, *Between Two Worlds* (Grand Rapids: Eerdmans, 1982), 7.

WHAT IS PREACHING?

Preaching occurs when a holy man of God opens the Word of God and says to the people of God, "Come and experience God with me in this text." *Encountering God through Expository Preaching* is an explanation of this sentence.

PART ONE

The Holy Man, the Holy Text, and the Holy Spirit

THE MAN MATTERS

God Shoots Out His Word
with Crooked Arrows, But . . .

It is a sweet and comforting thought that God is willing to use imperfect preachers. James, the brother of Jesus, is a prime example of this. God used him to lead the church in Jerusalem and to author a book of the Bible; but in the book that bears his name, James confessed, "We all stumble in many ways" (Jas 3:1). We all sin, and even preachers are stumblers. No preacher is perfect. The apostles James and John could be overly concerned about their status (Mark 10:37). Peter could be a coward (Gal 2:11–14). Despite these stumblings, God our Father used these men, and others like them, to lead thousands to the Lord and to convey to us the "faith that was once for all delivered to the saints" (Jude 3).

While it is sweet and comforting to know that God uses imperfect men to preach his Word, this sweet truth will turn sour if we use it to excuse our sin and to slacken in our fight for Christlikeness. We must be clear: God's grace will never encourage us to be less concerned about our sin. In fact, according to James, the reality that "we all stumble in many ways" should make us pursue preaching not with a complacent presumption but rather with greater fear and trembling. He writes, "Not many of you should become teachers, my brothers, for you know that we who teach will be judged with greater strictness. For we all stumble in many ways" (Jas 3:1–2). Since we stumble, we should be cautious about entering into a teaching ministry. We should be cautious because great stumbling will incur greater judgment, and it will undermine the goal of great teaching.

Bad men undermine good sermons. Paul knew this, and it is one of the reasons he wrote to the Romans, "You then who teach others, do you not teach yourself? While you preach against stealing, do you steal? You who say that one must not commit adultery, do you commit adultery? You who abhor idols, do you rob temples? You who boast in the law dishonor God by breaking the law. For, as it is written, 'The name of God is blasphemed among the Gentiles because of you'" (2:21–14). When people who talk about God live godless lives they put a bad taste in the mouths of their listeners. They make unbelievers want to spit and swear. Bad men preaching good sermons produces blasphemy. A preacher may proclaim the grace of God with glorious orthodoxy, but if his life contradicts his doctrine he will disgrace the gospel of Christ (1 Tim 3:7).

The Man Matters

These considerations underscore one vital point: when it comes to preaching, the man matters. Our definition of preaching specifies that it is *a holy man of God* who says to the congregation, "Come and experience God with me in this text." Good preaching is more than the sum total of rigorous exegesis, orthodox theology, and engaging homiletics. Good preaching is not simply a skilled act that can be done by any man. No, God desires that preaching be a skilled act that is done by a certain kind of man. So what kind of man must the preacher be? The aim of this chapter is to sketch out the kind of man God wants to use in the pulpit. God desires the ministry of preaching and teaching to be done by men who are holy, qualified, and progressing.

A Holy Man

The godly Scottish pastor Robert Murray M'Cheyne famously said, "A holy man is an awful weapon in the hands of God." That sentiment is backed up by Paul's words in 2 Timothy, where he clearly teaches that if a man cleanses himself from sin, he becomes useful to God. Paul wrote, "Now in a great house there are not only vessels of gold and silver but also of wood and clay, some for honorable use, some for dishonorable. Therefore, if anyone cleanses himself from what is dishonorable, he will be a vessel for honorable use, set apart as holy, useful to the master of the house, ready for every good work" (2 Tim 2:20–21). We will benefit from briefly unpacking this passage.

In this passage Paul compares Timothy's local church to a great house. Like every house, this one had some honorable vessels and some dishonorable vessels. Our houses today have both cheap plastic plates (which we usually use for the kids) and nicer ceramic plates (which we bring out to honor guests). Great houses in Paul's day would have had both dishonorable plates made of wood and clay and honorable plates made of silver and gold. From the context, we can tell that the two types of vessels are meant to represent two different kinds of church leaders. Honorable vessels are those who cleanse themselves by fleeing youthful passions and pursuing righteousness (2 Tim 2:22). A dishonorable vessel would be one of the false teachers Timothy was dealing with. They were men who "quarrel about words," "irreverent babblers," and those who do not flee "youthful passions" (2 Tim 2:14, 16, 22). Such men are dishonorable vessels whom the master of the church will not use.

Notice this: those who will be used are clean, and they are cleansed from sin. That is why they are called "holy" in verse 21, and it is why Paul explains what it looks like to cleanse oneself by commanding Timothy to "flee youthful passions and pursue righteousness, faith, love, and peace, along with those who call on the Lord from a pure heart" (2 Tim 2:22).

See what the Lord says about the person who is holy: such a man is "set apart," "useful," and "ready for every good work." Like the articles of the temple, the preacher who fights sin and flees sin is set apart, holy, devoted unto God. He is also useful. He can speak to others about sin and our Savior because he deals in these realities constantly. Like a chef knows knives, and a professor knows books, godly preachers know the ins and outs of what it looks like to fight sin and to apply Christ's saving grace. Like a guide familiar with a path he has walked a thousand times, the preacher is useful to those he guides because he knows well the pathway to holiness. He can help others since he has himself been helped along the path. Finally, he is ready for every good work. A man who is indulging in sin is grieving the Spirit, and when the frown of the Spirit is on a man he is not ready to preach the smile of heaven that comes to us through the cross of Christ. I (Fullerton) have the privilege of pastoring near an excellent seminary, and many students are under my pastoral care. That means I have the privilege of meeting and shepherding many men who aspire to be good preachers, and most of them are men who are following hard after God and pursuing godly character. Sadly, a few seem more eager to conquer the original languages than to conquer their carnal lusts. Some seem more eager to master homiletics than to manage their own homes. The result of their distorted values is that they will never be used mightily by God. They might be used occasionally in spite of themselves, like Balaam's donkey, but they will never know what it is to feel the abiding blessing of God on their ministries. The blessing of God is reserved for those who cleanse themselves and pursue holiness.

Because God blesses holiness, the preacher of God's Word must adopt certain vital community habits. He must stay close to God's people. Paul tells Timothy to "flee youthful passions and pursue righteousness, faith, love and peace, *along with those* who call on the name of the Lord from a pure heart" (emphasis added). Notice that Timothy is to stay close to other believers (those who call on the Lord from a pure heart). Preachers must not be distant from the communities they teach; rather, through friendships, accountability relationships, and small groups, they must be actively fighting sin along with the people. Too many preachers convince themselves they must hide their struggles from their people. This sometimes leads to preachers who hide their sin behind a veneer of holiness. But God does not bless veneers of holiness. He blesses men actively seeking holiness in all of life's struggles right alongside God's people.

Over the years, I have found that this commitment to holiness calls for costly decisions. Many times on Saturday evening, when I felt I needed every minute to prepare for Sunday, I have laid my studies aside to make a phone call, pay a visit, or write an e-mail to someone I may have sinned against. I have always felt that if I were going to be used of God, I would be better off having a more holy life than a more highly polished sermon. And I have been right; God has never disappointed. I can testify that He has always made up for any lack of polish in my sermon by the blessing He adds to the preaching as I imperfectly seek to be a pure vessel ready for every good work. Brother preacher, we eagerly want to help your preaching! The rest of this book is aimed to help you prepare your preaching, pray for your preaching, and then to preach in the power of the Holy Spirit. But, ultimately your preaching will need God's smile upon it if it will be successful, and that blessing comes as we pursue holiness.

And do not fear confessing your sin to your people. Unless your sin is disqualifying and scandalous, your confessions to them individually and corporately will not undermine your ability to minister the Word to them; rather, honest, humble confession will help your ministry to them.

A Qualified Man

God not only desires holy men, but he also desires qualified men. What do I mean by *qualified* men? I mean that the preaching ministry is ordinarily done by elders who meet the qualifications laid out for pastors in 1 Timothy 3:1–7 and Titus 1:1–9. I realize that not everyone reading this book will be a pastor in a local church. And I am not saying that only ordained pastors can ever preach. But I will say that qualified men are responsible for the preaching ministry of the church, and that those who aspire to preach God's Word regularly should also aspire to be qualified leaders in the local church. If you are not yet qualified to lead God's church, you should be working toward becoming qualified if you hope to exercise a fruitful preaching ministry.

So what are these qualifications? What lifestyle does God desire for preachers? We will survey the qualifications laid out in Titus 1. My goal in doing this is not to say all that could be said about the qualifications for ministry, but to notice specifically how these qualifications (or lack thereof) will affect your preaching ministry. I think the qualifications Paul lays out for the elder in Titus 1 remind us that *the man matters*.

God, in his wisdom, has commanded that His Word be preached, and He has told us by whom it should be preached so that it will be the most powerful. The seventeenth-century poet George Herbert said that when the Word of God is preached by a holy man of God it is like the light of the sun shining through a beautiful stained glass window:

> Doctrine and life, colours and light, in one
> When they combine and mingle, bring
> A strong regard and awe: but speech alone
> Doth vanish like a flaring thing.
> And in the ear, not conscience ring.[1]

Herbert is making an astounding assertion: just as the beauty of the light of the sun is enhanced by passing through a stained glass window, so the beauty and effectiveness of God's Word is enhanced when it is preached by a holy man. If you would have your preaching bring "strong regard and awe," you must be a man of good doctrine and a qualified life. Otherwise, your words will hit people's ears only to immediately "vanish like a flaring thing." So, what qualifications does God want to characterize your life?

First, an elder must be "above reproach" (Titus 1:1). To be above reproach does not mean you are perfect, but it does mean that there is no charge of persistent sin and especially of scandalous sin that can legitimately be charged against you. This call to be above reproach really sums up the thrust of all the other qualifications that follow. If the charge of being a drunkard or a greedy man can stick to you then your preaching will not stick to people's consciences. Instead, every time you call people to holiness, they will merely dismiss your words since you do not practice what you preach. On the other hand, I know of a preacher who, after he preached a sermon, was serving the Lord's Supper. As one of the members of the church filed up to him to take the bread, he whispered in the preacher's ear, "I have a love/hate relationship with your preaching." The man meant that he loved the preacher's presentation of the gospel

---

1. Jim Scott Orrick, *A Year with George Herbert: A Guide to Fifty-Two of His Best Loved Poems.* (Eugene, OR: Wipf and Stock, 2011), 69.

but he also felt pinched, convicted, and called to change by the preacher's stand for righteousness. This is what we want our preaching to do: simultaneously to wound and to heal, to pinch in a way that points to Christ. But it will not do any of this if every time we speak against sin our people can merely dismiss us as hypocrites.

The elder must be "the husband of one wife" (Titus 1:6). If he is married, an elder must be faithfully committed to his own wife in a monogamous marriage.[2] As preachers, our goal is to cultivate godly marriages among those we shepherd (Eph 5:22–32). How can we possibly do this if our own marriages are in shambles? I once heard of a church where the pastor and his wife divorced, and within two years, six more couples in the church also divorced. When the pastor's marriage fell apart, so did much of the fruit of his preaching ministry. On the other hand, when a preacher continually cleaves to his bride, his example joins with his preaching to declare God's faithfulness to His bride. As the pastor commits himself to his wife in marriage, he is providing his people a clear picture of Christ's commitment to the church. Our marriages matter to our preaching.

Paul's next qualification involves how a pastor manages his home. He writes, "His children are believers and not open to the charge of debauchery or insubordination" (Titus 1:6). The word translated "believers" can also be translated "dutiful," or "faithful." I think it should be translated "faithful" here, since that accords more with the parallel passage in 1 Timothy 3, and it also harmonizes more clearly with the theological reality that no elder has the power to make his children believers.[3] So

---

2. The phrase translated "the husband of one wife" has been understood in various ways. Some understand this phrase to be forbidding a polygamist from occupying the office of elder; others understand it to be forbidding a divorced man from occupying the office of elder. For a helpful overview of the various positions taken on this text as well as an excellent defense of the position taken above, see Andreas Köstenberger and David Jones, *God, Marriage, and Family* (Wheaton, IL: Crossway, 2010).

3. Justin Taylor points out that "the term *pistas* can mean either 'believing' or 'faithful' in the Pastoral Epistles (for the former with a noun, cf. 1 Tim 6:2; for the latter with a noun, cf. 2 Tim 2:2). Therefore, word studies alone cannot resolve the question." Justin Taylor, "Unbelief in an Elder's Children," Desiring God, February 1, 2007, http://www.desiringgod.org/articles/unbelief-in-an-elders-children.

here the elder is called to have a well-managed home where his children are submissive to him and not living scandalously and riotously.

Many godly men have fallen into the fault of not calling their children to the same standards to which they call others. Eli honored his sons above the Lord (1 Sam 2:29). David would not displease his son by asking him hard questions and calling his actions to account (1 Kgs 1:6). When we fail in the way that these good men did, we undermine our ministries and disqualify ourselves from New Covenant service. If we would have a church to trust our preaching, they must see that we are calling our children to the same standards to which we are calling the church. In our preaching we are called to "Declare these things; exhort and rebuke with all authority. Let no one disregard you" (Titus 3:15). If we do this to those in the pew while letting our children get away with murder (or maybe just immodesty), we will undermine our preaching.

He must not be "arrogant" (Titus 1:7). Hypersensitivity about your preaching is an indication of arrogance. If you cannot handle having your sermons critiqued and questioned, get out of the ministry. If you cannot handle having your imperfections exposed, do not pursue the pastorate. Furthermore, impatience is also often an indication of arrogance. The ministry of preaching is not for men who want everyone around them to "get it the first time." Rather, it is for men who have the humility to teach with all patience. Paul told Timothy, "Preach the word; be ready in season and out of season; reprove, rebuke, and exhort, with complete patience and teaching" (2 Tim 4:2). Patience is essential for effective preaching, and arrogant men are not patient men. Jesus showed His patience by explaining Himself over and over again even when He was misunderstood. Paul showed his patience by answering myriads of questions about what he had already taught. Both these men were misunderstood and criticized, and had they lashed out in pride they would have forfeited their ability to be heard. Humble men are able to absorb people's misunderstandings, false accusations, and constant (sometimes inane) questions. On the other hand, the impatience that grows out of arrogance will alienate people and ruin a preaching ministry.

An effective way to teach a young, untrained, unruly horse to be led by a halter is to put the new halter on him, then attach one end of a rope to his halter and the other end to the halter of a patient, old donkey. The horse may buck around and tug for a while, but the patient donkey stands his ground. Within a day or two the horse has settled down, and a little child can then lead the horse by its halter. Sometimes the Lord brings wild and unruly people into our ministries, and he tethers them to us and says, "Settle him down for me, so that he becomes willing for me to lead him." It requires patience.

A qualified pastor must not be "quick-tempered, or a drunkard, or violent" (Titus 1:7). A quick-tempered man belies his arrogance. A drunkard indicates that comfort and joy are to be found in substances and practices that dull our capacity to reason. A violent man uses his strength to bully people into doing what he wants. We may not be tempted to hurt people physically, but we may be tempted to use our intellectual abilities or even our theological expertise to overpower people by mental force. The ministry is full of pressures that may tempt us to resort to ungodly styles of leadership. There are pressures from the outside, such as persecution and worldly siren songs that call us to compromise. There are also pressures from inside, such as false teachers and false converts. There are pressures on our time from the demands of the home, the office, the study, the meetings, and the hospital visitations. There are pressures from dealing with the remaining sin in believers' lives. The ministry can be as pressurized as a piston in a diesel engine, and the man who is not full of trust in the Lord will explode. If we are prone to fly off the handle, drink away our problems, or punch our opponents, we will be unable to commend the Prince of Peace and our sermons will extol virtues that are as surreal to us as are fairy tales. No, we must meet pressures with a trust in God that avoids anger, drunkenness, and violence so that people can believe us when we speak of God's supernatural power to help them overcome sin.

He must not be "greedy for gain" (Titus 1:7). The minute your people sense that you are "in it for the money," your preaching ministry is over.

You may be as orthodox and eloquent as was George Whitefield, but if people think you are out for a buck, even your orthodox eloquence will be viewed as a "money grab." The apostle Paul sometimes refused to be paid for his ministry so that no one would mistake his motive as greed and consequently ignore his preaching (1 Cor 9:12). We too must be free from the love of money. The godly preacher may have to work a second job to provide for himself; he may need to suffer an unbearably low wage; he may need to suffer material loss so that others can gain a spiritual profit from his sermons. I am not saying there is never a time to discuss your needs with the church that pays you, but this must be done with great care and obvious freedom from greed so that no obstacle is placed in front of your people hearing the Word. Your attitude toward money deeply affects your preaching ministry.

He must be "hospitable, a lover of good" (Titus 1:8). Our home lives and our personal lives speak volumes that either commend or detract from our preaching ministries. Our homes should declare the same welcome that our gospel proclamation declares. People should feel in our homes the warm welcome of God that we proclaim to them when we preach the reconciling cross of Christ. Pastors of larger churches may not be able to host everyone in their homes, but they still must have a reputation as warm and hospitable men. They must also be lovers of good. If a preacher teaches purity but loves every seedy new show on television, his people will learn to dismiss his exhortation to love "whatever is pure, whatever is lovely, whatever is commendable" (Phil 4:8). It is my fear that this current generation of preachers diminishes the effect of their preaching by an inappropriate familiarity with sordid elements of pop culture. They want to be culturally engaged, and they do not want to risk being called fundamentalists by condemning pop culture, so they go along for the pop culture ride. They commend much that purports to be insightful and savvy on their Facebook pages, but in so doing they inadvertently commend things that are base and titillating. In one scene in the *Inferno*, Dante represents himself listening hungrily to a gossip-filled spat between two shades. Virgil, his guide, rebukes him, saying, "It is vulgar to enjoy that sort of thing."[4] If we consider ourselves simply as human beings created in the image of God, we ought to have a sense of dignity and discretion in our refusal to be conversant with the banality of much pop culture. How much more ought we to have a sense of humble dignity as holy men of God! Brothers, it should be clear from what we put on social media that we are not charmed by anything immoral, but instead we are lovers of good.

He must be "self-controlled, upright, holy and disciplined" (Titus 1:8). A preacher often works under minimal supervision. Sadly, some preachers are men who are "invisible six days a week and incomprehensible on the seventh."[5] With all of that unsupervised time, it is vital that our people know we are working hard as unto the Lord. There are times when you are invited to someone's home for dinner, and when you sit down at the table, you have no doubt that your hostess has put a lot of time and effort into the meal that is set before you. Our hearers ought to have the same sort of confidence when we feed them the Word of God. Our sermons, the fruit of our study, should be full of meat. They should be made so easily digestible that it is clear that we have been living self-controlled, disciplined lives of study. Incomprehensible preaching is not an indication of too much study; it is an indication of too little study and prayerful meditation. We ought to be able to preach with the confidence that a man can have only when he is actually living the kind of upright and holy life he is commending. In this way our lives will commend our preaching.

Finally, "He must hold firm to the trustworthy word as taught, so that he may be able to give instruction in sound doctrine and also to rebuke those who contradict it" (Titus 1:9). He must be an orthodox man—a man who is neither novel nor inventive, but who is faithful to the trustworthy word he has received. If he does this, a preacher will be able to give people the healthy food of sound doctrine and keep them

---

4. Dante, *The Divine Comedy I: Hell,* canto 30, line 148, trans. Dorothy L. Sayers (London: Penguin, 1949), 262.
5. Eugene Peterson, *Working the Angles: The Shape of Pastoral Integrity* (Grand Rapids: Eerdmans, 1987), 63.

from the poison of false teaching. I do not need to explore this verse in detail since it is a major focus of this book, but I will say one thing: when a man places himself under the authority of the Word of God, and shows that he is giving to others what he himself has submissively received, he has far more authority than he would otherwise have. If you get a reputation as an inventive man, or a creative man, many may admire you for a season. But if you are known as a "Bible man," you will have the reputation you need to command people to believe in our King who, regarding his own preaching ministry, persistently asserted, "My teaching is not mine, but his who sent me" (John 7:16).

A Progressing Man

Finally, as preachers we should be progressing men. Yes, we must constantly pursue holiness, and we must be qualified, but we should be progressing in the skill of preaching as well. Part of our holiness consists in loving our people enough to get better at presenting God's Word to them. Paul put it this way: "Until I come, devote yourself to the public reading of Scripture, to exhortation, to teaching. Do not neglect the gift you have, which was given you by prophecy when the council of elders laid their hands on you. Practice these things, immerse yourself in them, so that all may see your progress" (1 Tim 4:13–15). Notice something here: Timothy was to be continually reading and preaching the Bible without neglect. In fact, he was uniquely gifted to do this. Given the context, it would seem that the gift given to him by the elders was the gift of teaching. That is what he was not to neglect. Though he was to give himself to the routine practice of teaching, and he was gifted to do it through a prophecy, Timothy still needed to make progress. He needed to improve, and he needed to keep improving.

I love this verse because it takes the wrong kind of pressure off young preachers. It is expected that when you start, you will have room for improvement. It is okay to start badly, or at least not so well. Only a handful of preachers will ever sound like Spurgeon, and basically no one sounds like Spurgeon on his first sermon. But it is normal—and expected—that you will improve, and those who hear you ought to notice that you are improving. Your progress ought to be something "all may see." The old ladies in the pews should say, "That young man is getting better." And the people who have not heard you preach for five years should say, "You've gotten much clearer."

How do you improve? It is accomplished by practice and immersion in the task. Obviously, we hope you will read this book, but reading this book will only help you to practice better. Great basketball players probably started out with some basic instruction on how to shoot, dribble, and pass, but ultimately the really great players get their skills through playing the game on playgrounds. They did not play only in comfortable gymnasiums during the months of the basketball season; they played year round wherever they could get into a game. It is much the same with preaching. Do not wait until you are asked to preach in a nice church on Sunday morning. Start a nursing home ministry. Preach at the rescue mission. Just do it over and over and over and over, always aiming to improve. You practice, and while nothing will make a perfect preacher, practice will make a better preacher. You immerse yourself in these things. You do not study the bare minimum required to "have a sermon"; you study until you understand the text, until you understand the contours of the Bible, the story of Scripture, and the theology of the whole Bible. Like an Olympic athlete, you focus on one thing until you do it with excellence. And be sure of this: God knows where you are, and he knows when and how he wants to use you. As an ancient proverb asserts, "The stone that is fit for the wall will not be left to lie in the ditch."

While it can be assuring to younger preachers that they have room for improvement, it is an ultimatum for preachers young and old that we continually improve. Sadly, this is not always the case. We can start well but not end well. We may not make progress. We can start gripped and fiery in our youth and end up progressing little and slipping into a dead monotony in our preaching. I spoke once to a seasoned and very gifted preacher who told me that he had seen many men go from being excellent preachers in their thirties to becoming mediocre preachers in their fifties. Just like manna did not keep fresh overnight, but required daily replenishment, so too preachers must get fresh manna every day. We must constantly devote ourselves to preaching so that we continue to progress in a way that everyone can see. Below are a few tips for doing just that.

A Pathway toward Progressing as a Preacher

First, continue to read the Bible daily for your personal spiritual nourishment. Over the years, your knowledge of the Bible will grow richer and deeper. In due time you will be able to illustrate your sermons with just the right Bible verses and Bible stories. Your preaching will begin to bleed "bibline,"[6] as C. H. Spurgeon said in commendation of John Bunyan's writings.

Second, guard your sermon study time throughout your ministry. At the start of my ministry it took me more than twenty hours to prepare one sermon. If I had not had the twenty hours, I do not know if I would have had anything to say! As time has passed, I am now able to preach with much less preparation; but the temptation is to study too little because now I can "get away with it" (I speak as a fool). If you allow yourself to do this, over time you will become thinner and thinner in your preaching instead of fuller and fuller. To avoid this, I schedule and protect ample time to study and prepare my sermons. I avoid making appointments during these times. If at all possible, I deal with emergencies outside of these times. I seek to set myself aside for study and preparation so I can make progress serving the Lord and his people.

Third, never stop studying theology. Some who are reading this are in the middle of a course of undergraduate study. Others may have had the privilege of a seminary education. Still others may have gone through an intense season of independent study, but none should ever think he is finished studying. Continue to challenge yourself to read the best theologians and pastors. Their insight into the character of God and the living of the Christian life will sharpen your own thinking and will serve the people you love.

---

6. A "Spurgeonism."

Fourth, listen to and read good preaching. I was once told that I should never miss hearing an anointed man of God preach. It was good advice. Sitting under the preaching of an anointed preacher will fuel your own desires to be used powerfully of God. On top of this, make use of the many excellent preachers on the radio and the Internet. What a privilege to have access to so many godly preachers! I love to listen to them, learning not only from their observations and interpretations, but also from their style. I have learned much about Bible-saturated preaching from listening to John MacArthur. I learned how to pay attention to the exact details of the text from John Piper. I learned about illustration and spiritual application from Charles Leiter. I learned how to tell a story from Crawford Lorritts. I have learned how to knead one simple point into the affections of the heart from C. J. Mahaney. I have gleaned much about the appropriate use of humor in preaching from Alistair Begg. I could go on and on. I do not slavishly copy any of these men, but I have profited from listening to each of them.

Fifth, listen to bad preaching. I am not saying listen in order to ridicule it, or to feel superior to a bad preacher. Not at all! No matter how bad the preaching, we should try to get something out of it. As one friend told me, "The mature worshipper is easily edified." Do not be one of those people who sits in the congregation with their arms folded and a look on their face that says, "Well, say something to impress me. I dare you to try." We should seek to be easily edified even by bad preaching, but at the same time we should listen to it so that we can get better. What made the preaching bad? Was it too dense? Did the man speak in a "preacher voice" so that we never felt we were hearing from a real man? As preachers, if we hear bad preaching, we should try to discern why it was bad so that we can seek to avoid the same errors. I have learned so much over the years from hearing bad preaching and from hearing about bad preaching.

Sixth, ask for feedback on your preaching. Perhaps your wife is a helpful critic, or you have a trusted friend in the congregation. Or perhaps when you preach at different events with more seasoned preachers you might make use of their insights. I have learned much from the insights of others over the years. Church leaders have critiqued me about my pace (I tend to rush at the start), my poor choice of illustrations (I won't share it here), and my lack of theological precision. All of these critiques have helped me progress as a preacher. I want the help of those with more experience than myself. Years ago I heard a story of an older preacher teaching a younger preacher, and it has never left me. The older preacher was a southern gentleman, and the younger preacher was what they sometimes call a "boy preacher." Apparently this boy preacher had a pretty sharp mind but did not know how to use it discreetly in the pulpit. The older gentleman said to him, "Boy preacher, you is one of the finest doctrinal preachers I has ever heard. But you are giving the people too much meat. You are going to leave them constipated. You need to throw in a little boonana pudding." For years this story has reminded me to throw in something a little lighter, a little more digestible, a story or a proverb, to help the doctrine "go down." Who knows what kinds of wisdom you will get as you ask for helpful critique.

Seventh, pray. Always pray! Pray each and every week that God will give you power, and that he will make your service "acceptable to the saints" (Rom 15:31). Pray that you will preach "in a demonstration of the Spirit and of power" (1 Cor 2:4). Never take an opportunity to preach without taking opportunity to pray. It saddens me to think how often I have been invited to preach somewhere and the organizers did not think to set aside any time to pray before the sermon. A brief minute was devoted to prayer before I preached, and that was all. Brothers, I encourage you to set aside a good time when you can really plead with the Lord for his help on your preaching. I currently try to pray daily for my preaching, I meet with a number of our pastors to pray before I preach each Sunday, and I am always looking for time to pray with others when I travel somewhere to preach. I commend this practice to you. I am sure that as the Lord answers those prayers, He will make your progress evident to all.

Conclusion

Brothers, the man matters. *You* matter to the success of your preaching. This does not mean that the success of our ministries is up to us; it means that we must look to our faithful Savior to transform us more and more into His image. We must look to Him to make us holy, we must work out our salvation with fear and trembling so that we are qualified men, and we must do this in humility under our good master so that our progress may be evident to all (Phil 2:12; 1 Tim 4:15).

A DEFENSE
OF EXPOSITORY PREACHING

*We have somehow got hold of the idea that error is
only that which is outrageously wrong; and we do not seem
to understand that the most dangerous person of all is the one
who does not emphasize the right things.*[1]

When I (Payne) was a year and a half into my current pastoral ministry, we had a divisive controversy at the church, and some sixty-five to eighty people exited. One of the prevailing complaints was that my sermons were too long (45–50 minutes), too doctrinal, and "over their heads." It was a devastating critique, especially for someone who teaches preaching for a living and has devoted his life to the task.

The upshot to this, besides the great benefit of having idols exposed in my heart, is that I began to question my convictions on preaching. Is expository preaching effective anymore? Can churches that are not catechized and not trained to follow tightly woven arguments benefit from expositional preaching?

---

1. D. Martyn Lloyd-Jones, *Studies in the Sermon on the Mount*, reprint (Eastford, CT: Martino Fine Books, 2011), 2:244.

It was during that time period that one of our new members, Steve, who had moved from Seattle, Washington, took me to lunch. I shared with him a bit of my discouragement and how it seemed that no matter how much I worked and prayed in preparing for a sermon, glazed looks and criticism were the only fruits for my labors.

Steve listened attentively as I shared my burden with him. Then he responded to my laments in a way that took me completely off guard. "Keep doing what you are doing," he said. He added, "You are faithfully expositing the text. That's why we joined your church. Let me tell you a brief story to give you some perspective." He began to tell me that he and his wife had lived in Louisville before they moved to Seattle. In Louisville, they had attended a large church that had twenty-minute "felt needs"-oriented messages. They had enjoyed the messages and loved the church. When Steve's company relocated him to Seattle, one of their struggles had been leaving their church in Louisville.

When Steve and his family got to Seattle and settled in a home, they discovered that the only conservative, evangelical church within driving distance was a Bible church. So they attended the first Sunday and loved everything but the preaching. The preacher preached sixty minutes, and it was over their heads. They thought that it might be an anomaly, so they attended again the following Sunday and the same thing happened.

They recognized that this was the only church that was feasible for them in the area, so Steve set up a meeting with the teaching elder. He told the elder that they enjoyed everything about the church but one thing: his sermons. The elder responded by challenging Steve to give him six months. After six months they would talk again. The elder reasoned that during the six months Steve and his wife would grow into being able to process and digest the sermons.

Steve looked at me as he continued his story and said, "And that's exactly what happened. Over the six-month time period, our appetite for the Word of God began to grow by leaps and bounds. At the end of those six months, not only were we processing his sermons, we were hungering for them—delighting in them."

After five years in Seattle, Steve's company moved him back to Louisville. And naturally, the first Sunday back, they attended their old church. After all, it was where their friends were and where they had long enjoyed the preaching. But a strange thing happened. After listening to the sermon only a few minutes, they both recognized that they now had a different "spiritual palate." They longed for more—something deeper. They wanted to hear the Word of God. What Steve had experienced under faithful exposition was a reformation. Their view of spirituality had shifted from an almost selfish concern for their own private well-being to an adoration for the living God, his character, his will, and his works.

I cannot overstate the encouragement that Steve's testimony was to me. The Lord had used Steve to confirm my convictions on preaching. Indeed, "God, who comforts the downcast," comforted me through Steve (2 Cor 7:6). Before our conversation was over, Steve made a prediction that has proven true. He told me that if I continued preaching the way I had been preaching, more church members might leave, but the ones who remained would begin to grow in new life as the Word of God nourished and nurtured them.

The question that I will seek to answer for the remainder of this chapter is this: What is it about expository preaching that can accomplish the kind of growth that Steve and his family enjoyed in Seattle? That is, what is it about expository preaching that can take a person who is an inordinate "self-lover" (2 Tim 3:2), whose primary goal in listening to a sermon is the sermon's subjective usefulness, and transform him into someone who exults in and places his repentant, doxological faith in the Living God?

The Word of God is God's active, authoritative energy in the world. When the Word of God is preached, God himself is active. And when God the Lord is actively working through his Word, he comes with his authority, power, and presence.[2] God's work in salvation is accomplished

---

2. I am significantly indebted to John Frame's *A Theology of Lordship* series of books for my insights on God's lordship and the Word of God, especially *The Doctrine of the Word of God* (Phillipsburg, NJ: P&R, 2010), 50–68.

through his Word. Stated succinctly, God's *working* is found through his *wording*.[3]

Since this is the case, "it is the first business of an interpreter to let his author say what he does say, instead of attributing to him what he thinks the author ought to say."[4] Consequently, the more the interpreter (the preacher) drifts from the author's mind revealed in the text of Scripture, the more he diverges from the author's purpose. And what is the divine Author's overall purpose for Scripture? To teach, rebuke, correct, and train in righteousness (2 Tim 3:16–17), so that we might magnify the Living God by knowing and loving him. Preaching takes place when a holy man of God opens the Word of God and says to those hearing him, "Come, experience God with me *in this text*." The best way to experience God and lead others to experience him is through encountering him in the texts in which he reveals himself. God is alive in his Word.

First, the Word of God is God's very energy and self-expression as Lord. To say it another way, "God's Word is God's active presence in the world. . . . When God's Word goes out to act it means God himself has gone out to act. Thus (we may say) God has invested himself with his words, or we could say that God has so identified himself with his words that whatever someone does to God's words . . . they do to God himself. . . . God's . . . verbal actions are a kind of extension of himself."[5]

Second, if this is the case, in order to ensure that God works by his Word, the preacher must make it his main task to make the meaning of the text of Scripture clear to his hearers. This task is most effectively accomplished by consistently preaching in an expositional manner.[6]

---

3. Michael Horton, *The Christian Faith* (Grand Rapids: Zondervan, 2011), 574.

4. Preface to John Calvin's *Commentary on Romans*. This is a refreshing contrast to many today who seem to believe that a text may have "polysemy"—the coexistence of several possible meanings of a text, some even contradictory to others.

5. Timothy Ward, *Words of Life* (Downers Grove, IL: IVP Academic, 2009), 25, 27.

6. We devote an entire chapter to topical preaching, so we acknowledge that topical sermons are sometimes beneficial. We maintain, however, that expository preaching is most conducive to revealing the whole counsel of God, and therefore preachers ought primarily to preach expository sermons. Furthermore, as will become clear in the chapter on topical sermons, even good topical preaching is an assemblage of several mini-expositions.

The Word Is the Lord's Energy in the World

When my daughter Ava was five years old, she asked me on my day of departure for a mission trip why I was going to Africa. I told her that Africans need Jesus. She looked at me and said with all the sincerity of a five-year-old, "You aren't Jesus." And she was certainly right about that. But I was going to Africa to preach the gospel, and when the gospel word is rightly preached, Jesus the Lord is there.

The ancient Hebrews considered God's name, Yahweh,[7] too holy to pronounce. So when a Hebrew reader came to the name Yahweh in the text, instead of saying the name, he substituted the Hebrew word *Adonai*, which is translated Lord. Most English translations follow this convention, utilizing the word Lord (capitalized and with small capital letters following) for virtually all occurrences of Yahweh. Scholars are not exactly sure what the name Yahweh means; but since usage determines meaning, it is clear that "Lord," while not a translation, is an excellent interpretation.[8] A lord is the one who gives the orders. A lord expects to be honored and obeyed. As *the* Lord, Yahweh asserts his absolute sovereignty. The Lord does as he pleases. Yahweh, or Lord, is God's "name forever" and the name by which God wants "to be remembered throughout all generations" (Exod 3:15). In Scripture, the fundamental confessions of faith are confessions of God's lordship (Deut 6:4–5; Rom 10:9; 1 Cor 12:3; Phil 2:11). In fact, after Exodus 3, you could rightly say that the rest of Scripture is a revelation of God living up to his name. He performs all his works so that people *will know that I am the Lord* (Exod 6:7; 7:5, 17; 8:22; 10:2; 14:4; et al.).

In thinking about Yahweh's lordship, it is helpful here to note that while we are able to distinguish between God's essence and God's

---

7. Yahweh, the divine name revealed to Moses and the name by which God wants to be known forever (Exod 3:15), sounds in Hebrew like a form of the verb "to be" (*hayay*), and so is connected with that verb in Exodus 3:14. The four consonants that make up this name are referred to as the tetragrammaton (the "four letters"). Depending on how the consonants are pronounced, the tetragrammaton may be pronounced either "Jehovah" or "Yahweh."

8. In fact, the Holy Spirit must have approved of this convention, because there is not a single instance of the name Yahweh appearing in the New Testament. When Old Testament passages containing the word Yahweh are quoted in the New Testament, the Greek word for Lord is always used. This ought significantly to influence our understanding of the assertions that Jesus is Lord.

energies, they are, in fact inseparable, and we know about God's essence because of his energies. For instance, the sun's rays are not the sun itself, obviously, but they are the shining forth of the sun. We know about the sun because of its rays. Likewise, God's energies are neither God's essence nor a created effect but God's lordship shining on his creatures.[9]

Now if God's energies, workings, and acts are expressions of his lordship, then we come to know the *essence* of God as Lord through the *energy* of God the Lord. Consequently, God's speech, like all his actions and energies, expresses his lordship. A number of biblical passages focus on ways God expresses his lordship through his Word; and in these various passages there are three recurring themes: God's Word not only expresses but embodies his power, his authority, and his personal presence.[10] Let us explore how God's Word expresses and embodies these three qualities of divine lordship.

First, the Word of God is God's *expression* and the *embodiment* of his power. When God speaks, he speaks as Lord, for that is who he is; and the Word of God is the *power* by which the Lord brings all things to pass according to the counsel of his will (Eph 1:11). That is why it is correct to assert that when the Lord *speaks*, and when the Lord *acts*, it is essentially one and the same thing; when he speaks, he does (Ps 29:5, 8; Isa 55:10–11). He creates by his Word (Gen 1; Ps 33:6, 9). He governs by his word (Ps 147:15–18; Heb 1:3). He brings judgment by his Word (Ps 46:6). He saves by his Word (Luke 7:7–9). It is the Word that changes hearts and edifies and nourishes believers (Rom 16:25). That is why it is called the "word of life" (Phil 2:16). The Word is never powerless; on the contrary, the Lord's very omnipotence is communicated through the energy of his Word. It creates, controls, convicts, performs God's purposes, and overrides human weakness.

Second, the Word of God is the Lord's *authoritative speech*. That is, the Word not only informs us of the Lord's will, but it produces in us the qualities and desires required for us to submit to his will. We submit to the Lord when we obey his Word, and we rebel against the Lord when we

---

9. Horton, *Christian Faith*, 130.
10. John Frame, *Doctrine of the Word of God*, 50–68.

disobey his Word. For instance, Adam's first experience was that of hearing the word of God (see Gen 1:28ff). His life or death depended on his response to that word (Gen 2:17). When Adam disobeyed God's *spoken command*, he ruptured his relationship with God. After the fall, Adam's only hope was that God would fulfill the promise of his word (Gen 3:15). Other biblical saints illustrate that the blessing of knowing and enjoying God is contingent on knowing and obeying his authoritative word. Noah had no ground to believe in a coming judgment—except God's word. Abraham, as the New Testament model of faith (Romans 4; Gal 3:6–9; Heb 11:8–19; Jas 2:21–24), had faith in God's promised word. Israel was bound to the commands God had spoken (Deuteronomy 6; Josh 1:8ff; Psalm 119). When holy men of God spoke in God's name, their words were not to be regarded as merely the words of wise men; *God* spoke through Moses and the prophets (Deut 18:15–22; Jer 1:6–19; Ezek 13:2, 17). Furthermore, in the New Testament, Jesus is revealed as the Lord's ultimate authoritative speech. Jesus came as the Word of God made flesh (John 1:1, 14). Believing and obeying Christ as the living Word is the ultimate criterion of discipleship. If anyone hears the words of Christ but does not keep them, that person will be judged (John 12:47–50). So to hear Jesus's words is the same as hearing the words of the Father (John 8:47). And Scripture asserts that the apostles' words bear the same level of authority (John 14:23–26; 15:26; 16:13; Rom 2:16; 16:25; 1 Cor 2:10–13; 4:1; 2 Cor 4:1–6; 12:1, 7; Gal 1:1, 11, 16; 1 Thess 4:2; Jude 17). So when God speaks, he speaks with authority; and God's image-bearers are responsible to hear his Word, to understand his Word, and to obey whatever God commands through his Word. If we would submit to God himself, we must submit to his Word.

Third, the Word of God, because it is the very energy of God, is a manifestation of God's *personal presence in the world*. In Deuteronomy 4:7, the Lord says that he is "near" to Israel. Then in Deuteronomy 30:11–14, in virtually the same terms, it is God's Word that is *near*. Gloriously, Paul quotes this Deuteronomy passage and applies it to Jesus. The nearness of the Word in Deuteronomy is the nearness of Jesus Christ (Rom 10:6–8). And this is true because God's Spirit is present with his Word:

where the Lord is, the Word is; and where the Word is, the Lord is. This organic union of the Lord with his Word is further demonstrated by the biblical correlations between Word and Spirit (Gen 1:2; Ps 33:6; Isa 34:16; 59:21; John 6:63; 16:13; Acts 2:1–4; 1 Thess 1:5; 2 Thess 2:2; 2 Tim 3:16; 2 Pet 1:21).

Consequently, in light of the fact that God's Word is the supreme energy of God, it should not surprise us that his Word does things that only the Lord can do. For instance, in the book of Hebrews we read that the Word discerns the most hidden recesses of our being (4:12); and without any indication that he has changed the subject, the writer says virtually the same thing of God. "No creature is hidden from his sight, but all are naked and exposed to the eyes of him to whom we must give account" (4:13).

Further strengthening the identification of the Lord himself with his Word, note that the Bible credits the Word of God as possessing the attributes of God: it is righteous (Ps 119:7), faithful (119:86), wonderful (119:129), upright (119:137), pure (119:140), true (Ps 119:142; cf. John 17:17), eternal (Ps 119:89, 160), omnipotent (Gen 18:14; Isa 55:11; Luke 1:37), perfect (Ps 19:7ff), and holy (Deut 31:26; 2 Tim 3:15). Indeed, where the LORD's word is, there the LORD is present in power and authority.

In summary, the LORD has *invested* himself in his words. Or to say it another way, he has so identified himself with his words that to say that the LORD spoke, and to say that the LORD did something, is often one and the same thing.[11] This connection is established in the first chapter of the Bible where God creates by speaking (Gen 1:3ff.).

Since the Word of God is God's energetic expression and embodiment of his power, his authority, and his personal presence in the world, the questions arise, with such a rich written manifestation of God, what more would a minister of the Gospel need beyond the Word of God, and why would he preach anything else? And how could he possibly have greater influence than through expositing the very "oracles of God" (1 Pet

---

11. Ward, *Words of Life*, 27.

4:11)? Indeed, it is an obligation of faithful stewardship "in order that in everything God may be glorified through Jesus Christ" (1 Pet 4:11).

The Necessity of Expository Preaching

Al Mohler tells a story that hails from his days as a Boy Scout in Florida. He and his scout friends were fascinated with snakes. Most poisonous snakes in North America have unique markings that distinguish them from non-poisonous snakes, but there is one poisonous snake in Florida that is not so easy to identify—the coral snake. It has red, yellow, and black stripes. It is a beautiful snake, but it is one of the most poisonous snakes in the United States. The problem is that it looks almost identical to the scarlet king snake, which is harmless. The only difference in their appearance is the order of their colors. So if you are going to be a good Boy Scout in Florida, you need to know the difference between the king snake, which you can pick up and safely handle, and the coral snake, which can kill you. There were legends of kids who had picked up the coral snake thinking it was a king snake and putting it in their pockets and meeting their demise. To help you distinguish between the two snakes, they teach you a poem: "Red on black, a friend of Jack. Red on yellow, kill a fellow." One day when Mohler was around thirteen years old, he saw one of those multicolored snakes, and it had red rings touching black rings. He remembered, "Red on black, a friend of Jack." But as he was about to pick it up, he thought, *Just how much faith do I have in a poem? Not enough.* So he let the snake go.

As I heard him tell this, I thought, *What an appropriate question for the preacher to ask concerning the Word of God: Just how much faith do I have in the Bible?* When it comes to eternal things, the stakes are infinitely higher than discerning whether a snake is poisonous. People are lost and going to hell. Men and women are in rebellion against God. The Bible claims to have the answers to humanity's deepest woes. I want to help. Just how much faith do I have in the Bible?

Thus far we have seen in this chapter that the Scriptures' testimony is that you ought to have complete faith in it. When we speak to humanity's spiritual woes, the Bible has the answers that we need, and it is all that we need. And perhaps there is no better place to defend this assertion than from 2 Timothy. It was written while Paul sat in prison awaiting almost certain martyrdom. It is included in a group of Pauline letters that are collectively known as the Pastoral Epistles. In each of these letters, Paul demonstrates the role the Word plays in the pastoral ministry and in the church. Each letter has its unique emphases. In 1 Timothy, the accent is on *protecting* the Word (cf. 1 Tim 1:3). In Titus, the weight is on *practicing* the Word (cf. Titus 2:11–14). And in 2 Timothy the stress is on *preaching* the Word (2 Tim 4:2). Now let us explore the case that the Holy Spirit inspired Paul to make in 2 Timothy for the preaching of the Word.

In 2 Timothy 3, Paul begins a section that will end up being his final recorded words. In fact, he knows his death is imminent (2 Tim 4:6–8). And so, not only are his words breathed out by the Spirit of God (2 Tim 3:16), they are the last words from a spiritual father to his son in the faith concerning ministry in the local church. So these last words promise to be crucial words, weighted with solemnity and earnestness.

The unit begins with a dire warning. These last days will be "times of difficulty" (3:1). And in 3:2–5, Paul tells us why: people! Paul describes these people with eighteen descriptors in verses 2–4, with a nineteenth added in verse 5. Importantly, the first two words in the list, translated "lovers of self" and "lovers of money," begin with the Greek prefix *phil* (related to love). And the two nouns in the last phrase of 3:4 have the same *phil* prefix as in 3:2 ("lovers of pleasure more than lovers of God," KJV). So the list begins and ends with words expressing misdirected love. This suggests that what is centrally wrong with the human condition is that our love is misdirected and that all other vices flow from this misdirected love.[12]

What makes this list so sobering is that Paul is not merely speaking about the world outside of the church. It is a given that the world is "alienated and hostile in mind, doing evil deeds" (Col 1:21). But Paul says the people he has in mind have "the appearance of godliness," but

---

12. In this paragraph I am indebted to ideas I encountered in George W. Knight III's book *The Pastoral Epistles*, The New International Greek Testament Commentary (Grand Rapids: 1992), 428–30.

deny "its power" (2 Tim 3:5). These people are in the church! He goes on to give specific examples of the kind of people he is speaking of (3:6–8), namely, "Men corrupted in mind and disqualified regarding the faith" (3:8).

At first glance, Paul paints what appears to be a hopeless situation for the church in the "last days" (3:1). How can a minister succeed in these "times of difficulty"? When a people's love is misdirected, that is no superficial, easy-to-fix problem; it is a fundamental problem at the core of human existence. This is the polluted fountain from whence flow all poisonous streams. How can that change? Can a minister actually say or do anything that can change a person's loves—his deepest commitments and affections? It is one thing merely to stir the listeners' emotions. But emotions may be fleeting and superficial, and emotions often fail to produce action. It is another thing to change what a person loves. Love is long-lasting and deep. Love involves the mind and will as well as the affections.

Gratefully, Paul does not end on a pessimistic note. He is convinced that these professing Christians with misdirected love "will not get very far" (3:9). Paul believes "God's firm foundation stands" (2:19). But God uses means to assure the stability of his foundation and to overcome brokenness in a church.

What is the most fundamental means that God uses? The Word of God. Timothy saw Paul model commitment to the Word in Paul's own life and ministry (3:10). The aged apostle was so convinced of its veracity and efficacy that he was willing to suffer for it (3:11). Indeed, everyone whose "aim in life" (3:10) centers on Christ and his Word will be persecuted (3:12), and it will only get worse (3:13). But Paul's commitment to the preaching of the Word was unwavering.

Considering the problems that Timothy was dealing with and was likely to encounter in the future, many church growth gurus might say that Timothy needed to be innovative and do something novel, hide the church's *otherworldliness,* and become slickly *this worldly.* This approach makes sense from a secular marketing perspective, and we do want to be relevant and influential, but the irony is that churches can influence the culture for godliness only *by distancing themselves from the culture.* They influence the culture, not by offering what can already be had from the world, but by offering an alternative that only God can provide. Central to this countercultural ministry is the preaching of the Word, which confronts and transforms *this worldly* thinking. Paul tells Timothy that when it comes to addressing sin in a church or in the culture, and when it comes to building a people for his own name, God cares about our method as well as our message. The method should match our message, and proclaiming the message is our method.

In particular, our participation in God's redemptive purposes is directly tied to the gospel. Cooperating with God requires cooperation with his method, namely preaching the Word. We ought to value God's Word the way he values it; and if our view of Scripture is lower than God's own view of Scripture, we are likely to adopt some alternative expedient that will supplant the simple preaching of God's Word. Predictably, our alleged improvements to God's own methodology will ultimately fail to bring about God's Kingdom, and they may actually cause great damage and devastation.

That is the message of 2 Timothy 3:14–17: we will be tested and tempted to think there is a better way to engage the *difficult days—* especially when the promised persecution comes for our faithfulness (3:12). But Paul tells Timothy, continue in the Book! That is God's only strategy. And Paul gives three reasons: Scripture's ability, Scripture's author, and Scripture's aim.

Scripture's Ability

In our earlier discussion on the Word of God as God's active presence in the world, we noted the Scriptures' ability to achieve God's purposes in redemption. In 3:15, Paul says they "are able to make you wise for salvation through faith in Christ Jesus." Protestant theologians have stressed four essential attributes and characteristics of Scripture: the sufficiency of Scripture, the clarity of Scripture, the authority of Scripture, and the necessity of Scripture. One we see here: the *sufficiency* of Scripture. That is, the Scriptures contain everything we need for knowledge of salvation and godly living. To "make . . . wise" means to teach wisdom to someone who doesn't presently have that wisdom.

And this statement echoes a glorious promise of the Scripture's ability, asserted in Psalm 19:7, for "making wise the simple." Even simple, inexperienced persons can receive wisdom from Scripture. This *clarity of Scripture* is a second attribute that theologians have pointed out. That is, the saving message of Jesus Christ is plainly taught in Scriptures and can be understood by all who have ears to hear.

Scripture's Author

Of course, when Paul is thinking of the "sacred writings" (2 Tim 3:15), he has in mind what we know as the Old Testament. But 3:16 confirms that it is not just the Old Testament that has ability. The New Testament has this ability as well because they both share the same *author*. Indeed, "all Scripture is breathed out by God" (3:16a). All Scripture has its source in God, and this is its essential characteristic. The Holy Spirit worked through the biblical writers to pen God's Word entirely and exactly as he intended. And this brings us to a third attribute that theologians have identified: the *authority of Scripture*. Because the Scriptures are breathed out by God, the last word always goes to Scripture. We must never allow the teachings of culture, human experience, science, or church councils to take precedence over it.

Scripture's Aim

Because "all Scripture is God-breathed" and is authoritative, clear, and sufficient, Paul can categorically state that it is profitable (3:16b). In other words, when God speaks, he has an aim in mind, and that ultimate aim will be accomplished. It "shall succeed in the thing for which I sent it," says the LORD (Isa 55:11).

When we preach God's Word, it goes out to act as God's authoritative, all-powerful presence in the world; it profits in "teaching, reproof, correction," and "training in righteousness that the man of God may be complete, equipped for every good work" (2 Tim 3:16b–17). That is, Scripture teaches us about ultimate reality, about the living God and his person, worth, works, and ways. Scripture, as the plumb line by which every thought, deed, word, belief, and motivation is measured, reproves and corrects us for wrong thinking, misplaced love, and idolatrous motivations and desires. And it trains us in righteousness, provoking in us an unswerving commitment to uphold the worth of the Lord's glory. The result: competence and equipment for "every good work" (3:17).

This is why the Protestant theologians were right with the fourth attribute of Scripture as well: the *necessity of Scripture*. The Bible is profitable and therefore necessary for everything that needs accomplishing in a broken world.

In 2 Timothy 4:1–5, Paul tells Timothy what to do with this Word: *preach it.* "I charge you in the presence of God and of Christ Jesus, who is to judge the living and the dead, and by his appearing and his kingdom: preach the word" (2 Tim 4:1–2a). Preach the Word—not *a* word, but *the* Word—the very Word that he calls "the good deposit" (2 Tim 1:14), the "sound teaching" (4:3), the "truth" (4:4) and the "faith" (4:7).

"Preach the word." It is an imperative, or a command, and the imperative *preach* is the first of nine commands in 4:2–5. "Preach" is from *kerusso*, which means "to herald." In ancient days, the herald acted as an imperial messenger. He would go through the streets announcing the victory of the king, new government policies and actions, or the appearing of the emperor. The Christian herald announces the victory of Christ our King, his policies and actions, and his pending appearance.

Preaching the Word is God's method of transforming a culture plagued by misdirected love; and remember, misdirected love is the root of the problem. The fact that the Holy Spirit led Paul to give Timothy this command to preach the Word implies at least two things. First, the church has a natural tendency to lose sight of the centrality of preaching the Word. Second, the people of God need to hear the Word preached. The preached Word centered on the gospel is the only God-ordained method we have to prepare sinners for that Day—the Day of Christ's appearing, judgment, and kingdom.

This is why the preacher is to preach "in season and out of season" (4:2)—that is, when it is convenient and comfortable, and when it is inconvenient and costly. When the culture does not think it is relevant, or when it sees its message as archaic, preach the Word! This is the church's method.

When we preach the Word, we are to "reprove, rebuke, and exhort with complete patience and teaching" (4:2). We are to *reprove*. This word is used elsewhere of reproving one who continues in sin (1 Tim 5:20) and of correcting an opponent (Titus 1:9, 13). We are to *rebuke*. This means to prevent an action or bring it to an end. Whereas reproving is to speak to show who is in error and to attempt to convince them of that, rebuking means to tell those doing wrong to stop. A third goal in preaching is to *exhort*. This is a call to urge truths upon hearers. It's a responsibility to exhort the listener to respond. And when we reprove, rebuke, and exhort, we are to do so "with complete patience and teaching." Change doesn't happen overnight. It requires persistence and forbearance. Patience and teaching must go together. The preacher is to be patient in his teaching, and he is to teach in his patience.

Patient teaching is necessary, "for the time is coming when people will not endure sound teaching, but having itching ears they will accumulate for themselves teachers to suit their own passions, and will turn away from listening to the truth" (4:3–4). Under these dire conditions, what must a preacher do? Paul tells Timothy in 4:5. First, "be sober" (NASB). That is, keep your head. "Endure suffering." The presence of pushback and conflict in no way invalidates the method or message of preaching. In fact, faithfulness in method and message may invite suffering. "Do the work of an evangelist." Whereas preaching primarily pertains to the church, and evangelism pertains primarily to the world, there is overlap. And "fulfill your ministry," a mandate that is clearly dependent on the faithful presentation and application of the Word of God. A preacher most fundamentally fulfills his ministry by "rightly handling the word of truth" (2:15). This is the preacher who is "approved, a worker who has no need to be ashamed."

In light of this, it should not surprise us that of the ninety-seven verbs in the New Testament for communicating God's Word, at least fifty-six are verbs that indicate declaration, verbs such as *kerusso* to "herald," *didasko* to "teach," or *laleo* to "speak." Alec Motyer correctly asserts that this emphasis should have pride of place before such verbs as *parakaleo* "to appeal," *deomai* "to plead, beseech," *peitho* "to persuade," or *noutheteo* "to counsel." "Our primary task is to make the truth plain."[13]

Conclusion

Making the *truth plain* is what an expository preacher does. When the main point of the text is the main point of the sermon, the preacher has the assurance that the Lord himself is coming to speak and act. That is, the Lord's power, authority, and presence are erupting to make things new. How else do you explain the change in affections that Steve and his wife experienced as they sat under a faithful expositor for five years? Because their pastor in Seattle was faithful to communicate the Divine Author's intentions in the Word and was clearly under the authority of God and his Word, he carried that authority as God's spokesman. And that is the only hope for bringing about enduring individual and corporate transformation and reformation. Martin Luther was asked how he accomplished what he did during the Reformation. His response: "I simply taught, preached, [and] wrote God's Word; otherwise I did nothing. . . . The Word did it all."[14]

---

13. Alec Motyer, *Preaching? Simple Teaching on Simple Preaching* (Fearn, Ross-shire, Scotland: Christian Focus, 2013), 103.

14. Quoted in Gordon Rupp, *Luther's Progress to the Diet of Worms* (New York: Harper and Row, 1964), 99, from *Works of Martin Luther* (Philadelphia: Muhlenberg Press, 1915), 2:399–400.

CONTEXT MATTERS: PART ONE

I should think myself in the way of my duty to raise the affections of my hearers as high as I possibly can provided that they are affected by nothing but the truth.[1]

Some time ago I (Payne) received a surprise e-mail from David, a friend from college. All he said in the e-mail was "You are the man." I knew that David had a purpose behind his statement; I just did not know what it was. So I responded, "David, I am not sure what you meant by your statement. Without a context it could mean several things. You could be accusing me of adultery, like Nathan did King David, 'You are the man!' But I have not committed adultery, so that cannot be it. You could be affirming me as an alpha male. However, I already know that, so that makes your e-mail pointless. Or, you may just be reaching out as a way of reestablishing contact. Could you please clarify?" He responded by telling me that I was overanalyzing.

I likely was. The e-mail was not that important, but it does serve to illustrate the point that without some context, I really could not

---

1. Jonathan Edwards, *The Works of Jonathan Edwards*, ed. Edward Hickman, 2 vols. (Carlisle, PA: Banner of Truth, 1992), 1:391.

accurately interpret his e-mail message. In fact, there was no certain meaning apart from context—only several possible meanings. Was David warning me or encouraging me? I understood the vocabulary and grammar of the brief sentence that David sent. However, I did not have context for that sentence, and when it comes to determining meaning, context is king. Since I had no accompanying context to his brief e-mail, I had no basis for knowing his meaning with any certainty. I assumed that he really did mean something, and a bit more context would have made his meaning apparent. In this case, the only way that I could know the context of his e-mail was to ask him to provide it. In the Bible, however, the Lord has provided us with context for all that he says. If we are inviting our hearers to "come and experience God with me in this text," we must always allow the God-given context to inform our interpretation of any and every Scripture; and when we do this, we have taken the first step in expository preaching.

Unfortunately, there are many preachers who do not honor this principle in their interpretation of the Bible. There are four ways that preachers violate the truth that a biblical author has a discernable meaning that is revealed through context. First, there are some who take a text, and then they stray off into saying something that has nothing to do with the text. Second, there are others who take a text, yet focus on some matter in the text that has little to do with the overall message of the author.[2] Third, there are those who teach the text, but they consistently preach without reference to the gospel, which is the overarching theme of the entire Bible. Therefore, they preach in such a way that would not get them expelled from a synagogue or offend the religious sensibilities of those who do not believe in Jesus Christ as Lord. Such preaching lacks

---

2. E.g., I recently heard a preacher on radio preaching from Genesis 29 where Jacob thinks he has married Rachel, but awakens in the morning, and "behold it was Leah!" The essence of the preacher's sermon was "when you think you married the wrong person." Now there is no doubt that the preacher was addressing a situation that many listeners may have had. However, was this really Moses's intention as he wrote this when Israel was making their way through the wilderness en route to the promised land? Did Moses think ahead and consider that there may be those in the covenant community who might feel like they married the wrong person? If this is not the meaning of the author, we ought not to manipulate Scripture to make it mean something that the author did not intend.

gospel centrality. Finally, there are those who preach the gospel, but they do not adequately deal with what the text actually says. Consequently, every sermon sounds the same because they fail to deal with the nuances of the particular text. Each of these four errors in their own unique way misrepresent what the Word says and, make no mistake, this is the highest expression of "bearing false witness."

This widespread mishandling of the Word of God is why I believe this chapter is necessary. I intend to clarify what expository preaching is. To accomplish my goal, I think it is important to make a distinction between what might be called the "macro-message" of Scripture (the message of the Bible as a whole) and the "micro-message" of any particular text. Why is this important? Again, the answer has to do with context. "The context of the word is the sentence. The context of the sentence is the paragraph. The context of the paragraph is the chapter. The context of the chapter is the book,"[3] and the real context of any Bible text is the whole Bible.[4] In other words, every verse has several contexts: the verses that appear on each side, the book of which it is part, the section of Scripture in which it is found, other texts dealing with the same theme, other books by the same author, and other books of the same genre. Ultimately, the most crucial context of any verse is the whole Bible.

The implication of this is that when I am interpreting a particular text, I start with the presupposition that the message of the text will complement the message of the whole Bible. In fact, if the Bible as a whole has a central theme (and it does) then every particular text in some way supports that theme. So, "The Scriptures in their entirety and in their particularity clarify which questions are important and which questions are not."[5] This is a significant point. A faithful expositor should seek

---

3. Bernard Lonergan, *Method in Theology* (Toronto: University of Toronto Press, 1971), 161.

4. Graeme Goldsworthy, *The Gospel and Kingdom* in *The Goldsworthy Trilogy* (Waynesboro, GA: Paternoster, 2000), 31. Richard Lints says, "The canon is a single work of God with diverse parts. It is not a single work of any human author, but divine authorization of the canon entails that it be read as a single work whose unity is complex. It must be read as a totality in order to understand it. Richard Lints, *Identity and Idolatry: The Image of God and its Inversion*, New Studies in Biblical Theology, ed. D. A. Carson (Downers Grove, IL: InterVarsity, 2015), 24.

5. Richard Lints, *The Fabric of Theology: A Prolegomenon to Evangelical Theology* (Grand Rapids, MI: Eerdmans, 1993), 293.

answers from the text that the text itself is asking. That is, it might appear that a particular text is asking one set of questions, but if it were to be approached from the broader perspective, it is likely that a different set of questions is more fundamental to the passage itself.[6] If I lose sight of the macro-message of the Bible, I will be more apt to interpret the parts in a manner that does not fit with the whole. Conversely, if I consider only the whole, then I will likely mute the parts and compromise the particular text.

So, how do we avoid this? This is the challenge for the preacher. How does he faithfully preach the macro-burden of the Bible while allowing each passage to speak on its own terms? That is, how does the preacher use his exegetical "magnifying glass" and study a text's particular details while at the same time employing his exegetical "fish-eye" lens to see how the immediate text relates to the whole?[7] In short, how do we read the Bible in "stereo" and avoid reading it in "mono?"[8]

Four horizons need to be considered in this quest: the *contextual* (immediate context), *covenantal* (context of the period of revelation), *canonical* (context of the entirety of revelation)[9] and *contemporary*[10] horizons. We will consider the first two in this chapter and the last two in the next.

---

6. Ibid., 293–94.

7. A term used by Bryan Chapell. He asserts, "Accurate expositors use both a magnifying glass and a fish-eye lens, knowing that a magnifying glass can unravel mysteries in a raindrop but can fail to expose a storm gathering on the horizon." Bryan Chapell, *Christ-Centered Preaching: Redeeming the Expository Sermon*, 2nd ed. (Grand Rapids, MI: Baker, 2005), 275.

8. A term employed by Gary Millar and Phil Campbell, who remind of a time when we listened to music before "stereo" and all of the sound came through one speaker. This was called listening in "mono." *Saving Eutychus: How to Preach God's Word and Keep People Awake* (Kingsford, Australia: Matthias Media, 2013), 79.

9. This is largely dependent on the three interpretive horizons proposed by Richard Lints—the *textual, epochal*, and *canonical* horizons. Lints, *The Fabric of Theology*, 293–311.

10. Strictly speaking, it is the first three horizons that are necessary to answer the "what?" question: What does the text mean? Each of these three horizons must be seriously considered as each horizon regulates the other two. However, the preacher has a responsibility that extends beyond this question. He must also answer the two-fold "so what?" and the "now what?" questions. This is the importance of the contemporary horizon.

Contextual Horizon

When my children were younger, I introduced them to the *Wizard of Oz*. Afterward, if you had asked them what the movie was about, they would have told you "flying monkeys." Of course, there were flying monkeys in the movie, but to say that flying monkeys is the central point would be wrongheaded at best. A simple analysis of the overall context of the movie would expose their cute, but nevertheless wrongheaded, thinking. Obviously, the story is about an exiled young girl and her little dog who, along with their new friends, overcome evil and make their way back home.

That's the real point, correct? It certainly is as far as the movie goes. However, the movie is based on the book by L. Frank Baum, and there are many who contend that the movie got it wrong. That is, the story as it appears in the book is really a political satire.[11] At the time when Baum wrote this story, one of the central political debates going on at the time was over the issue of whether America should continue to use the gold standard as the basis for the U.S. dollar or whether the switch should be made to silver. This background perhaps makes sense of the central line of the book, "Follow the yellow brick road." Recall that though the yellow brick road led to the Wizard, it turns out he was a fraud. Dorothy's actual hope resided in her shoes, which were *silver* in the book. Along these lines, the characters in the story represent different segments of society. The Scarecrow represents the farmers (no brains). The Tin Man represents the factory workers (no heart). Perhaps the cowardly lion represents the political leadership; the Wicked Witch of the East, the East Coast establishment, and the Wicked Witch of the West the West Coast establishment. Who is the heroine? Middle America—Dorothy from Kansas.

Now if this book is truly a political statement, it clearly reveals the importance of context. Without an understanding of the genre or the purpose of a work, it is likely that the meaning will be compromised.

---

11. This insight on *The Wizard of Oz* comes from J. Scott Duvall and J. Daniel Hays, *Grasping God's Word: A Hands-On Approach to Reading, Interpreting, and Applying the Bible*, 2nd ed. (Grand Rapids, MI: Zondervan, 2005), 175–76.

In coming to terms with the contextual horizon of the Bible, the preacher should aim to read the particular text according to the grammatical-historical method where he discerns God's intent through the human author's intent. Again, every text has a context. It does not take place in a vacuum. Words and sentences are a part of a larger conversation that is set within a particular historical situation. In particular, there are two contexts to consider in this horizon: the historical context and the literary context.

Historical Context

Broadly speaking, to respect the historical context means that the interpreter must learn as much as possible about the world from which the particular text emerges. Perhaps the most important question here is "Why was the book written?" The reason for which it was written becomes the reason for which the preacher preaches it. When considering this context, the interpreter studies the author and his audience. The principle here is that Scripture was God's Word to other people before it became God's Word to us. This leads us to a basic interpretive principle: For our interpretation of a text to be right, it must be consistent with the historical-cultural context of the particular text.

Literary Context

This context concerns the passages immediately preceding and following the text as well as the genre of the particular text. Also involved is the ability to perceive relations to writings such as quotations or allusions to the Old Testament. Unless we can grasp the whole before attempting to dissect the parts, our interpretation is doomed for failure. Without a situation to give a particular verse or passage context, it becomes meaningless. This may be the most crucial principle of biblical interpretation because context determines meaning. The Holy Spirit directed the human writers to connect their words, sentences, and paragraphs into a literary whole in the normal way that people use language to communicate.[12]

Discerning the literary context of any passage consists of three steps.[13] First, it requires the interpreter to identify how the book is divided into sections. There are signals, such as transition words (e.g. therefore, then, but); change of genre (e.g. from a greeting to a prayer); changes of topic or theme (main idea); changes in time, location, or setting; and grammatical changes (e.g. subject, object, pronouns, verb tense, person or number). Second, the interpreter needs to summarize the main idea of each section. Finally, the interpreter must explain how the particular passage relates to the surrounding sections.[14]

In short, "The meaning of words and phrases; the effort to understand the cultural distance between text and reader; the textual, historical, circumstantial, and social contexts; and the identification of genre, are the key elements" of this horizon.[15] We study the historical context of a text because God spoke originally to peoples living in cultures that are radically different from ours. In turn, we study the literary context of a text

---

12. Duvall and Hays raise the scenario of a man seeking counsel from Scripture about whether to propose to his girlfriend. As he dances around the Bible, he finds two verses that provide the answer he desires: 1 Corinthians 7:36c: "They should get married" and John 13:27: "What you are about to do, do quickly." But context protects us from committing this error. Indeed, the 1 Corinthians context reveals that Paul is actually saying that it's better not to marry. And in the passage from John, the phrase refers to Judas's betraying Jesus and has nothing to do with marriage. Duvall and Hays, *Grasping God's Word*, 119.

13. Ibid., 128.

14. With regard to the literary context, chapter and verse divisions created one of the biggest hurdles to the process of interpretation. It wasn't until the ninth and tenth centuries AD that verse divisions began to appear in the Hebrew Bible of the Jewish Masoretes. "The chapter and verse references do help us identify and locate passages quickly. . . . But unfortunately they have also contributed to the widespread practice of elevating individual verses to the status of independent units of thought. Each verse is treated like a complete expression of truth that, like a number in a phone book, has no connection to what precedes or follows—each is a "quote for the day" or "proof text" considered in isolation from its biblical context. There is simply no justification for routinely treating individual verses as independent thought units that contain autonomous expressions of truth. As written communication, readers must understand biblical statements as integral parts of the larger units where they occur. Detached from their contexts, individual verses may take on meanings never intended by their writers. To qualify as the text's intended meaning, an interpretation must be compatible with the total thought and the specific intention of the immediate context and the book context." William W. Klein, Craig L. Blomberg, Robert L. Hubbard Jr., *Introduction to Biblical Interpretation* (Nashville: Thomas Nelson, 2004), 217.

15. Dan McCartney and Charles Clayton, *Let the Reader Understand: A Guide to Interpreting and Applying the Bible*, 2nd ed. (Phillipsburg, NJ: P&R, 2002), 158.

because to fail to do so violates the way people use language to communicate. The contextual horizon is crucial. It is not, however, sufficient by itself. We also must consider the covenantal horizon that we might rightly understand the contextual horizon.

Covenantal Horizon

One of my childhood joys was going to Disney World, and one of the things I remember most about Disney World is its monorail system. In fact, this system is one of the most heavily used monorail systems in the world with over 150,000 daily riders. Now, why is this the case? Certainly there are better rides at Disney World than the monorail. Well, there's one reason: the monorail will take you to any place in the park. Analogously, you could say that in Scripture the covenants function somewhat like those monorails. They will take you to your desired destination—as long as your desired destination is Jesus Christ.

Thus far, we have considered the contextual horizon. Additionally, since God is the ultimate author of all sixty-six books of Scripture, it is crucial to discern what God is communicating in a particular text by relating that text to what God is communicating in the whole Bible. God did not accomplish his ultimate purpose all at once. He did not send Christ to be born of Eve by the gates of Eden, nor did he give the whole Bible to Moses at Sinai. Instead, God revealed himself to be the Lord of times and seasons (Acts 1:7), so the story of God's saving work is framed in periods of history that God determines by his word of promise.[16] In this horizon, we are seeking to read a particular text in light of where it is in redemptive history and in terms of the unfolding divine plan. In order to do this well, we need to know how to relate a particular text to the biblical covenants.

In an art museum, beautiful paintings are displayed in appropriate frames. Sometimes the frame is as beautiful as the painting! Someone who understands art has chosen an appropriate frame that complements the work of art that it contains. Understanding the covenants can

---

16. Edmund P. Clowney, *The Unfolding Mystery* (Phillipsburg, NJ: P&R, 1989), 12.

help you to frame a text in a setting that complements the message of the text.

Simply stated, a covenant is an agreement between two or more persons. Marriage is a covenant. The warranty on a new car is a covenant. An insurance policy is a covenant. In covenants between humans, each person involved has something that the other person(s) in the covenant wants or needs. So usually there is some bargaining that takes place between the persons involved. But since humans have nothing that God needs, that bargaining aspect of covenants is absent when God initiates the covenant. He imposes the regulations and conditions of the covenants he makes, and he graciously commits himself to bestow certain blessings when the obligations of the covenant are met. In the Bible, we read of various covenants that God has established with specific humans. We have texts of Scripture that God gave us when a particular covenant was or is in effect. Naturally, some of the requirements specified under a particular covenant may be unique to the covenant that was in effect when a text of Scripture was written. The same is true concerning some of the blessings. So, to give a couple of simple examples, under several of the covenants described in the Old Testament, God required animal sacrifices to be offered. With the coming of the new covenant, that requirement is no longer in effect. Since Jesus has offered himself as a sacrifice to satisfy divine justice and reconcile us to God, the practice of animal sacrifice has been abolished. Again, one of the blessings promised to Abraham was the inheritance of a physical land. Under the new covenant, God does not promise that Christians will inherit a particular plot of land in the world.[17] What he does promise is much better—Christians will inherit the earth—but the point here is that the promises made to Christians are based on a different covenant.

If you do not have a pretty good idea of the various covenants, it is likely that you will make some significant mistakes in your exposition and application of Scripture. Throughout history and right up

---

17. The covenants refine and extend the scope and nature of God's redemptive program, but they do not necessarily abolish all past covenants. For example, the new covenant does not abolish the Abrahamic covenant.

to this very day, within Christianity there have been sects and sometimes entire denominations whose distinguishing trait has emerged from a failure to distinguish between the covenants. The "health and wealth" denominations sometimes extract promises of the Old Covenant and misapply them to Christians. Some Christians maintain that the covenant with physical Israel is still in effect, while others insist that the promises made to physical Israel were fulfilled, and God is now concerned exclusively with spiritual Israel. And the disagreement between those who baptize only believers and those who baptize infants is a disagreement that is founded in the question regarding who is included in the new covenant.

As we saw in the preceding section of this chapter, coming to terms with the contextual horizon is foundational, but that horizon alone is insufficient. It is also crucial to determine the time of redemptive history in which the particular text is found and the notable sequences of events that distinguish a particular period of time from others. The key to marking out the crucial stages is by way of the covenants. The importance of covenants in the Bible is illustrated by the fact that we divide the Bible into two testaments, and *testament* is simply an old term for *covenant*.

The covenant is one of God's chief acts of self-revelation.[18] There are common ideas that are found in virtually all of the covenants, and the focal idea in comprehending the covenants is God's promise, "I will . . . be your God, and you shall be my people" (Lev 26:12). Having said this, there are several covenants in the Bible, and the potential for confusion exists. Yet, these complexities must not deter the preacher who desires to handle the Scriptures rightly. The covenants establish a framework that holds the biblical storyline together and helps set the context to understand the significance of Jesus Christ. So, while acknowledging the complexities, we assert that it is the notion of *promise* that is basic to the covenants. And, like a monorail system that leads to a centralized location, all the covenants ultimately find their fulfillment in Christ.

---

18. A helpful resource on the covenants is Peter J. Gentry and Stephen J. Wellum, *Kingdom Through Covenant: A Biblical-Theological Understanding of the Covenants* (Wheaton, IL: Crossway, 2012).

Although it is not within the parameters of the chapter to get too detailed on the discussion of the covenants, it is important at least to mention the covenants that God makes with humankind. The storyline moves from Adam, through Abraham, to Sinai, and issues in a promise of a *new covenant* whose advent is tied with the cross (Luke 22:20; 1 Cor 11:23–26). The major covenants in Scripture are as follows.[19]

Edenic Covenant (Gen 2:16–17)

In the Edenic covenant, Adam was assigned the responsibility of representing humanity. The word "covenant" is not used in the story of Adam, but the essential parts of a covenant are there: a definition of the parties involved, a legally binding set of provisions that stipulates the conditions of their relationship, the promise of blessings for obedience, and the condition for obtaining those blessings. As further evidence that there was a covenant with Adam in Eden, Hosea refers to the sins of Israel and says, "But like Adam they transgressed the covenant" (6:7). If Adam had obeyed this covenant, he would have been able to continue on as God's covenant servant, delighting in the favor of God.

Since Adam was the representative of the entire human race, every human who has descended from Adam in the ordinary way bears the consequences of Adam's failure to keep the terms of this covenant. "Sin came into the world through one man, and death through sin, and so death spread to all men because all sinned" (Rom 5:12).[20] This covenant makes clear that by simply being a descendant of Adam, every human already stands in covenant relationship with God, and that covenant has requirements that no one but Jesus has kept. It also speaks to why the Hebrew prophets would preach not only to Israel, but to the Gentile nations as well since they had broken the requirements of this first covenant. This is a crucial starting point for the gospel because unless a person knows that he is accountable to his Creator, there is no making

---

19. This section on the covenants is dependent on John Frame, *Systematic Theology: An Introduction to Christian Belief* (Phillipsburg, NJ: P&R, 2013), 62–84.

20. Should someone object that it is unfair that the consequences of one man's disobedience should plunge all humans into a state of sin and misery, remember that the way of salvation is offered to us through one man's obedience (Rom 5:19).

sense of the need for the Messiah. That is, since Adam was the representative head of the human race, we have all sinned through him (Rom 5:12–21). This means that Adam's sin is our sin (Rom 5:19), and his guilt our guilt (Rom 5:16–17). It is understanding this bad news that makes sense of the good news of the "last Adam."

Covenant of Grace

Humans cannot be saved from sin and its consequences by keeping the Edenic covenant because such obedience can never erase Adam's sin, and no one but Jesus ever comes even close to perfect obedience. Early in Genesis, God reveals his intention to save a people through a man who will come from the seed of the woman. This man will crush the head of Satan (3:15). This becomes the mother promise of the Bible, and is evidence that God has already initiated a covenant of grace.

Noahic Covenant (Gen 6:8, 18; 9:9–17)

God's covenant of grace continues for the remainder of Scripture, until the final judgment. The Noahic covenant is a promise of a new creation and embraces all humanity. This covenant promises a stage for God's redemptive drama to play out until the "seed" of the woman comes. In that sense, it is a covenant of saving grace. Yet, it is also a covenant of common grace, in that God's forbearance toward all humanity is essentially embedded in the overall promise.

Abrahamic Covenant (Gen 12; 15; 17; 22)

This covenant illumines the way in which God will fulfill the blessing promised to Noah for all flesh and bring about the promise of Genesis 3:15. The covenant comes off the heels of God's judgment on the nations (Gen 11:1–9). Now the question is raised: How will this blessing come to the nations? The answer is clear: through a promised son. In an awe-inspiring covenant ceremony, God swears to Abraham that he will not forget his promises to him and to his seed (Gen 15; 17:2; Jer 34:18–20). Abraham received God's promises by faith, and it was counted to him as righteousness (Gen 15:6).

The Covenant with Israel (Mosaic Covenant)

Importantly, this covenant begins with the sovereign grace of God who delivered Israel from Egypt and redeemed her for himself. This deliverance was not based on Israel's brilliance (Deut 7:7–8) or her righteousness (Deut 9:5–6), but on divine love. Importantly, God's establishing his covenant with Israel was in fulfillment of the promises made to Abraham. It is as the God of Abraham, Isaac, and Jacob that God calls Moses to deliver his people from Egypt (Exod 3:6). The covenant was *dependent* on the Abrahamic covenant; but unlike the Abrahamic covenant, which was largely unconditional, the obedience of Israel was the *means* to experience covenant blessing in their lives, and disobedience brought about covenant curses. In this sense it republishes the covenant with creation and makes life conditional upon obedience. In doing this, it anticipates and leads men to Jesus, who delivers from the curse and brings life through his obedience. Israel, through fidelity to the covenant, was to be God's witness to the nations of the world (Isa 43:10–12; 44:8), which will ultimately bring Israel together with the other nations (Isa 19:23–25).

The Davidic Covenant (2 Sam 7; 1 Chron 17; cf. Pss 89; 110; 132)

God had promised Abraham (Gen 17:6, 16) and Jacob (Gen 35:11) that their family would include kings. The office of king would be a natural development in the conquest of the land (Deut 17:14–20), and divine requirements were placed on the office. The king must be an Israelite (Deut 17:15), and must be faithful to God's law (Deut 17:18–20). In time, and in fulfillment of the promise made to Judah (Gen 49:8–12), God makes a covenant with David.

The Davidic covenant is also a partial fulfillment and means of fulfillment of the Abrahamic covenant. Like the Abrahamic, the Davidic covenant consists of promises to David and is *unconditional*. God's intention to fulfill the promise is repeated in the subsequent history of the Davidic kings despite constant rebellion (see 1 Kgs 11:11–13, 34–36; 15:4–5). Yet, an uninterrupted reign in Israel by David's descendants was *conditional* (see 1 Chr 28:5–6; 1 Kgs 2:2–4). The great *name* promise of the Abrahamic covenant has been passed to the Davidic king (2 Sam 7:9; 1 Chr 17:8) as well as the promise of a great nation (cf. Gen 12:2). Hence, under the *Davidic king*, the Abrahamic promise of a "great nation" and "name" come together. The ultimate fulfillment of the Abrahamic covenant corresponds with the ultimate fulfillment of the Davidic. The final fulfillment of the Abrahamic promise of blessing in a land will take place under the rule of a Davidic king. David's greater Son will be King over all, the promised seed of the woman crushing the serpent and ruling the lands of the earth, extending God's promised blessing to the nations (Gal 3:16–29). Thus the Davidic king becomes the mediator of the covenant.

The New Covenant (Jer 31:31–34; cf. Heb 8; 10; see Ezek 34; 36–37; Isa 40–66)

When we turn to the New Testament, we pass from the context of prediction to that of fulfillment. The things that God had promised through types and promises he has now brought to accomplishment in Jesus Christ, who is the seed of the woman, the seed of Abraham, and the seed of David. The foundation-stone of the New Creation is now in place. Jesus Christ is the central theme of the Bible, and the *new covenant* is the name for the new relationship that we have with God through Jesus.

This new covenant will have a purpose similar to the Mosaic covenant in that it brings the blessing of the Abrahamic covenant into the present experience of the new, spiritual Israel. And unlike the Mosaic covenant, that blessing comes through the obedience of the True Israel, Jesus Christ. The new covenant will also be different from the old. Everyone now in the covenant will know God in a saving way (Jer 31:31–34).

How can this be? How can God forgive sin without going back on his word that sin must be punished? In an enlightening passage, God revealed himself to Moses and said to him that he was a God full of *steadfast love and faithfulness* (Exod 34:6), which obligates him to bring to fruition the blessings that he has promised, whatever it may cost him personally to do that. He will forgive "iniquity, transgressions, and sin" yet, interestingly, he "will by no means clear the guilty." How is this tension resolved? The righteousness *of* God, which is our judgment, must become the righteousness *from* God, which is our hope.

That is the essence of the new covenant: Jesus our substitute was faithful to God's covenant, and he bore the curse due to our disobedience in order that God's blessing might be ours (Gal 3:13–14). God's *steadfast love* has been poured out upon us, whatever the cost to himself—even his Son's death. That brings us to the third and fourth horizons: the canonical horizon and the contemporary horizon.

CONTEXT MATTERS: PART TWO

Canonical Horizon

On November 22, 1963, President John F. Kennedy died. Why did he die? That could be answered in a "thin" way, which so oversimplifies the reason that the answer is compromised. Or, it could be answered in a "thick" way, where a more robust meaning is found. A correct but thin answer may assign the cause to the pulling of a trigger, the impact of a bullet, or the anatomical damage caused by the bullet. A more thorough and thick answer might take into account the various persons and events that led up to the tragic assassination of a president. Both answers would be descriptions of the same act, but they work on different explanatory levels. The first answer is thin when compared to the last. Thin descriptions result from using too narrow a context to interpret a particular action. It is possible to interpret texts, like actions, at various levels of complexity. Thin descriptions of particular texts "suffer from a poverty of meaning."[1] While each level produces helpful descriptions, we cannot claim to have come to terms with the true meaning until we consider the

---

1. Ideas in this paragraph were influenced by Kevin Vanhoozer, "Exegesis and Hermeneutics," in *New Dictionary of Biblical Theology: Exploring the Unity and Diversity of Scripture*, eds. T. Desmond Alexander, Brian S. Rosner, D. A. Carson, Graeme Goldsworthy (Downers Grove, IL: InterVarsity, 2000), 61–62.

text in its context of the completed canon. Considering a text this way is what we mean by thick description. It is only in the final form of the text that we understand the divine speech act in its completeness. Therefore, the overall context of the entire Bible is crucial for determining what the authors, human and divine, are ultimately saying in individual texts.[2] In order to understand each text, we must always consider how it fits in the canonical horizon.

Canon is the term scholars use to refer to all the books of the Bible, so the canonical horizon is the context of the whole Bible. The meaning of any text can be fully understood only in the context of the Bible as a whole. Texts that might be interpreted in one way when isolated from the rest of Scripture are seen to have a different meaning when considered in the canonical horizon. As noted in the preceding chapter, coming to terms with the contextual horizon is the means of finding the original, basic meaning of a text. Yet understanding that contextual horizon establishes only the initial core meaning of the text and not the total meaning of a text. Ultimately, the entire Bible leads up to God's redemptive work accomplished through Jesus Christ, and the revelation of Christ is progressive throughout the Old Testament. Later revelation reflects earlier revelation and brings it to completion.[3]

In confirmation of this concept, consider that the New Testament asserts that "all the promises of God" find their "yes" in Jesus (2 Cor 1:20). That is, Jesus constitutes the defining chapter of the entire biblical narrative, the basis upon which everything else in creation makes sense. There is continuity between the promises that God has made and his fulfillment of those promises. This is crucial to our understanding of Scripture in its canonical horizon.[4]

---

2. Ibid., 62.

3. The Christian interpreter of Scripture ought to be able to see truth that may not have been evident to the original human author or audience. A helpful illustration is that of an acorn that grows into a mighty oak tree. By merely looking at an acorn, no one can see the full end result. But from a later viewpoint, one can look back and recognize how the oak tree gradually grew out of an acorn. It is important to clarify, though, that the divinely intended meaning of any particular text is organically related to the human author's intention. See McCartney and Clayton, *Let the Reader Understand*, 162–65.

4. Lints, *Fabric of Theology*, 303.

This is one main reason why the interpreter of the Old Testament must think in terms of the *promise-fulfillment* theme. We have already considered the importance of the covenants, and the covenantal horizon is studded with the bright stars of God's fulfilled promises; but let us proceed to consider eight other ways that the Old Testament points beyond itself to Jesus Christ: prophecies, pictures, presence, providence, people, precepts, problems, promises fulfilled.[5]

Prophecies

These are explicit promises that find their fulfillment in some way in Jesus.[6] Anthony Hoekema summarizes the Old Testament prophetic hopes:[7]

1. The expectation of the coming Messiah (Gen 3:15; 22; 49:10; Deut 18:15; 2 Sam 7:12–13; Psalm 110; Isa 7:14; 9:6–7; 11:1ff; 42:1–4; 49:5–7; 52:13–53:12; 61:1ff; Dan 7:13–14; Ezekiel 34).
2. The coming kingdom of God: (Isa 9:6–7; 11:1ff; Dan 7:13–14).
3. The new covenant (Ezekiel 36; Jer 31:31ff; cf. Heb 8; 10:16–17; Rom 11:27).
4. The restoration of Israel (Isa 11:11; 49:8ff; cf. 2 Cor 6:2).
5. The outpouring of the Holy Spirit (Ezekiel 36; Joel 2:28ff; cf. Acts 2:17ff).
6. The approach of the Day of the Lord (Obad 15–16; Joel 1:15; 2:1–17; Isaiah 13; Amos 5:18–20).
7. The creation of a new heaven and new earth (Isa 65:17; 66:22; cf. Revelation 21–22).

Pictures

There are pictures of Christ in the Old Testament. These pictures are often called types, and they function in a way similar to prophecies. You

---

5. Murray offers the first seven, I (Payne) add the eighth. David Murray, *How Sermons Work* (Carlisle, PA: Evangelical Press, 2011), 53–56.

6. Many of these promises are fulfilled inaugurally in Jesus's first advent and will be fulfilled consummately in his second advent.

7. Anthony Hoekema, *The Bible and the Future* (Grand Rapids: Eerdmans, 1994), 3–12.

might call types "incarnational prophecies." Sometimes, historical persons are pictures or types of Christ. For example, consider how many correlations there are between Joseph and Jesus. We only scratch the surface when we note that both were betrayed by brothers, both endured a time of deep humiliation, both were exalted to positions of authority, and both brought great joy to their fathers. Moses, too, is a type of Christ. Moses led Israel out of political slavery in Egypt, and Jesus saved his people from sin's bondage. Moses led Israel into a land flowing with milk and honey, and Jesus leads his people into the new Eden,[8] that is, the new creation, which has both a present and future reality. Melchizedek, David, Solomon, and others are clearly types or pictures of Christ. Many of the Old Testament rituals, and even objects, are also clearly typological, and identified to be such in the New Testament. Christ is the rock that followed Israel in the desert (1 Cor 10:4), the manna (John 6:31–35), our Sabbath (Matt 11:28; 12:8), our Passover lamb (1 Cor 5:7), and on and on. Typology rests on the reality that the way God moved in the Old Testament was preparatory and anticipatory of the work of Christ. So as people note the "type" of thing God has done, and interpret these patterns in light of the promises God has made, they are provoked to expect God to act in the future as he has acted in the past.[9]

Presence

There are occasions in the Old Testament when God appears and speaks to man, and these appearances point forward to the incarnation of Immanuel, God with us. For instance, in Exodus 3, the "Angel of the LORD" appears to Moses at the "mountain of God" (Exod 3:1–2), and this very person is called "Yahweh" and "God" in 3:4. Earlier, in Genesis 16:7–13, Hagar has an encounter with the angel of YHWH, and she responds: "You are a God of seeing" (Gen 16:13). Later, in Genesis 22:11–12, the "angel of YHWH" calls out to Abraham and says, "You have not withheld your son . . . from me" (in context, "me" is God). One final example

---

8. James M. Hamilton Jr., *What Is Biblical Theology?: A Guide to the Bible's Story, Symbolism, and Patterns* (Wheaton, IL: Crossway, 2014), 77–79.

9. Ibid., 79.

is Judges 13:21–22, where Manoah realizes he has been speaking to the "angel of YHWH" and cries, "We have seen God." At the same time, the angel of YHWH is described as subordinate to YHWH in Zechariah 1:12, where it is recorded that the angel of YHWH prays to YHWH. The angel of YHWH is equal to YHWH yet submissive to YHWH. Do you think the people were being prepared for someone? These Christophanies (pre-incarnate manifestations of Christ) are clearly preparing God's people for the incarnation.

Providence

"God's works of providence are his most holy, wise, and powerful preserving and governing all his creatures and all their actions"[10] In his providence, God governs everything and every person in creation; and in the Bible we read especially of how God has been at work in history to prepare the world for Jesus and his ministry. All of redemptive history has an end that finds its fulfillment in Jesus. God has a plan for both his creation and his creatures. To be concise, the supreme revelation of God's purpose in history is the coming of Jesus into the world. This truth is affirmed by John, who asserts that Jesus is the "alpha and omega" (Rev 1:8; 21:6; 22:13), the "beginning and the end" (22:13), and the "first and the last" (1:17; 2:8; 22:13). Indeed, "the person and work of Christ constitute the defining chapter of the whole narrative, the hinge of history; the basis upon which everything else in creation makes sense."[11]

Therefore, in short, when preaching about Old Testament characters and events, it is crucial to remember that redemptive history has unfolded according to a specific purpose. It is on a trajectory that leads to Jesus.

Persons

Jesus said, "Your father Abraham rejoiced that he would see my day. He saw it and was glad (John 8:56). John writes that Isaiah saw Christ's glory

---

10. The Baptist Catechism.
11. John Stackhouse, Jr., *Evangelical Landscapes: Facing Critical Issues of the Day* (Grand Rapids, MI: Baker, 2002), 166.

and spoke of him (John 12:41). Hebrews 1–10 reveals Jesus in all of his glory and sufficiency. Hebrews 11 then sets forth the gospel faith of the Old Testament believers. Implicitly and explicitly it is communicated that their faith was in Christ (11:26). Therefore, when preaching about Old Testament saints, it is crucial to remember that they, like us, were saved by grace alone through faith alone in Christ alone.

Precepts

God's precepts (or his law), were never intended as the way of salvation. Its purpose was to show the people's need of a Savior and to foster grateful obedience in response. That is why God's law is framed in a redemptive context in both Exodus 19:4 and Exodus 20:2. In other words, "The Lamb came before the Law. The pattern was redemption, relationship, response and reward."[12] That is always the order of the divine saving economy with humankind.

Problems

Another way the Old Testament points beyond itself to Jesus is that it presents problems that only Jesus can solve or fix: the curse, our moral inability to keep the law, our alienation from God and neighbor, and more. In fact, it is not an overstatement to say that one of the central purposes of the Old Testament is to make the definitive case that we need the Messiah.

Promises Fulfilled

Jesus began his public ministry by announcing that *the time has been fulfilled, and the kingdom of God is at hand* (Mark 1:15). Nowhere did Jesus define what he meant by the phrase "the kingdom of God," and this indicates that he assumed the idea was familiar to his listeners. So this concept would have been a broad way of saying that all of the Old Testament hopes and promises fall under this realm, the kingdom of God, which is the saving rule of God as expressed in his conquering messianic Davidic King.

---

12. Murray, *How Sermons Work*, 55.

In the New Testament we discover that the *fulfillment* of the great event of "the last days"[13] predicted by the Old Testament has *already* occurred. Because of Jesus's coming, the New Testament writers express a clear consciousness that they are already living in "the last days" (Mark 1:15; Acts 2:17; Gal 4:4; 1 Cor 10:11; 2 Tim 3:1ff; Heb 1:1; 9:26; 1 John 2:18). The "mystery" revealed in the New Testament is that what the Old Testament writers seemed to portray as one movement must now be recognized as involving two stages: there is an overlap of two ages—that is, "the age to come" has intruded into the "present age." The New Testament claims that when Jesus came to earth he inaugurated the "last days" by bringing into the "present age" the "powers of the age to come" (Heb 6:5). But the New Testament also affirms that the "not yet" is still to come (see John 6:39; 11:24; 12:48). The relation between these two stages of the "last days" is that the present blessings *already* brought by Jesus guarantee the greater blessings *yet to come* (Acts 1:11; Titus 2:11–13; Heb 9:27). Yes, Christian expectation and hope is rooted in what God has already begun in the past in Jesus. Additionally, the New Testament writers expect a future consummation of God's purposes based upon Christ's victory in the past. This is at the heart of the canonical horizon.

Summary of the Three Horizons

We have been discussing the importance of interpreting Scripture in light of the first three interpretive horizons—the contextual, covenantal, and canonical. Doing so will help our interpretation to progress from a "thin" understanding of a particular text to a "thick" understanding. This may seem a bit abstract, so an example would likely help in order to make the overall argument a bit more concrete.

Consider the episode of the golden calf, recorded in Exodus 32. We read that Moses pleads with God and changes God's mind.[14] This narra-

---

13. "The latter day"/ "last days"/ "days to come" refers to a future that reverses the present situation and at the same time brings to a fitting outcome that toward which it is striving (Bruce Waltke, *An Old Testament Theology*, 154). This is synonymous with the kingdom of God.

14. This is the example Lints gives in his *Fabric of Theology*, 293–94.

tive is intimately linked with the covenantal significance of Moses as a mediator of the covenant and the canonical significance of his action as a foreshadowing of Christ. These horizons help the preacher define which questions are important to the particular narrative and which are not. If I fail to consider the covenantal and canonical horizons, this might lead me into the error of reading the narrative too narrowly, that is, too "thinly." For example, I might focus on the issue of prayer and its efficacy. Sure, effectual prayer is an important application of this narrative, but it is not the ultimate message. Or, I might focus on the issue of whether prayer can actually change God's mind. Again, this is an important discussion. Yet, this is not the fundamental meaning of the text. So, what the preacher might see as central to a text may actually be a peripheral issue when the text is considered from the viewpoint of the covenantal and canonical horizons.

We do not want to be "peripheral" preachers. We desire for the message of the text to be the message of the pulpit, and the message of the text and of the Bible as a whole centers on the person and work of Jesus as the goal of history. It is this "thick" understanding of the Bible as a unified story of redemption centered on the person and work of Jesus Christ as the ground of God's grace to us that primes the listener to respond with the obedience of faith.

That is why after his programmatic passage in Titus 2:11–14, where he speaks of Jesus giving himself "for us to redeem us" as a "people for his own possession who are zealous for good works," Paul instructs Titus to "declare these things" (Titus 2:11–15). Moreover, in Titus 3, after speaking of God's "goodness," "loving kindness," "mercy," and "Holy Spirit" being poured out on us "through Jesus Christ," Paul again wrote, "I want you to insist on these things, so that those who have believed in God may be careful to devote themselves to good works" (Titus 3:8). It is clear that these glorious truths that are "in accordance with the gospel of the glory of the blessed God" (1 Tim 1:11) demand a response from the listener. Furthermore, these are the realties that the preacher is to "declare" and "insist on" as the message of his pulpit. This leads us to the fourth and final horizon for preaching, the contemporary horizon.

Contemporary Horizon

When I was about to begin my ministry at the current church I pastor, someone encouraged me to read William Still's book, *The Work of the Pastor*. I did read it, and I have not regretted doing so. In chapter one, Still issues a call to pastors to feed the sheep of God. In that remarkable chapter he asserts: "Israel's sheep were reared, fed, tended, retrieved, healed and restored for sacrifice on the altar of God. This end of all pastoral work must never be forgotten that its ultimate aim is to lead God's people to offer themselves up to Him in total devotion of worship and service."[15] This is the goal of all preaching. In other words, preaching is not sufficient if all the preacher has done has answered the "what?" question of meaning. He must also answer the "so what?" (why this text is important) and the "now what?" (how the listeners should respond) questions as well.

The first three horizons have centered on the task of interpreting Scripture. Yet, if we become proficient only at interpreting Scripture, we will miss the point for which our lives were given to us: glorifying Jesus with our *lives*. That is, if our exegesis of a text is accurate but we do not tell our people how to apply it, then we have fallen short as preachers. When we remember to preach in light of this contemporary horizon we assert that Scripture is as relevant to our people as it was to the original audience.

Ultimately, this horizon is intended to communicate that in light of what God has done supremely in his Son, we have responsibilities to live in light of the gospel. As Paul exhorts: "Only let your manner of life be worthy of the gospel of Christ" (Phil 1:27). The gospel informs behavior. We need to preach with a special eye to connecting the Gospel with behavior. For instance, in 1 Corinthians 6, Paul appeals to the church to flee sexual immorality (6:18). He reminds them of the Gospel as the supreme motivating fact for their sexual purity (1 Cor 6:20).

---

15. William Still, *The Work of the Pastor*, rev. ed., (Fearn, Ross-Shire, Scotland: Christian Focus, 2010), 17.

Another example is found in 2 Corinthians 8:9. Paul is collecting funds for Christians who were in financial need. He desires for the church to contribute to the fund. He writes, "I say this not as a command" (8:8). In this case, he does not insist with the authority of an apostle; rather, he cites the gospel as a motivation towards generosity: "You know the grace of our Lord Jesus Christ, that though he was rich, yet for your sake he became poor, so that you by his poverty might become rich" (8:9).

When contemporizing a text, in some way the gospel answers the "what?" question with regard to ultimate things for the believer, and that very gospel demands a further response. There are the "so what?" and the "now what?" questions that the preacher must answer.

Without connecting the contemporary listener to the gospel, admonitions will ultimately prove ineffective because the listener will either not be sufficiently motivated to respond, or he will be wrongly motivated. Without connecting the gospel to the contemporary listener's behavior, the listener could be deluded into thinking that practical response is unnecessary. A big part of the preacher's job in preaching is to make the connection from the truth of the text to the practical response of the listener.

Conclusion

As preachers our aim is not to be clever moralizers; we desire to be expositors of God's Word and to preach the message of the text of Scripture. We believe the authority of God is in the text, not in our creative imagination. We have looked at four horizons that are necessary to understanding the text: the contextual, covenantal, canonical, and contemporary horizons. Studying God's Word with these horizons in view helps us to make the message of the ancient text fresh, relevant, and practical to our listeners. We are getting ready to invite them, "Come and experience God with me in this text."

PREACHING THROUGH BOOKS

The unfolding of your words gives light;
it imparts understanding to the simple.[1]

Recently, I (Payne) visited an elderly lady who was in the hospital. She had broken her hip the night before, and her husband had called me with deep concern. Upon entering her hospital room, I immediately saw that she was in great pain. She had beads of sweat across her forehead and face. When she saw me, she forced a smile and said, "Hello, pastor, thanks for coming to see me." It was her follow-up words for which I was unprepared. "Pastor, can I ask you a question?" "Sure," I responded. She then asked, "Why do you keep preaching on elders?" After the initial shock of the question, my first thought was, *Obviously there are more painful things to endure than broken hips.* For this lady, the subject of elders was clearly a concern. After I recovered from her surprising question, I was able to respond to her, "Well, it's not that I have an ax to grind; it's just that I keep coming to the subject of elders in the text, and the text drives my sermons." She nodded her head, and the issue was dropped.

---

1. Psalm 119:130.

At the time of this hospital visit, I was near the end of a year-long sermon series in the Pastoral Epistles, and obviously, there is much to be said in those epistles on the office of elder. At the time of this writing, my church has a single-pastor model of leadership, and it was evidently concerning to at least one person that we might transition to the plural-elder model of church leadership. But here is the point: after numerous sermons through 1 Timothy, 2 Timothy, and Titus, no one can deny that the subject of elders is a subject that commonly occurs in the Pastoral Epistles, and no one can rightly accuse me of having a bully pulpit concerning the subject of elders. Why? Because my approach to preaching is to preach consecutively through books of the Bible, a method that has historically been called the *lectio continua*[2] method of preaching. In following this method, the text has not only set the agenda for my pulpit, it has established the content of my pulpit as well.

A qualification is in order here. Expository preaching does not require the preacher to preach through books. One can preach faithful expositions *textually*, where the preacher may, for instance, preach a passage from Matthew one week, and one from Exodus the following week. Expositors do this all the time when they preach as a guest somewhere. But having granted this concession, it is our conviction that as a general rule, the congregation will benefit from a *main diet* of preaching consecutively through books. In this chapter, my goal is to convince you of this. I will lay out six broad benefits of preaching consecutively through books. There is no particular order of importance to these arguments, but I hope that through all these arguments, you will become convinced that preaching through books is the best way to preach the whole counsel of God. If you already hold to this position, I hope I can strengthen you in your convictions. I will consider the preacher's personal benefits, pastoral benefits, prophetic benefits, priestly benefits, preaching benefits, and the practical benefits.

---

2. Translated literally, "continuous reading."

Personal Benefits

A first argument for the *lectio continua* method is that it helps the preacher personally to grow in knowledge and obedience by his disciplined encounter *with* and immersion *in* God's Word. Because the under-shepherd cannot lead his flock where he himself is not going, this may be the most fundamental argument for this method. This is not to say that preachers who do not employ the *lectio continua* method are not immersed in God's Word; but in the proposed method, immersion in the text is virtually inevitable. By definition, you are seeking to come to terms with what the author is saying in the particular text and how it fits with the overall argument of the book, and why it matters. In other words, you are asking and answering the "what?" of the text, the "so what?" of the text, and the "now what?" of the text; and this discipline, week in and week out, brings enormous benefit to the preacher even before it benefits the congregation.

Although my own experience is simply anecdotal, I believe that many expositors would share the same testimony that preaching through books teaches us more and challenges us more personally than does any other discipline in our lives. For instance, although I spent nine years as a full-time seminary student, nothing has contributed to my growth as a Christian and a minister like preaching through books of the Bible. Each week, as I prepare for a new sermon(s), I am graciously confronted anew with a text that addresses my fallen condition and reminds me of the lordship of God over my condition. Because this is a weekly, indeed a daily, discipline, it has grown me exponentially in the knowledge of Scripture and in my own sanctification.

My experience is consistent with the apostle Paul's counsel to his son in the ministry, Timothy. In 1 Timothy 4, he speaks to Timothy, his protégé, on how to "be a good servant of Christ Jesus," which is parallel to "being trained in the words of the faith and of the good doctrine" (1 Tim 4:6). The word *trained* (*entrephomai*) can be translated "nourished." The good servant is actually *nourished* in the "words of the faith" and "good doctrine."

In fact, "good doctrine" is so crucial in the formation of the preacher that Paul adds in 4:7 that the good servant is not to invest in trivial matters not taught in Scripture. Instead he focuses on only those things that can promote godliness for both the preacher and the church. And godliness is not automatic. It is something we grow into (cf. Titus 2:11–12). It happens through the means of *training*—similar to the sort of vigorous training that might go on in a gymnasium. In fact, our word *gymnasium* comes from the same Greek words that are used in 1 Timothy 4:7–8. When we train in a gymnasium, we might use barbells or exercise machines to help us gain strength, stamina, and other features of a healthy body. In the realm of spiritual health, the context of this passage clearly reveals that the training is centered on "the words of the faith" and "sound doctrine." It is this teaching that "accords with godliness" (1 Tim 6:3; Titus 1:1), and "godliness . . . holds promise for the present life and also for the life to come" (1 Tim 4:8).

So to summarize, the "good servant of Christ Jesus," which is clearly the elder/overseer, is *nourished* and *trained* by the "words of the faith" and "sound doctrine." It is to "this end we toil and strive" (1 Tim 4:10). Toiling and striving will involve "devoting" oneself to "exhortation," and to "teaching" (1 Tim 4:13). Moreover, the preacher is to "practice these things," and he is to "immerse" himself in these things to the point that his progress is evident to everyone (1 Tim 4:15). In short, Timothy, and every pastor/elder after him, is to keep a "close watch" on himself and "on the teaching." Pastors are to "persist in this, for by so doing you will save both yourself and your hearers" (1 Tim 4:16).

Paul says there are two things to which Timothy must give attention: the first is himself (cf. 4:7b); the second is the *teaching*. Paul is connecting Timothy's salvation and the listener's salvation with faithfulness in "teaching." It is not just any teaching that the pastor arbitrarily devises. *Teaching* appears fifteen times in the Pastoral Epistles and involves a systematic explanation of the word (cf. 2 Tim 3:15–4:2).

Therefore, one reason for preaching through books is that it is a prime way for the preacher to keep a close watch on himself and on his teaching. This is how it personally benefits him. Paul says the stakes are high here—salvation (1 Tim 4:16). There is no greater personal benefit than that.

Pastoral Benefits

When you pastor a church, you are privy to issues in the church body that may be highly sensitive in nature. In fact, members will confess issues to you that they do not want to be widely known. It may be issues with their children, their finances, private sins, or their marriage—highly charged issues or delicate concerns that you, in your weak humanity, likely would not address from the pulpit if they could be avoided. As Derek Thomas perceptively asks, "Why would a preacher desire to choose as his subject divorce, or polygamy, or incest other than the fact that they arise naturally in the course of exposition?"[3]

However, you cannot play the avoidance game when you preach through books. The text sets the agenda and no one can justly charge you with insensitivity when they know this is your method. For instance, a few years ago, I was pastoring in Cincinnati, Ohio, and one of our leading laymen was arrested for a horrible crime. It made the front page of the local paper and was the lead story on the local news. I was preaching through Joshua at the time, and I happened to be in a text that very next Sunday that addressed the very nature of his sin and crime. It was a remarkable providence. God let me deal with the issue without the appearance that I was piling on my friend. This allowed our church to renew our minds in the Word of God concerning the issue, without the concern of being charged with callousness. If I had been a topical preacher or a preacher who chooses a different text each week, I would not have addressed that sensitive and potentially volatile issue that week, and maybe not at all. But because I happened to come to that very issue in the text that I came to in my exposition that week, I was able to address that particular issue in a pastoral way that ministered to the church in a timely manner.

---

3. Derek Thomas, "Expository Preaching," in *Feed My Sheep: A Passionate Plea for Preaching*, ed. Don Kistler (Morgan, PA: Soli Deo Gloria Ministries), 89.

When it comes to sensitive issues, one issue that has increasingly become a hot topic in the culture is homosexuality. I am aware of several families in my church who have loved ones who are engaged in that lifestyle. In my frail humanity, I might not have the courage to address this controversial issue if I were a textual or topical preacher. But because I preach through books, I have addressed that sin several times and no one can rightly accuse me of insensitivity.

In fact, there may come a day in the future when preaching for repentance from certain sins could be considered a "hate crime." If a preacher picks and chooses his topics and texts in an arbitrary fashion, it will be very easy for him to rationalize his neglecting to address those issues that are deemed taboo. But short of that potentially dangerous future, even now a caring pastor does not want to give the impression that he is trying to deal with a member's private and embarrassing issue in a public manner from the pulpit. In the average church, it is possible that someone might mistake your motive, since most churches are relatively small in number. According to the Barna Group, the average Protestant church size in America is eighty-nine adults, and 60 percent of Protestant churches have fewer than one hundred adults in attendance. So if you are a pastor in one of these smaller churches, and you know sensitive information, it is possible that you may not broach many issues that might come across as hurtful or insulting to someone in the congregation. But if you preach through books of the Bible, then sooner or later you will have the opportunity (and obligation) to forthrightly address the issues that come up in the text. So there are pastoral benefits to preaching through books.

Prophetic Benefits

P. T. Forsyth perceptively argued that the church has historically been most effective when "she did not lead the world, nor echo it; she confronted it."[4] But it is one thing to confront the culture in general, it is

---

4. P. T. Forsyth, *Positive Preaching and the Modern Mind* (Milton Keynes, Exeter, UK: Paternoster Press Reprint, 1998), 73. Quoted in Timothy Keller, *Preaching: Communicating Faith in an Age of Skepticism* (New York: Viking, 2015), 96.

altogether another thing to prophetically confront the issues in your local church with the people you know and interact with on a daily basis. And when it comes to controversy, the church is no stranger. Typically, controversy comes to the local church when members disagree over doctrine or when some carnal, sinful situation arises that must be addressed. Preaching through books is a tempered and patient way to prophetically address both types of controversies without appearing reactionary and paranoid to your flock.

For instance, one of the doctrinal controversies I had early on in my ministry was the issue over election and predestination (even though when the controversy started, up to that point I had never addressed either doctrine in a sermon). A couple who had joined our church three months earlier (and had been through a new members' class with me where I addressed doctrine and answered questions about doctrine) sent out a broadcast e-mail to the other members of the church accusing me of having a theological agenda concerning these doctrines. It was untrue, except I would gladly confess that my agenda is that our people grow in the grace and knowledge of our Lord Jesus Christ.

I called for a special meeting on a Wednesday night to address the charge, and I was able to say at the time, "I have preached eighty-nine sermons in this church so far, and if I had an agenda like this couple claims, it would have shown itself by now." The following Sunday, I stayed on task in the book I was preaching at the time, the Gospel of Luke. In time, I did come to a text that addressed the issues this couple raised, and I was able to approach the text without any pushback because it just happened to be the next text in the passage. The church saw it for what it was: the Word of God.

We have also had other kinds of controversial drama in our church. Early on in my ministry at my present church, there were those who actually complained about the type of people who were starting to attend the church. In fact, a lady and her husband sat in my office one evening, and she looked at me with tears and said, "I don't like the new people. It's affecting the chemistry of the church." Had this been an isolated incident, it could have been dealt with then and there; and I did address it at the time. However, this couple represented a large group within our church. How does a relatively new pastor of a church deal with this without using the pulpit as a bully pulpit? I kept preaching through Luke, trusting that the Lord at the right time would give me the text I needed to address the issue.[5]

In time, God did just that. I came to Luke 5:27–32, where Jesus calls Levi, a tax collector, to follow him. As is well known, there was virtually universal hatred toward tax collectors. And here Jesus is calling one to follow him. To add to the scandal, Levi threw a party for Jesus and invited all his tax collector friends. The Pharisees grumbled at Jesus and his disciples for eating and drinking with the tax collectors and sinners. When preaching from this text, I was able to say, without looking reactionary, insecure, or bitter, "If you are appalled by the kind of people Jesus is attracting, that is the spirit of Pharisaism. And if you are unrepentant in that self-righteousness, you, like these Pharisees, are under the judgment of God." There was utter silence and stillness in the room when I said this. Later, the chairman of the deacons came up to me astounded at how perfectly the text fit the situation at the church. He told me that there was not a better text to deal with the nonsense. He was right. Furthermore, because I waited to come to the right text, it allowed me to address the issue without all the emotion that I originally felt when the crisis first surfaced.

Priestly Benefits

One of the awe-inspiring realities of our Great God and Savior Jesus Christ is that he is the Great High Priest (Heb 4:14), "for us and for our salvation" (to use a glorious phrase from the Nicene Creed). The Baptist Catechism beautifully enlarges on the implications of this truth: "Christ executeth the office of priest in his once offering up himself a sacrifice to satisfy divine justice (Heb 9:14, 28) and reconcile us to God (Heb 2:17),

---

5. Sometimes the preacher needs to break from his preaching schedule to address an issue that has arisen in the church, culture, or world. However, if a preacher does this every time there's a crisis, his pulpit will be primarily a reactionary one that does not best serve the long-term spiritual health of his church.

and in making continual intercession for us (Heb 6:24–25)." In other words, the work of Jesus Christ as our Great High Priest gets at the heart of the gospel, which is the essential message of the Bible, indeed, the message of "first importance" (1 Cor 15:1–4) and the message by which the believer stands. Any persistent emphasis from the pulpit that in some way does not have gospel implications is alien to the Bible.

It is not an overstatement to assert that in the evangelical church today, biblical and gospel illiteracy abounds. In my estimation, there are two main factors at work here. First, most preaching is done at the horizontal level rather than the vertical. That is, preaching is aimed more at helping people get along with one another in this world rather than being aimed at helping people to glorify God and enjoy him forever. The congregation hears the predictable "how-to" series on finances, marriage, anxiety, parenting, friendship, depression, fear, self-image, and business success, but too little preaching is centered on "doctrine in accordance with the gospel of the glory of the blessed God" (1 Tim 1:10–11).

Second, the gospel is largely assumed, which implies that the listener can fix his own problems without need of the Savior. In this case, the preacher is teaching the listener to be his own messiah. The implication from this is that the doing, dying, rising, and ruling of Jesus Christ did not need to take place in order for these kinds of sermons to work.

As we have argued in other chapters, we need God to exercise his lordship over our lives or we are hopeless. We need the power of the gospel to awaken us from our spiritual slumbers. We need an "awe" rescue. We need the triune God our Savior!

When we preach through books of the Bible, we have opportunity on every page to emphasize man's desperate need and God's abundant grace. The "melodic line"[6] or "vibe,"[7] that is, the central theme of the Bible, is

6. David Helm's term. David Helm, *Expositional Preaching: How We Speak God's Word Today* (Wheaton, IL: Crossway, 2014), 47.

7. Gary Millar and Phil Campbell's term. Gary Millar and Phil Campbell, *Saving Eutychus: How to Preach God's Word and Keep People Awake* (Kingsford, Australia: Matthias Media, 2013), 31. An anecdote about Mark Twain and his wife says that one time Twain's wife got angry with him and did something she had never before done: she started cursing at him. He started laughing, which made her even angrier. She then asked him what he thought was so funny. He said, "My dear, you know the words, but you don't know the tune" (source unknown).

God's purpose to glorify himself by establishing his saving reign, authority, and covenantal presence over all created order through the person and all-sufficient work of the Messiah, the God-Man Jesus Christ. This glorious and all pervasive theme is most ably picked up by preaching consecutively through books. When this is emphasized week after week, the Holy Spirit uses that gospel-centric word to rescue the listeners' awe and transform their being as they are encountered by the Living Christ.

Preaching Benefits

The reality is I am a finite and fallible person, pastor, and preacher. I simply do not have the personal wherewithal to always know where everyone in my church is struggling. And even if I had the capacity to know all the issues and concerns in a church body, it would be impossible to address them all from the pulpit.

When a pastor allows contemporary crises and urgent felt needs constantly to determine what he preaches, he is like a physician whose whole approach to medicine is pain management. Pain management is important, but a good physician will try to determine what is causing the pain and seek to heal the cause. A good physician treats the disease and not just the symptoms. Like a doctor who encourages his patients to maintain healthy lifestyles, a preacher who consistently preaches the whole counsel of God as revealed in books of the Bible will promote overall spiritual health, and many personal crises that might otherwise occur will be fended off by a healthy spiritual immune system. I have heard that before Martyn Lloyd-Jones would agree to personally counsel someone, he insisted that the person first listen to his preaching for six months. He believed that the preached word would cure the fundamental ills of humanity. Similarly, as Timothy Keller argues, we need not only the Bible's prescription to our issues but also its diagnosis of them.[8] In other words, if we analyze our people's issues without allowing the Bible to be the grid by which we do so, we will likely treat the symptoms rather than the problems behind the symptoms.

---

8. Keller, *Preaching*, 97.

Furthermore, unless we preach through the whole counsel of God, the vacillating concerns of the congregation rather than the teaching of Scripture may become the preponderant emphases of the pulpit. So another crucial preaching benefit of the *lectio continua* method is that it allows the Bible to define the issues in your church body, rather than allowing the contemporary issues themselves to be the starting point. As Dick Lucas once said, "The pew cannot control the pulpit. We cannot deliver 'demand led' preaching because no one demands the Gospel."[9] The gospel and its necessary implications are always the remedy for the fallen human condition.

There are other homiletical benefits to preaching through books as well. A second preaching benefit is that it balances the preacher's area of "expertise" and preferred topics with the breadth of God's thoughts in the Bible. The reality is that every preacher has favorite topics and doctrines that represent only a small percentage of the Bible. Our knowledge and our perceptions of what is important are limited by our creaturely perspective. Our narrow, finite perspective must be broadened to become as robust and expansive as is God's. That is why the preacher, with his limitations, has a fundamental need for God's absolute, infinite perspective as revealed in Scripture if he is going to serve as an effective change agent for his people. Ironically, the preacher who recognizes his finite nature as a created being, and who commits to working his way through the books of the Bible, will end up addressing more "topics" than the topical preacher. God knows more about people and their problems than we do! Faithfully preaching what God reveals in his Word forces the preacher to address a greater number of issues than what would otherwise occur to him. In fact, "Only by the discipline of consecutive expository preaching will a congregation be exposed to the full range of Scripture's interests and concerns."[10]

Related to this benefit, preaching through books of the Bible gives the preacher accountability not to avoid skipping over what does not suit his taste or temperament on any given day. It will stretch both him and

---

9. Quoted in Alistair Begg, *Preaching for God's Glory* (Wheaton, IL: Crossway, 2010), 23–24.
10. Thomas, "Expository Preaching," 88–89.

his congregation to have to deal with subjects that would not be typically or naturally chosen.[11] If you are a preacher who chooses topics and texts in a random manner, you will likely never preach certain books or passages. How many topical preachers have preached Genesis 36, the genealogy of Esau? Or, how many have preached Judges 19, the "Levite and his concubine"? But are those texts also the Word of God? Are those texts profitable? According to the apostle Paul, they are (2 Tim 3:16–17).

Practical Benefits

One of the practical benefits of preaching through books is that it helps the preacher conserve time and energy that would otherwise be used in choosing a sermon for each week. Furthermore, much research time can be saved because each new sermon does not require a new study of the book's or passage's author, background, context, and purpose.[12]

My preaching mentor once told me, "Sunday comes every seven days." At the time, I thought this was a bit too obvious to be of any practical help in ministry. I have since learned that it may have been an understatement (if that is possible). When I awaken on Monday morning, I

---

11. I recently read a great example of how a text that does not seem to profit at face value actually does. Jack Klumpenhower is a children's Sunday School teacher and author who was teaching through Joshua. But the curriculum he was using skipped the story of Achan in Joshua (Josh 7:10ff.), likely due to the graphic nature of the narrative. Here you have a man who wrongfully takes some of the plunder of Jericho for himself. His sin is uncovered and the people stone him, his wife, kids, and livestock. Then they set them on fire and heap stones on their charred bodies. Only after that was God's anger appeased. Well, naturally speaking, it makes sense that the curriculum skipped the story. After all, it is a curriculum directed toward children. But Klumpenhower did not want to cherry pick, even though he found out the morning he was going to teach it that one of the moms who assisted him was worried because her daughter was prone to nightmares brought on by tense stories. Yet, Klumpenhower felt it was too late to change his plans. So he taught them. He taught them that because this one man sinned, many died. But later in the Bible, we learn that there was one man who never sinned but still got punished. Then he said: "Your sin is very bad. It can hurt many people. But God loves you so much that he sent his Son, Jesus, to become a man and die for your sin. Jesus was hurt most of all." He said to the children: "I wasn't sure I should tell you this story because I thought it might be too scary. It's about the scariest thing ever—getting punished by God. But when you know the whole story, it isn't scary. If you belong to Jesus, he took your punishment and God becomes your Father. So I hope you won't be scared. You don't have to be scared of anything. Jesus makes the scariest thing of all go away." The surprise came later: The mom told him a few weeks later that her daughter's nightmares had stopped. The girl insisted that it was because she knew that because of Jesus she did not have to be scared anymore. Jack Klumpenhower, *Show Them Jesus: Teaching the Gospel to Kids* (Greensboro, NC: New Growth Press, 2014), 4–7.

12. An additional benefit of this is that it allows the church to prepare ahead by reading and meditating on the passage.

am keenly aware that what just transpired the day before must take place again in six days. Since pastors must preach so often, I completely understand why websites exist to give preachers topical ideas for preaching.

However, the expository preacher who preaches through books does not have the challenge of choosing what to preach next. Once the expositor has determined the book that he will preach, he does not have to concern himself with that choice again for some time. From that point, the text sets the agenda. But this is not the case for many preachers who struggle under the yoke each week of whether this or that text, or this or that topic is best for Sunday.[13]

Another practical benefit of preaching through books is that it promotes biblical literacy in the congregation by setting them an example of how to study their Bibles. That is, it teaches a reproducible method of Bible study. The old adage is true: "Give a man a fish, feed him for a day. Teach him how to fish, feed him for a lifetime." For better or worse, the preacher shapes the way his church reads the Scriptures.

An additional practical benefit is that it increases the trustworthiness of the pastor's preaching in the eyes of the congregation. One of my seminary professors once told me that before you can lead your church to make necessary changes in structure and direction, you need to earn their trust as someone who faithfully interprets the Word of God. Once you have earned their trust in this way, they trust you in other areas. When a church discerns that you take the Word of God as your authority, it establishes credibility with them. It is one thing for a preacher to say that the Bible is his authority, but what you really believe is revealed by how you handle the Scriptures. A preacher who preaches line by line and word by word, considering the parts in light of the whole, and the whole in light of the parts, demonstrates by his actions and method that he believes the Bible is his all-sufficient, authoritative script. It reveals that he actually believes in verbal, plenary inspiration. When this faith in the sufficiency and veracity of Scripture is modeled week after week, over

---

13. I have faced this dilemma when I am guest preaching. The Saturday night before I preach, I am often doubting whether the particular text I have chosen is the right one. It can be distracting and lead to second-guessing.

time another benefit is that it increases the congregation's conviction in the inspiration, inerrancy, clarity, and sufficiency of Scripture. And once the church members recognize this about the preacher and grow to a greater faith themselves, they begin to willingly trust him as he seeks to take the church in a biblical direction.

One last practical benefit is that this method increases the likelihood of the pastor preaching the whole counsel of God over time.[14] At the end of his ministry, the Apostle Paul was able to say that he had preached the whole counsel of God while in Ephesus (Acts 20:27), and it should be the heart cry of every preacher. My own personal desire is that at the end of my ministry, I will have preached every passage from every book of the Bible. I do not know if I will have the time to accomplish this, but it is my heart's desire. I cannot think of a better investment of my life. The preacher who begins deductively with topics rather than inductively with the Word of God will be hard pressed to say this at the end of his ministry. But for the one who aspires to this, what better way is there to communicate and model that we need all 1189 chapters and 31,102 verses of the Bible so that we can more adequately glorify God and enjoy him forever?

Conclusion

I have given six broad reasons why preaching through books is the best method: there are personal benefits, pastoral benefits, prophetic benefits,

---

14. The Reformers, in their desire to expose their congregations to the whole counsel of God, most effectively developed the *lectio continua* method of preaching. For example, Luther and his clergy colleagues "undertook an extensive campaign of religious instruction through the sermon. There were three public services on Sunday: from 5–6 A.M. on the Pauline epistles, from 9–10 A.M. on the Gospels . . . On Wednesdays on the Gospel of Matthew, Thursdays and Fridays on the apostolic letters, and Saturday evening on John's Gospel" Roland Bainton, *Here I Stand*). John Calvin's method was similar to Luther's. From 1549 he preached in Geneva two times every Sunday and in alternate weeks at a daily evening service. He tended to preach the Old Testament on weekdays and the New Testament or Psalms on Sundays. In the fifteen-year period from 1549 until he died, he expounded Genesis, Deuteronomy, Judges, Job, some Psalms, 1 and 2 Samuel, 1 Kings, and all the prophets, and from the New Testament a harmony of the Gospels, Acts, 1 and 2 Corinthians, Galatians, Ephesians, 1 and 2 Thessalonians, and the Pastoral Epistles. A century later, Matthew Henry in his twenty-five-year ministry (1687–1712) focused on the Old Testament on Sunday morning and on the New Testament each Sunday afternoon. In doing so, he worked through the whole Bible twice and during his midweek lectures expounded the whole Psalter no less than five times. These expositions are the basis of his commentary.

priestly benefits, preaching benefits, and practical benefits. In light of the weighty benefits of this method, one wonders why a preacher would employ any other. We admit that there are some preachers who have honestly considered the advantages of this method, and they are nevertheless convicted that each week they need to come up with an independent text that has been specifically chosen with their particular congregation in mind. We respect that. On the other hand, let me suggest four not-so-good reasons that preachers do not adopt this expository method. First, it is hard work. It is a rigorous exercise to exegete and exposit passage after passage, week after week. A second reason is that deep down the preacher is not convinced that his people will find it compelling.[15] Could it be that this is due to the fact that the preacher does not find it compelling himself? After all, is it not human nature to center on the things we are excited about? A third reason is that the preacher may not trust in the sufficiency of Scripture. If he did, then he would believe that all Scripture is profitable and important. A fourth reason is that the preacher has not been adequately taught.

It is my prayer that this chapter has at least addressed the last reason and the other parts of this book address the former reasons. Whatever the preacher's method of preaching, it is simply inexcusable for the Word not to be the centerpiece and mainspring of the preacher's sermon. Consider that in the twenty-eight chapters of Acts, there are around thirty-seven references to the growth of the church. Of these references, six link growth with the quality of church life and Christian character. Seven connect growth with the evidence of "signs and

---

15. For instance, Andy Stanley has recently argued that expository preaching was effective in a time when the culture esteemed the Bible. Stanley believes that does not work anymore. So rather than starting inductively with the Bible and drawing practical application from that, Stanley argues that the preacher should start with a current human need or contemporary question and then bring in the Bible for a solution. He asks, "To what extreme are you willing to go to create a delivery system that will connect with the heart of your audience? . . . Are you willing to abandon a style, and approach, a system that was designed in another era for a culture that no longer exists?" Andy Stanley and Lane Jones, *Communicating for a Change* (Eugene, OR: Multnomah, 2006), 89. Tim Keller points us to Hughes Old to debunk this perspective. Old points out that expository preaching was the norm during the first five centuries of church history, at a time when the culture was not only non-Christian, but often violently anti-Christian. Hughes Oliphant Old, *The Reading and Preaching of the Scriptures in the Worship of the Christian Church*, vol. 1, *The Biblical Period* (Grand Rapids: MI: Eerdmans, 1998), 299, in Keller, *Preaching*, 96.

wonders." And an astounding twenty-four references associate growth with the preaching of the Word of God. In fact, in Acts 12:24 the growth of the church is actually called the growth of the Word.[16]

---

16. These statistics are found in Alec Motyer, *Preaching: Simple Teaching on Simply Preaching* (Fearn, Ross-Shire, Scotland: Christian Focus, 2013), 19.

CHAPTER

6

TOPICAL
PREACHING

This chapter may seem a little out of place. After all, this book argues that preaching should be expository. Aren't topical sermons and expository sermons opposites? Aren't the biblical riches of expository preaching supposed to deliver us from the shallow waters of topical preaching? What is this chapter on topical preaching doing here?

Well, the reason it is here is simple: topical preaching is biblical. How biblical? Let me (Fullerton) put it to you this way: every sermon in the New Testament is a topical sermon. That's right, all of them. Think of Peter in Acts 2. A striking public event has occurred. Amidst the bustling multicultural crowds gathered in Jerusalem for the celebration of Pentecost, Peter and a small band of Christians were powerfully declaring "the mighty works of God"; and miraculously, they were being heard in multiple languages (Acts 2:11). And as they preached in these different languages, people were talking. They were asking questions like, "How is it that we hear each of us in his own native language" (Acts 2:8)? And, "What does this mean" (Acts 2:12)? Some were speculating, "They are filled with new wine" (Acts 2:13). The outpouring of the Holy Spirit raised a lot of questions and a lot of eyebrows. How did Peter respond? Well, he did what any freshly Spirit-filled preacher would do in his situation. He preached a topical sermon. It had one point, one application, and three texts. Peter's one central point was to show that this miraculous situation was not the result of drunkenness but rather it was the result of the risen Lord Jesus Christ having poured out the promised Holy Spirit. It had one application. Since Jesus has been raised, everyone who could hear Peter was called to "repent and be baptized every one of you in the name of Jesus Christ for the forgiveness of your sins, and you will receive the gift of the Holy Spirit." The sermon was based on three texts: Joel 2, Psalm 16, and Psalm 110. It was a topical sermon.

What about the preaching of our Lord? Topical again. Think about the Sermon on the Mount. In one sermon Jesus deals with the blessed-ness of God's people (Matt 5:1–12), the purpose of God's people (5:13–16), the fulfillment of the Law (Matt 5:17–20); and then under that heading he addresses murder, adultery, divorce, oaths, retaliation, and love. I could go on, but you get the point. Why is Jesus dealing with all of these different issues? Were they all clear applications of a particular text he was expositing? Not exactly. In fact, in the Sermon on the Mount, he quotes multiple texts. So what binds this sermon together? It is all about the kingdom of God. The entire sermon tells us about the people and the ways of Christ's Kingdom. It was a topical sermon.

The New Testament clearly models topical preaching for us. This does not mean all preaching should be topical. In fact, as stated in the previous chapter, we believe the best way to open up the whole counsel of God on the most issues while helping the preacher and his people get to know the text of the whole Bible is by preaching through books of the Bible. We believe that, and we practice that. But the New Testament witness keeps us from altogether rejecting topical preaching because the New Testament models topical preaching. In fact, since the New Testament models topical preaching we would be well advised to follow that lead and sometimes utilize this biblical method of preaching.

Why Such a Bad Reputation?

I know that for many people topical preaching is the main diet of preaching they have received. But in the circles I frequent, expository preaching through books is the norm, and topical preaching has a bad name. Its reputation is tarnished because topical preaching is often associated with preachers who find an idea they want to preach and then find texts to support it. Topical preaching is often associated with taking verses out of context. Topical preaching is also associated with preachers who preach their favorite doctrines (often the ones that make people feel good) rather than preaching the whole counsel of God (which includes lots of parts that make people feel bad). Or, worse still, preachers can use topical sermons to avoid doctrinal issues altogether. In other words, topical preaching can be associated with not listening carefully to what God says (taking verses out of context), not listening to all that God says (failing to preach the whole counsel of God), and placing the thoughts of man over the thoughts of God (as when a preacher goes looking for texts that will allow him to preach his sermon idea). We should want to reject any method of preaching that puts the mind of man over the mind of God. We should want to embrace ways of preaching that clearly put the Word of God over the words of man. Any man of God with a true reverence for God will not want to preach God's Word in a way that hides God's precious voice rather than amplifying it. So for this reason no real man of God will want to give his life to the kind of topical preaching I have criticized above.

Topical Preaching Is Not the Problem

The problem with the kind of topical preaching we have been discussing is not the fact that it is topical. The problem is that it is bad. Bad topical preaching highlights man's wisdom over God's Word and then plays fast and loose with God's voice in an attempt to communicate man's message. This is despicable, but that is not the way it has to be. Topical preaching can be done in a way that honors God and follows the New Testament model. In order to do this, topical preaching must be three things. It must be biblical. It must be expository. It must be balanced.

Topical Preaching Must Be Biblical

When I say that topical preaching must be biblical, I mean something more than it must use verses of Scripture. I mean that the topic it seeks to address must actually arise from the Bible, and the answers it seeks to provide must actually emerge from those same Scriptures. Recently, I preached a short series on unity. The first sermon expounded Psalm 133 verse by verse. We explored the beauty of unity: "Behold, how good and pleasant it is when brothers dwell in unity" (Ps 133:1). We explored the strange imagery of oil on Aaron's beard and the dew on Mount Hermon. It was an expository sermon on one text of Scripture. But when I was done I wanted to think with my people more about how God produces that unity and how we as his people are called to protect it. So, for the next two weeks we looked at a number of topics related to God's producing and our protecting the unity of his people. We explored our common experience of the new birth, and our common salvation at the foot of Christ's cross. Then we explored how character, corporate disciplines, and hospitality all promote unity. For each of these topics I opened and explained a particular text, but that is not my point here. My point here is that each and every idea I explored was about a topic the Bible itself had raised. I was not thinking up a topic and then explaining it using the Bible. No, the Bible had raised a topic and I was filling out that topic biblically. We must make sure that the topic we are aiming to preach is actually a topic that is raised in the Bible itself.

Why is this so important? Because if we do not start with topics the Bible raises, then our preaching cannot be biblical no matter how many verses we use. Take for example the topic of alcoholism. A preacher may want to address alcoholism because it is relevant to so many in the congregation and it is so destructive to those in its clutches. If he looks at alcoholism as a genetically transmitted disease (which many do in our day) then he must speak God's Word about disease to his people. He would explain that disease is a product of the fall (Genesis 3); disease is not always our fault (John 9); Jesus can heal disease (all four gospels); God uses the suffering of disease for our sanctification (Rom 5:1–5); and finally, all disease will be destroyed in the new heavens and the new earth (Revelation 21). Such a sermon would meet his people where they are, it would touch the deepest pains of their hearts (who doesn't know someone ravaged by alcohol abuse?), and it would draw upon the riches of Scripture. It would do all of this, and it would be entirely unbiblical.

What's the problem? The problem is that the Bible does not deal with the disease of alcoholism; it deals with the sin of drunkenness (1 Cor 6:9–10). While I do not deny that a tendency toward drunkenness could be genetic, the Bible does not treat this sin primarily as a genetic issue but as a sin issue. Since drunkenness is an act of rebellion against God, a topical sermon dealing with drunkenness would look very different from a topical sermon dealing with alcoholism. In preaching the sermon against drunkenness, the preacher would call men and women who fall into the sin of drunkenness to repent and believe the gospel (Mark 1:15). He would warn them that drunkards will not inherit the kingdom of God (1 Cor 6:9–10). He would tell them of the cross of Jesus that is sufficient to pay for all their sins and to deliver them from the wrath of God (1 Thess 1:10). Finally, he would tell them about the marvelous gift of the Holy Spirit, who can help them overcome their sin as they walk toward the goal of heaven (Gal 5:16–18, 6:8).

In order to make sure our topical preaching (and really all of our preaching) is biblical, we must be sure to allow Scripture itself to define every topic we address. The Bible must be allowed to define the problems we have and the solutions to those problems. We must not go from a problem we invent to a cure the Bible gives. Similarly, neither should we start with a nonbiblical solution and work back to a problem exposed in the Bible. Only when we allow the Bible, and not science, philosophy, sociology, psychology, or any other discipline to define our problems and our goals will our topical preaching be biblical.

Topical Preaching Must Be Expository

Our goal in writing this book is to cultivate and equip better expository preachers. We want to encourage all preachers to expose the text and to labor, above all else, to say what God has said when they preach. We believe this is best done by consecutively preaching through books; but as

Brian Payne has written earlier in this book, "Expository preaching does not require the preacher to preach through books." The essence of expository preaching does not consist in consecutively preaching through books but in exposing the text. Since this is the case, good topical preaching is not the enemy of expository preaching. In fact, when topical preaching exposes many texts, it is a kind of expository preaching. If topical preaching were a species it would be *Preachus Expositorius Topicalis*. It is part of the family.

This means that when you decide to preach a topical sermon you must not forget that your primary goal is to expose texts. If you are dealing with the topic of sanctification then your job is to expose the texts that deal with sanctification. Your primary aim is not to give a summary of what various theologians have said about sanctification, nor is it merely to describe the believer's experience of growing in grace. Rather, you must aim to explain Romans 6, Philippians 2, 2 Corinthians 3–4, and other texts like these. When you preach topically you must never forget that you are primarily preaching textually.

Failure to practice this is the real reason why topical preaching is often so negligent. Men simply do not do the work it takes to do it well. Good topical preaching does not entail less work than good expository preaching; often it entails more. In order to preach a topical sermon well you must study not just one text in a week, but many texts must be understood and synthesized in one week. If you do not understand a topic very well, and if you do not understand many of the texts on that topic, then a topical sermon is not the sermon you want to prepare for during a busy week.

It is my general conviction that topical preaching will be done best by those who do it occasionally. Ironically, the hard weekly work of studying to preach one text per sermon is the best equipping you can get for occasionally preaching a topical sermon. Men who consecutively exposit books of the Bible will be the ones who are best equipped to handle various topics from different passages of the Bible.

Topical Preaching Must Be Balanced

It is very possible for topical preaching to be fully biblical and expository but not balanced. This is especially true if you preach a topical series. It is possible to explain in a wonderful topical sermon how Christ justifies believers by giving us His righteousness, but if it is never followed up with a sermon on how God always sanctifies those who are justified, it could give a very distorted picture of the Christian life.

The New Testament writers labored to avoid this kind of imbalance. Many of the New Testament letters deal with a topic or multiple topics, but it is amazing how they do this with such wise, pastoral balance. Large portions of James explain how "faith without works is dead" (Jas 2:17), but in the balance of the letter he adds, "we all stumble in many ways" (Jas 3:2). He avoids the sin of antinomianism but does not fall into the sin of perfectionism. Paul shows the same kind of balance in the book of Galatians. The whole book revolves around the topic of justification by faith alone, and Paul spends chapters establishing his authority (Galatians 1–2) and arguing for this precious doctrine (Gal 2:16–5:12), but he does not end there. He also explains how the Christian life is lived by the Spirit and that failing to live by the Spirit will lead to death and hell (Gal 5:16–19, 6:8). He explains the full and free justification of God but not in such a way that he denies or diminishes the work of the Holy Spirit in producing holy lives.

Our topical preaching should follow this lead. It is fine to emphasize a particular topic in one sermon, but it should not be done is such a way—or with such frequency—that another truth is deemphasized or denied.

Now, having said what topical preaching must be in order to avoid being bad, I want to emphasize why topical preaching can be very good.

Topical Preaching Can Allow You to Respond to Cultural Events in a Balanced Way

There are certain events that come along in the life of a church that require a comprehensive response. Topical preaching can enable a preacher to help his people respond with that appropriate balance.

Take, for example, the legalization of same-sex marriage that occurred in the United States in 2015. Is there one text that would allow a preacher to give a full response to this sad event? Preaching from Leviticus might make it clear that homosexuality is a sin, but it might not be the best text for showing that Christ loves homosexuals. On the other hand, preaching on "such were some of you" from 1 Corinthians 6:11 could have the opposite effect. It might allow you to help Christians see that they too were great sinners, but it might not help a congregation feel the great weight of the evil that the sin of homosexuality is and the tragedy that this sin has been sanctioned in our courts. How can we help people respond biblically to the legalization of same-sex marriage? How can we help people feel the depths of God's hatred for sin? How can we help them feel God's disapproval of judges who call evil good? Furthermore, how can we show God's desire for us to love sinners, and our responsibility to live as aliens in a culture that does not share our values? How can we answer all of these questions that are on our people's minds? We can do this through a well-thought-out, well-crafted topical sermon.

Topical Preaching Can Allow Us to Respond to Congregational Events in a Balanced Way

Two years ago, the congregation I pastor was passing through a trial. Mark, who had formerly been a very wayward Christian who had repented and turned into a delightful follower of Christ, was about to die. Our dear brother had been diagnosed with a brain tumor about a year and a half earlier, and now the hour of his death was approaching. Sadly, he would leave behind a precious wife and three children. Our congregation was bracing for our brother's death, and the family of his wife, Anna, was also preparing for his death. Her mother was set to be Anna's rock following Mark's death. But then, just six weeks before Mark's death, Anna's mom died suddenly and unexpectedly. It was a Saturday night.

I knew that on Sunday morning many of my people would be discouraged. This event would tempt many of them to doubt the goodness of God. Not only was Mark going to die, but Anna was going to be widowed, and the children would be without a father, and now this. I knew I had to speak to their hearts. That morning, I found that a topical sermon would allow me to do just that. It would allow me to inform, comfort, challenge, and turn their eyes to Christ. So I put together a sermon using passages that I already knew well—remember, we don't want any bad exposition in our topical preaching. The outline ran like this:

Ten Truths about Death

Death Is . . .
1. *Death Is Unnatural—Genesis 1:27–28, 2:16–17*
2. *Death Is Right—Romans 2:15, 6:23*
3. *Death Is Certain and Soon—James 4:13–15*
4. *Death Is Frightening and Enslaving—Hebrews 2:14–15 (This is a harder passage, but I have thought a lot about it over the years.)*
5. *Death Is Hated by Jesus—John 11:32–37*
6. *Death Is Defeated—1 Corinthians 15:54–57*
7. *Death Is Never Seen by the Believer—John 8:51*
8. *Death Is Gain—Philippians 1:21*
9. *Death Is Not All—John 5:28–29*
10. *Death Is Going To Die—Revelation 21:1–4*

I believe using this topical outline allowed me to capture this moment and to do all I could in the power of the Holy Spirit to set apart the hearts and minds of God's people to God. I also believe that it would have been unwise to continue in the consecutive Bible exposition I was engaged in. Similar to the story that Brian Payne related in an earlier chapter, I have heard other testimonies about how God had just the right text lined up for just the right event because of consecutive exposition. This was not going to be one of those stories. My planned text was Deuteronomy 13, which deals with executing your wife if she turns to idols. This, too, is an inspired text of sacred Scripture, and I preached it the next week, but I believe it was good in this hour of pain to turn to a topical sermon on death and the Christian.

Topical Preaching Can Serve
Consecutive Preaching Through Books

It is commonly noted that preachers will be helped by systematic theology. Well, systematic theology is topical theology. Systematic theology tries to arrange, organize, and explain the teaching of the entire Bible on various particular topics. Systematic theology answers questions like "What does the Bible say about sin?" and "What does the Bible teach about the person of Christ?" Systematic theologians study many texts and seek to understand how they fit into the whole story line of the Bible, and then they seek to present them in a way that will summarize the whole counsel of God. This knowledge helps preachers because it helps them balance out certain texts.

Knowing that justification is always accompanied by regeneration will help a preacher explain justification in a way that does not lead to antinomianism. If a preacher understands the full doctrine of election it will help him to present it in a way that does not lead people into fatalism and does not quench their evangelistic zeal. Knowing systematic theology is a great help to preachers. So why wouldn't it be a great help to our people? Topical preaching can make that help a reality.

If you are going to preach through the book of Galatians you will be asking your people to think through some very complicated arguments (see especially Galatians 3–5). Before they jump into those complicated arguments, it might help if you laid out the central doctrine of the book for them. A single sermon explaining the full doctrine of justification could help orient your people as they proceed through the knotty arguments in Galatians.

Or what about utilizing a topical sermon to introduce a ministry of expository preaching? Many men who are committed to expositionally preaching through books face a great deal of opposition. Perhaps their people would be more eager to receive their expositional ministry through books if they heard a topical sermon on the value of expository preaching. An outline could go something like this:

Expositionally preaching through books . . .
Helps me preach the whole counsel of God (Acts 20)
Helps us understand the way God reasons (Isaiah 1)
Helps us honor the fact that all Scripture is God-breathed
(2 Timothy 3)
Helps all of us to follow the example of the Bereans (Acts 19)
Helps us see all the glories of Christ (Luke 24)

A sermon such as this one could greatly benefit a congregation that is being introduced to consecutive verse-by-verse exposition.

One final way that topical preaching can serve consecutive preaching is by helping people see where the book they are about to study fits into the "big picture" of Scripture. A few years ago I began an extended exposition of Deuteronomy. I knew that my preaching would be constantly referring to events with which my people might not be very familiar—events like the exodus, the wilderness generation, the giving of the Law, etc. I also knew that I would be showing people how these events pointed forward to Jesus Christ. I knew that my preaching would be constantly going from the events of Deuteronomy to the events of our salvation through Christ. I knew that I would be constantly moving from the old covenant that came through Moses, and I would be pointing to the new covenant that came through Christ. I wanted my people to be as oriented as possible before I repeatedly travelled those connections with them. In order to accomplish this I preached a topical sermon. I used an excellent curriculum called *The Bible Overview*[1] to trace out the whole story of the Bible from Genesis to Revelation, from Eden to the new creation, and from Moses to Christ. We looked at the whole Bible in an hour. By doing this I was able to say, "Here is where Deuteronomy fits into the big picture" before I dived into the details of Deuteronomy. In this way I think a topical sermon served a consecutive series.

---

1. Matthew Brain, Matthew Malcolm, Greg Clark, *The Bible Overview* (Sydney, AU: Matthias Media, 2001).

Topical Sermons Can Help in the Equipping of the Saints

A number of years ago our pastors were thinking about how to help our people grow in evangelism. We planned to teach our small group leaders about evangelism. We prayed about evangelism. But we also preached on it. We preached a simple five-point gospel presentation (most of which was not original to us). We explained to all of our people that evangelism could be summed up in five words: Connect, God, Man, Christ, Response. I preached these words as my outline. Not only did the sermon outline the gospel for our people (always a good thing), but it gave them a simple, memorable gospel outline that many of them actually used in their own evangelistic endeavors.

Topical Preaching Is a "Special Forces Unit"

The point of this chapter is not to make topical preaching the dominant preaching diet of your ministry. No! We hope the vast array of your sermons will use consecutive Bible exposition, but we do hope that topical preaching will be seen as a "special forces unit" in your army that can be called upon at appropriate times to expose God's Word and to help your people.

THE SERMON
AND THE SPIRIT: PART ONE

The Wind of the Spirit
through the Preaching of the Word

The preaching of the New Testament was powerfully effective. It "cut to the heart" and moved its hearers to ask, "What shall we do?" (Acts 2:37). Not only did this Spirit-empowered preaching make hearers beg for personal application, it also fostered deep commitment. Those who responded to the first sermon, "devoted themselves to the apostles' teaching and the fellowship, to the breaking of bread and the prayers" (Acts 2:42). This remarkable reaction to God's Word did not happen only once; the preaching of the book of Acts repeatedly resulted in these kinds of dramatic conversions. In Acts 2, we read that as the apostles devoted themselves to teaching, "the Lord added to their number day by day those who were being saved" (Acts 2:47). As they suffered and witnessed, "those who had heard the word believed, and the number of the men came to about five thousand" (Acts 4:4). As they preached and performed miracles, "more than ever believers were added to the Lord, multitudes of both men and women" (Acts 5:14).

Repeatedly throughout the book of Acts, we see the power of the preached word and, "a great many people were added to the Lord" (Acts

11:24). "The word of God increased and multiplied" (Acts 12:24). "The churches were strengthened in the faith, and they increased in numbers daily" (Acts 16:5). "The word of the Lord continued to increase and prevail mightily" (Acts 19:20). It is a soul-stirring reality that the preaching of the early church brought thousands upon thousands into the kingdom of God. To be sure, there were sermons that did not result in conversions, and on at least one occasion Paul's sermon put a man to sleep (Acts 20:9). But on the whole, the preaching was extraordinarily powerful and effective.

Why don't we see as much of this powerfully effective preaching in our day? Someone might suggest that it is because we are not living in the age of the apostles. I concede this is partially true. That special season of widespread signs, wonders, and various miracles when God was confirming the testimony of Jesus and the apostles has passed. Nonetheless, I hardly think this is a sufficient reason to explain the lack of effective preaching in our day. The apostles may have enjoyed a special season, but we must never forget that they also ushered in an age of Spirit that continues to this very hour. Could there be other reasons we do not see this kind of effectiveness in our own preaching? I think there are.

C. H. Spurgeon famously told the story of one of his first students who complained,

> "I have been preaching now for some months, and I do not
> think I have had a single conversion." I said to him, "And
> do you expect that the Lord is going to bless you and save
> souls every time you open your mouth?" "No, sir," he replied.
> "Well, then," I said, "that is why you do not get souls saved. If
> you had believed, the Lord would have given the blessing."[1]

Do You Believe in the Holy Spirit?

I believe that one of the primary reasons we do not see anything close to the effectiveness of the preaching in the book of Acts in our day is because we do not expect it. Specifically, we do not expect the Holy Spirit

---

1. Charles Spurgeon, *The Soul Winner* (Lafayette, IN: Sovereign Grace, 2001), 17.

to be powerfully at work in our preaching and in the hearts of those to whom we preach. We preachers will labor for hours to make sure our exegesis of the text is right. We will meditate for hours looking for just the right applications. We will surf the web looking for just the right illustrations. We may even write for hours making sure that all of our doctrine is precise. But only fleeting moments are given to consciously seeking the presence and the power of the Holy Spirit on our preaching. As a result, our preaching is very different than the preaching of the New Testament authors. It is far too often orthodox but ineffective, polished but powerless. We may say the right words, but neither we nor our hearers are experiencing God in our preaching.

New Testament preaching was different. To be sure, the preaching of the apostle Paul was based on the soundest exegesis of the Old Testament texts. His applications were perfect, and His doctrine was impeccable; but there was something more. He preached, he tells us, "in demonstration of the Spirit and of power" (1 Cor 2:4). His preaching was not simply a transfer of knowledge, much less a display of personal learning, but it came in "power and in the Holy Spirit and with full conviction" (1 Thess 1:5). I imagine that when men and women heard Paul preach they asked, "Did not our hearts burn within us?" (Luke 24:32). I realize that not every church will relive the intensity of the book of Acts, and not every preacher has the gifting of the apostle Paul, but I fear that while his preaching saved many, infuriated others, and occasionally put a man to sleep, our preaching saves very few, arouses very little hatred, and puts many to sleep. We need something to change. We need the Holy Spirit.

The Paintings and the Lights

One of the reasons we may not value and seek the ministry of the Holy Spirit as we should is because of something good. We value God's book so much. It may be that in our attempt to honor the Holy Spirit's inspired Bible, we have neglected the gift of the Holy Spirit who was given to help us delight in and preach the Bible. Years ago, my father-in-law and I were having a conversation. I cannot even remember its exact topic, but I know we were talking theology. While I don't remember the details of most of our conversation, I do remember one of his final comments to me: "Ryan, you know a lot about the Bible, but you do not know a lot about the Holy Spirit." For years I recoiled at that statement. After all, to know the Bible is to know the Spirit's Word. The Bible was breathed out by him (2 Tim 3:16), and he is the author of Scripture; so if you know the Bible you know the Spirit, right? Well, partially right.

It is true that the Spirit authored the Bible and we cannot know the power of the Spirit of God apart from his Word, but it does not follow that just by knowing the Bible you have exhausted the ministry of the Spirit. You see, the Spirit of God who wrote the Bible is also the Spirit of God who illumines the Bible. The One who inspired the objective Word of God also illumines our darkened hearts to delight in it and proclaim it.

Think about a painting in an art gallery. It is always the same painting during the day as it is at night. The work of the painter does not change when the lights are off or when the lights are on. But when the lights are on, the painting can be seen. Similarly, the Bible does not change on days when we are spiritually dim and do not understand or delight in its message. It is always the Spirit's masterpiece. But, it is seen by us when the Spirit illumines the Word. It is when the Spirit gives us a spirit of wisdom and of revelation in the knowledge of God that we perceive the beauty and glory of the Word. He must turn on the lights.[2]

As preachers who would experience the work of the Spirit in our preaching ministries, we must seek the Spirit's illumination when we study the Word. We must pray with the Psalmist, "Open my eyes, that I may behold wondrous things out of your law" (Ps 119:18). We must plead with our God and Father to give us "the Spirit of wisdom and of revelation in the knowledge of him" (Eph 1:17). We cannot do justice to the texts and the topics we preach unless we have had "the eyes of" our "hearts enlightened" (Eph 1:18). The Spirit-filled preacher is one who has tasted and seen in the Word that the Lord is good. He is able to lead others to understand and experience God in the text because he has understood and experienced God in the text. His sermons are not just a

---

2. This illustration comes from William Still, "The Holy Spirit in Preaching," *Christianity Today*, September 2, 1957, 8–9. I encountered it in Arturo Azurdia's, *Spirit Empowered Preaching*.

lecture, but a lecture and a field trip rolled into one: a lecture in that they teach the subject matter clearly, and a field trip in that the subject matter is experienced. May God give us hearts to both read and preach his Word with the lights on!

Of iPods and Corpses

Of course, it is not just we preachers who need the Spirit's light on the Spirit's book. The people to whom we preach need his illumination as well. Without the Spirit they are spiritually dead and unable to receive the things we preach. I heard of a bizarre trend that illustrated this to me very well: many in our day are being buried with their ear buds in and their favorite playlist playing on their iPods. Now this is foolish for several reasons. The most obvious reason is that the batteries on these iPods are not going to last. Soon each of these caskets will be filled with the silence of the grave. However, the most profound reason this idea is folly is that even if the iPod batteries lasted forever the person listening could not hear a sound. Why? Because he is dead, of course! Such is the case with the unconverted to whom we preach. We may play the most beautiful music. Indeed, when we preach Christ crucified for sinners, we do play the most beautiful music, but it cannot be appreciated. The total depravity of unconverted sinners makes it so that they have stone hearts when it comes to experiencing God. What are we to do? We are to ask our Father for the Holy Spirit. He is the One who opens the eyes of our hearts so we can see the glory of God in the face of Jesus Christ (2 Cor 3:18; 4:6).

We need the Holy Spirit, and He has been promised to us by Christ:

> Nevertheless, I tell you the truth: it is to your advantage that I go away, for if I do not go away, the Helper will not come to you. But if I go, I will send him to you. And when he comes, he will convict the world concerning sin and righteousness and judgment: concerning sin, because they do not believe in me; concerning righteousness, because I go to the Father, and you will see me no longer; concerning judgment, because the ruler of this world is judged" (John 16:7–11).

He promises that the Spirit will convict men of sin. We may preach sin, persuade of its wickedness, and describe its degrading horror; but unless the Spirit helps us, men will never see themselves as guilty of sin. We can describe the righteous life of Christ: his hatred of hypocrisy, and his love for his disciples, his friends, and his enemies. We can show his glorious miracles and unpack his marvelous sermons, but if the Holy Spirit does not work they will never see the beautiful righteousness of Christ that people need credited to their guilty souls. We may talk about judgment, preaching hell fire and brimstone, but unless the Spirit teaches the fear of God and illumines to dead sinners the judgment of God they will continue in their sin. Never will a man or a woman give up their nonchalance or cynicism toward God until they have been taught the fear of God by the Spirit of God. Only the active work of the Holy Spirit upon our ministries will open the heart of a Lydia and cause the Philippian jailer to cry out, "What must I do to be saved?" (Acts 16:30).

How Could It Be Otherwise?

It is a sad state of affairs that any of us should forget our conscious reliance on the Holy Spirit of God. We can do absolutely nothing without him (John 15:5). Even the Lord Jesus Christ needed the Holy Spirit poured out on him in order to minister the Word of God to God's people. By the time Jesus embarked upon his earthly ministry he would have been saturated with the Scriptures. No doubt his mother, whose mind was intoxicated with Scripture (Luke 1:46–55), would have taught him the word. His Father would have taught this superlatively receptive child so that by the time he was a young man he was, "filled with wisdom. And the favor of God was upon him" (Luke 2:40). Nonetheless, the Lord Jesus Christ himself needed the power of the Holy Spirit. Before he would be tempted in the wilderness, before he would preach the sermon on the Mount, before his entire earthly ministry there was something (or rather, Someone) else Christ needed. That someone was given to him on the day of his baptism. On that day, John "saw the Spirit of God descending like a dove and coming to rest on him" (Matt 3:16). Jesus needed the Spirit of God to rest on him before he would be ready to minister, and it was in the power of the Holy Spirit that he did minister. That is why Acts 10 proclaims that "God *anointed Jesus of Nazareth with the Holy Spirit and with power*. He went about doing good and healing all who were oppressed by the devil, for God was with Him" (Acts 10:38). Jesus's ministry was not merely the ministry of a supremely holy man with an astounding grasp of Scripture; he was also empowered by the Holy Spirit.

The same would be true of his disciples. Though they were better prepared for ministry than any men before or since, they were still in need of something after their time at Jesus's side was over. Though they had heard his sermons personally, watched his example carefully, and even participated in the ministries that he had delegated to them, now that Jesus had gone back to heaven, they were not ready to go out alone and preach the gospel. That is why they were told, "And behold, I am sending the promise of my Father upon you. But stay in the city until you are clothed with power from on high" (Luke 24:49). They needed the power of God poured out upon them before they would be effective preachers. Once the Spirit was poured out on the day of Pentecost, they saw hearts "cut to the heart" and thousands saved (Acts 2:37). That is the difference the Spirit makes.

Do we need the Holy Spirit to accomplish what we are called to do? Obviously, we do. But how do we go about securing the power, illumination, and regenerating power of the One we so desperately need? First, we need a clear conception of what we are seeking. Second, we need a practical plan by which we can seek what we are after. To those two ends we turn in the next two chapters.

THE SERMON
AND THE SPIRIT: PART TWO

How Shall We Then Preach?

In the last chapter we saw that we need the Holy Spirit to empower our preaching in the same way that he empowered the preaching of our Lord Jesus Christ. In this chapter I (Fullerton) want to spend some time describing the Spirit's work in our preaching. Jesus promised the early church that they would "receive power when the Holy Spirit" had come upon them (Acts 1:8). My main questions in this chapter are "What is that power?" and "What does it look like in our preaching?"

Before we can pursue something, we must know what we are after. A sportsman must decide if he is after fish or deer before he chooses a rod or a rifle. In the same way we must understand what God's power in preaching looks like and feels like before we can think about how to pursue it. Thankfully, the Scriptures teach us by example and precept what the empowerment of the Holy Spirit looks like.

Boldness

The first mark of the Spirit's empowerment on a man's preaching is boldness. One of the dominant descriptors of the preaching in the book of Acts is that the apostles preached *boldly* (9:27–28; 13:46; 14:3; 18:26; 19:8;

26:26). *Boldly* is how New Testament preaching was done. This boldness was produced by the Holy Spirit of God. After their initial encounter with persecution, the apostles did not want to preach as if they were tamed lions, so they prayed, "And now, Lord, look upon their threats and grant to your servants to continue to speak your word with all *boldness*, while you stretch out your hand to heal, and signs and wonders are performed through the name of your holy servant Jesus" (Acts 4:29–30, emphasis added). This was a prayer request the risen Lord was more than happy to answer: "And when they had prayed, the place in which they were gathered together was shaken, and they were all filled with the Holy Spirit and continued to speak the word of God with *boldness*" (Acts 4:31, emphasis added).

It is important to realize that our boldness is enabled by the careful study of God's Word. If we know we are approved workmen, we will preach with the confidence that comes from knowing we have God's message. Having said this, we must make it perfectly clear that this boldness involves something more than scholarly assurance. It is the boldness that comes from a man who has lingered long in the presence of Jesus, the source of all true authority. It is the assurance that steels a man's soul when he has, like Joshua, spent time in the tent of meeting (Exod 33:11). This boldness comes by the Holy Spirit through a personal acquaintance with the risen King of kings and Lord of lords. When men hear such preaching they know it is more than just the authority of a scholar. Luke reports that when the Jews of his day "saw the boldness of Peter and John, and perceived that they were uneducated, common men, they were astonished. And they recognized that they had been with Jesus" (Acts 4:13). Something much greater than a scribe giving a lecture was happening here: the audience was hearing the boldness that comes from witnesses of Jesus who have seen him. Our preaching must have that boldness today. Though we will not see Jesus with the eyes of the flesh, we will see him as the Spirit illumines the Scriptures to us and moves us to speak with bold assurance.

Such boldness is still present in the world today, and it is still just as baffling as it was two thousand years ago. Hughes Oliphant Old, in his massive, seven-volume work, *The Reading and Preaching of the Scriptures in the Worship of the Christian Church*, concludes his assessment of John MacArthur's preaching with these words:

> "Why do so many people listen to MacArthur, this product of all the wrong schools? How can he pack out a church on Sunday morning in an age in which church attendance has seriously lagged? Here is a preacher who has nothing in the way of a winning personality, good looks, or charm. Here is a preacher who offers us nothing in the way of sophisticated homiletical packaging. No one would suggest that he is a master of the art of oratory. What he seems to have is a witness to true authority. He recognizes in Scripture the Word of God, and when he preaches, it is Scripture that one hears. It is not that the words of John MacArthur are so interesting as it is that the Word of God is of surpassing interest. That is why one listens."[1]

When the Spirit of God gives a man confidence in the Word of God, he imbues a man with a Spirit-wrought boldness in the act of preaching.

Such boldness can speak with authority in the face of opposing powers. The apostle Paul knew this; it is why he asked for prayer when he was imprisoned, that words might be given to him, in opening his "mouth boldly to proclaim the mystery of the gospel, for which I am an ambassador in chains, that I may declare it boldly, as I ought to speak" (Eph 6:19–20). Though he was in chains, Paul wanted to speak with authority to those who had imprisoned him. Such is the power of the Holy Spirit upon a man when he preaches. He does not fear the power brokers in the congregation, the sneers of the intellectual elite, or the guns of his persecutors. He is enabled to declare God's Word as a witness of the King. Oh, God-called preachers, we must believe that God loves to give an otherworldly boldness to his preachers.

---

1. Hughes Oliphant Old, *The Reading and Preaching of the Scriptures in the Worship of the Christian Church* (Grand Rapids: Eerdmans, 2010), 557–558.

Martyn Lloyd-Jones tells the dramatic story of one man to whom God gave this boldness. After hearing some particularly powerful preaching, a Welsh minister by the name of David Morgan reported, "I went to bed that night just David Morgan as usual. I woke up the next morning feeling like a lion, feeling that I was filled with the Holy Ghost." For an extended season after this experience, he preached "with such power that people were convicted and converted in large numbers." Such is the power and boldness God is able and willing to give to his ministers. We may not have an identical experience to David Morgan's (indeed, his own experience was not consistent over the years), but we should all be able to say that there is a noticeable boldness in our preaching.[2] When Paul said, "My speech and my message were not in plausible words of wisdom, but in demonstration of the Spirit and of power" (1 Cor 2:4), he meant exactly what he said. The power of God on his preaching was demonstrable. The boldness and power were not unseen realities his hearers "took by faith"; they were demonstrable, observable realities. Such is the boldness God gives to His preachers. May God allow us to see more of it in our day.

Light

In the last chapter we saw that the Spirit performs a distinct role of illumination in the lives of believers. This activity of illumination should be particularly pronounced in the act of preaching. As we preach, we should ask and expect the Holy Spirit to shed His marvelous light on the glorious truths we are preaching. Paul describes the effects of the Spirit's illumination on our souls when he prays for the Ephesians that "the eyes of your hearts would be enlightened, that you may know what is the hope to which he has called you" (Eph 1:18). What does he mean when he prays that they would know the hope to which God has called them?" He does not mean that he hopes they will be able to define the doctrines they believe. How could he mean that? In the first thirteen verses of the chapter he has burst forth like a geyser, extolling all the different doctrines of our salvation. He rattles off terms like *election, redemption,* and *sealing* without

---

2. Martyn Lloyd-Jones, *Preaching and Preachers* (Grand Rapids: Eerdmans, 1972) 322–24.

making the slightest effort to define them. Clearly, he assumed that these Ephesians knew their doctrine. So what does he mean by their "knowing the hope to which God has called them"? He means something experiential. In Ephesians 3 he will pray that they would know the love of Christ with a knowledge that surpasses knowledge. He is praying for experiential religion. Of course, as some have said, he is not referring to a knowledge that *bypasses* knowledge, but rather a knowledge that *surpasses* knowledge. Paul is speaking about a knowledge that goes beyond mere definition. A man may know a woman's address, her phone number, and her favorite color, but there is a knowledge of her that comes to a man only when that woman becomes his wife. It is an intimate and illumined knowledge. That is the sort of experiential knowledge we are looking for in preaching.

As preachers, we desire God's truth to be "lit up" in our souls while we preach. We are looking to the Spirit to help us taste and see that the Lord is good while we preach. We are looking for God to help us not only to define such doctrines as justification and the new birth, but also to feel afresh the thrill Charles Wesley felt when he wrote in one of his most beloved hymns, "Thine eye diffused a quickening ray—I woke, the dungeon flamed with light; My chains fell off, my heart was free, I rose, went forth, and followed Thee."[3] Oh, that our souls might flame with light in the pulpit when we preach.

Al Martin has written that when a man is illumined by the Holy Spirit in the pulpit, "the truth that flooded your soul in the study with 100 watts of a divine influence of spiritual light and 100 BTU's of spiritual heat—that very truth, not another (and certainly not an extemporaneously conceived error) is now augmented to 1000 watts of light in your mind and 1000 BTU's of heat in your own spirit. It stands out in bold three-dimensional relief in the act of preaching."[4] When the Spirit illumines us, he brings the truth to us in a sweet clarity. He takes truths that

---

3. Charles Wesley, "And Can It Be That I Should Gain," in *Psalms and Hymns*, 1738.

4. Albert N. Martin, *Preaching in the Holy Spirit* (Grand Rapids: Reformation Heritage Books, 2011), 19. Throughout this chapter, I am deeply indebted to Albert Martin's helpful outline of the experience of the Spirit in preaching. He helpfully describes the specific manifestations of the Spirit in preaching, as a heightened sense, unfettered liberty, an enlarged heart, and a heightened confidence in the Word.

looked black and white on the page, and he illumines the eyes of faith to see them in high definition and living color.

The Spirit-empowered preacher should be able to say from the depth of his being, "Oh, taste and see that the Lord is good! Blessed is the man who takes refuge in him" (Ps 34:8)! We are not like men recommending a restaurant at which we have never eaten. We are men commending water that has slaked our thirst, wine that has rejoiced our hearts, and bread that has satisfied our souls. Therefore, we should ask the Lord to come to us in the act of preaching and to give us manna for that very hour so that we can zealously invite men to come and to taste what we are tasting. Say, "Come and experience God with me!"

Love

It would not be possible to overestimate the importance of love in preaching. Preaching without love is worse than the sound of a toddler beating relentlessly on pots and pans. Paul says it best when he writes, "If I speak in the tongues of men and of angels, but have not love, I am a noisy gong or a clanging cymbal" (1 Cor 13:1). Loveless preaching is annoying; but worse than that, if a man habitually preaches without love, not only is his preaching irritating, but the man himself "is nothing." A loveless man is not even a believing man, let alone a helpful preacher.

Thankfully, the Spirit's chief fruit in our lives is love. "The fruit of the Spirit is love" (Gal 5:22). Nowhere is this fruit more important than in preaching. In preaching we must plead for God to make us lovers of men. Our Lord Jesus showed that the Spirit of love was on him because even when he spoke the hardest words, he spoke them from the softest heart. As he called the rich young ruler to the high cost of discipleship, he did so in love. "And Jesus, looking at him, loved him, and said to him, 'You lack one thing: go, sell all that you have and give to the poor, and you will have treasure in heaven; and come, follow me'" (Mark 10:21). What potency would come into our exhortations if we experienced more of the Spirit's supernaturally empowered love in our hearts while we preached!

Do we think it made no difference that when Paul spoke about the doctrine of election, he spoke of it as a weeping man? Before he spoke of Esau being hated and Jacob being loved, the apostle wrote, "I am not lying; my conscience bears me witness in the Holy Spirit—that I have *great sorrow and unceasing anguish in my heart.* For I could wish that I myself were accursed and cut off from Christ for the sake of my brothers according to the flesh, my kinsmen according to the flesh" (Rom 9:1–3, emphasis added). What love beat in this beautiful apostle's soul! Do we think it made no difference to the power of Paul's preaching that while he held out the Savior who died for men, his own heart beat with the Savior's dying love? We must cry out to God to pour out His love-producing Spirit on our souls.

We live in a day and age where we have every kind of method, strategy, and initiative to see people come to Christ. Many of these are good, but none of them alone, nor all of them together, are able to produce the kind of fruit we see in the book of Acts. For this kind of fruit we need love. In the early days of the Salvation Army, two young officers were seeking to establish a new work. They felt they had tried everything, but they had only tasted failure and frustration. They wrote to General William Booth saying they had tried everything and they were ready to quit. The general, who knew the importance of love, telegraphed back, "Try tears."[5] How we doubt the value of tearful love in the work of preaching! But our doubt only shows our lack of familiarity with the loving, powerful Spirit God has given to us. Tears of love were a vital part of New Testament preaching. The apostle Paul could call the Ephesian elders to remember "that for three years I did not cease night or day to admonish everyone with tears" (Acts 20:31). Were those tears not a mark of the Spirit of God at work in the preacher's life? Do we not need more of that work today?

Brother preacher, you and I may not yet know the depth of love felt by Jesus or by Paul, but I trust you know some of the Spirit's love beating in your soul when you preach! Does not your soul almost jump out of your chest for the man in your congregation who is on the edge of walking away from the faith? Does not your heart go out in love to the lost

---

5. This story is found in many places and can also be found in Dave Earley's *Pastoral Leadership Is . . .* (Nashville, TN: B&H, 2012), 90.

who visit your congregations on Sunday morning? If you have known a little of the love the Spirit produces and empowers in us then that is all the more reason to ask, seek, and knock to ask him to "do far more abundantly than all that we ask or think, according to the power at work within us" (Eph 3:20).

Words

The final way in which the Spirit moves upon us when He empowers us is in giving us words. The apostle Paul prays for this in Ephesians 6:17, "that *words* may be given to me in opening my mouth boldly to proclaim the mystery of the gospel." By words spoken in boldness he meant "that he might say the right thing in the right way, and do so without inhibitions."[6] Notice that saying the right thing in the right way is something that is given to us. It is the work of the Spirit to give us the right words for the communication of His truth.

Now we do not mean to suggest by this that the Spirit gives a preacher fresh revelation equaling what he gave to the holy men who wrote the Scriptures. No! What we mean is that the Spirit helps us to choose the right words to communicate His unchanging word to the audience before us. Paul always aimed to preach the mystery of the gospel: the truths God revealed in shadows in the Old Testament and now plainly revealed in the person and work of the Lord Jesus Christ. His message was fixed, but in every situation Paul needed fresh words to make the message known to his hearers.

In Ephesians 6, he is praying for words because even after we know the gospel we always need appropriate words to impress the truth upon the hearts of various people. In Acts 13, when Paul preached to Jews, he started with words from the Bible. In Acts 17, in Athens, he started with words from a Greek poet. The gospel preacher always needs to know which words to use to apply the gospel. Think about it: when Paul wanted to defend the truth that justification is by faith alone he needed to know the OT background, but also he needed to know how to use

---

6. F. F. Bruce, *The Epistle to the Colossians, to Philemon, and to the Ephesians* (Grand Rapids, MI: Eerdmans, 1984), 413.

the right arguments to keep people in the faith. He needed to use arguments that made sense to the people to whom he was writing. He needed to understand what they knew and where they were mistaken in order to correct them and to lead them on in the faith. In 1 Corinthians he needed to know the right words to keep people united around the cross. This is what ministry is: finding the right words to bring people to Christ. We need words to rejoice with those who rejoice and to weep with those who weep. We need words.

One of the things that I find so hard about the ministry is that you have to fill so many different roles and adapt to so many different situations. One minute you are at a funeral with the loved ones of the deceased, then you are in an elders' meeting debating a vision for the future, then you are at a prayer meeting, then a pre-engagement session, then a new member's interview where the person thinks the church is awesome, then a meeting with a member who is thinking about leaving, then sharing the gospel with a homeless man, then heading off to meet an atheist for lunch; and in all of those situations you need appropriate words. You need to know if you ought to share a word of encouragement, an intellectual worldview challenge, simple kindness and courtesy, laughter, tears, or all of the foregoing! In all of ministry you are looking for words. It is like this in preaching: we need the right words to bring the gospel home in each preaching situation. Each time we open our mouths to preach, we need the words to help the people in front of us. No doubt God helps us have this as we study the Bible and study our people, but it is also necessary that He give us wisdom to know the right words as we preach and prepare to preach.

The work of the Spirit in our preaching is not a fog or a mist. It is the work of a real person who gives us boldness, light, love, and words. Now we turn to how we should seek this help on our preaching.

CHAPTER
9

THE SERMON
AND THE SPIRIT: PART THREE

Seeking the Spirit

A friend of mine (Fullerton) tells a story that he attributes to the preacher Vance Havner. Once at a conference where many were discussing the Holy Spirit, Havner said, "I've been sitting around listening to all these scholars lecture about the Holy Spirit. It put me in a mind of a bunch of hobos sitting around the campfire talking about high finance, without a dollar between them." We do not want to be such hobos, and we do not want to be such scholars. We do not want merely to talk about what the Holy Spirit can do in preaching; we want to seek him, and ask him, and expect him to do his work in our preaching. And expect it we should! The Spirit who was poured out on the apostles in Acts 2 is the same Spirit who empowers preachers today. Yes, the events of Pentecost were unique in the history of redemption, but that should not quell our enthusiasm for the Spirit: it should instead excite it. As John Murray has written, "If Pentecost is not repeated, neither is it retracted. . . . This is the era of the Holy Spirit."[1] The Holy Spirit was uniquely poured out on the day of Pentecost, but this does not close the door to our receiving the Holy Spirit

---

1. Quoted in Arturo G. Azurdia, *Spirit Empowered Preaching*, 17.

in a similar way; it opens it. Just a short time after the initial and unique outpouring of the Holy Spirit as recorded in Acts 2, we find the apostles asking for and receiving the help of the Holy Spirit again. After facing their first round of persecution, the apostles gathered with other Christians and prayed, "Lord, look upon their threats and grant to your servants to continue to speak your word with all boldness, while you stretch out your hand to heal, and signs and wonders are performed through the name of your holy servant Jesus." And when they had prayed, the place in which they were gathered together was shaken, and they were all filled with the Holy Spirit and continued to speak the word of God with boldness" (Acts 4:30–31). This same Holy Spirit is offered to us today. So then the question we must ask is, "How should we seek the Holy Spirit's empowerment on our ministries?" I offer four ways we should seek him today.

With a Constant Reliance on the Spirit's Word

One of the things you find as you read the New Testament is that the Spirit is not just the one behind miraculous gifts or godly lives. He is the One who authored Scripture. When the Scripture speaks, the Spirit speaks. When I say this I do not merely mean that the Scriptures were inspired by the Spirit in the past. This is glorious and true, but what I am aiming to say is that when we read the Scriptures today, the Spirit is still actively speaking. The author of the letter to the Hebrews says it this way, "Therefore, *as the Holy Spirit says*, 'Today, if you hear his voice, do not harden your hearts as in the rebellion'" (Heb 3:7–8, emphasis added). In this remarkable passage the author of Hebrews (who is himself writing under the inspiration of the Holy Spirit), quotes Psalm 95 to the Hebrew Christians and reminds them that what they are reading is the active voice of the Spirit of God. As they read his letter they are hearing what the "Holy Spirit says."

The Holy Spirit speaks through the written Word. It is imperative to remember this when we think about preaching in the power of the Holy Spirit. There can be a temptation in all of us, when we come to understand the Spirit's active and personal ministry, to rely on his subjective guidance and empowerment apart from the written Word of God. We can begin to ask, "What is the Spirit saying to me today?" or "What does the Spirit want to say through me to his people?" We can ask these questions with our eyes strained toward heaven more than focused on the book. This is folly. If we do not seek the Spirit's word with our primary gaze on the Scriptures we will always miss his voice. Looking for a word from God with our Bibles closed is like gagging a man and then asking him to speak.

Brothers, do you want the Spirit to speak through you? Then you must devote yourself to understanding and explaining his word. The tasks of diligent Bible study, careful exegesis, and understanding biblical and systematic theology are not distractions that will take you away from the power of the Spirit. No, these are all disciplines that help us accurately discern the voice of the Spirit of God. The one who studies hard in order to "rightly handle the word of truth" is the one through whom the Spirit will speak. The Holy Spirit will provide his wind to our preaching only if we make sure we are raising the sail of his Word.

With a Constant Reliance on the Lord's Gospel

It is possible to preach the Bible without preaching the gospel. If there is such a thing as "rightly handling the word of truth," then there is such a thing as wrongly handling the word of truth (2 Tim 2:15). The false teachers Paul confronted in the book of Galatians were not trying to get the Galatian Christians to turn *away* from the Bible, but instead, to focus on *one part* of the Bible while neglecting the teaching of another part of the Bible. Their aim was to get the Galatians to embrace the Law of Moses, with its rites and rituals, instead of the fulfillment of all that Moses pointed to, which is found only in Jesus Christ. This is part of what made their teaching so insidious. Instead of abandoning the Bible, they were deceptively emphasizing one portion of God's Word to the detriment of another—the very part that could lead men to Jesus Christ.[2] They wanted

---

2. This deadly mistake of the false teachers in Galatia, which was, in fact, a spurious gospel, sprang from their failure to interpret Scripture in light of *the covenantal horizons* described earlier in this book.

to focus on the Law as a way to establish a righteousness of their own, rather than letting the law drive them to the saving righteousness of Christ (Rom 10:3).

As we pursue preaching in the power of the Holy Spirit, we must make sure we know just what the Holy Spirit is eager to say. What we find in the Scriptures is that the Holy Spirit loves to talk about Jesus! Our Lord Jesus Christ made that clear to the two disciples on the road to Emmaus. That day, as he walked with those two disciples, the risen Christ preached to them what must have been one of the most marvelous and warm expositions of the Scriptures ever given. Luke summarizes Jesus's message this way: "And beginning with Moses and all the Prophets, he interpreted to them in all the Scriptures the things concerning himself" (Luke 24:27). Jesus did not merely explain to these disciples that Genesis 3:15 pointed to him, or that Isaiah 53 looked to him. No, he opened to them "all the Scriptures" from the books of Moses to the end of the prophets. In all of this he showed them himself.

If the entire Bible points to Jesus (and it does), then this means that the Holy Spirit is always talking about him. Consequently, the faithful preacher will make the same resolve that Paul made to the Corinthian Christians: "I decided to know nothing among you except Jesus Christ and him crucified" (1 Cor 2:2). Paul had one message, and that message was Christ. Granted, he applied Christ to marriage, lawsuits, parenting, and every other area of the Christian life; but for Paul, preaching was always about Christ.

Arturo Azurdia in his marvelous little book, *Spirit Empowered Preaching*, calls the Holy Spirit the Christocentric Spirit.[3] The Spirit loves to talk about Jesus. If we would have his blessing on our ministries and his power on our preaching, then we must make sure our preaching always orbits Christ like the earth orbits the sun. We must be Christocentric if we would receive the Christocentric Spirit. After all, his promised power was given so that we could be his witnesses (Acts 1:8).

---

3. Azurdia, *Spirit Empowered Preaching*, 47.

With a Constant Reliance on God in Prayer

Often our lack of the Spirit's empowerment is not a complicated matter. James sums up our problem when he says, "You do not have, because you do not ask" (Jas 4:2). It is that simple. No prayer, no Spirit. God has determined to work through means. He not only decides what he is going to do (give us the Spirit), but how he is going to do it (through our asking). If we would have more of God's Spirit, we must ask! This is the clear teaching of Luke 11:9–13, where our Lord taught:

> And I tell you, ask, and it will be given to you; seek, and you
> will find; knock, and it will be opened to you. For everyone
> who asks receives, and the one who seeks finds, and to the
> one who knocks it will be opened. What father among you, if
> his son asks for a fish, will instead of a fish give him a serpent;
> or if he asks for an egg, will give him a scorpion? If you then,
> who are evil, know how to give good gifts to your children,
> how much more will the heavenly Father give the Holy Spirit
> to those who ask him!

Our Heavenly Father wants to give us good gifts. More than we want to see our children's faces light up when we give them gifts, God wants to enjoy our receiving delightful gifts from him. Above all other gifts, he wants to give us more and more of the empowerment of his Holy Spirit. Again, not only has he made clear *what* he wants to do (give us the Holy Spirit), but also *how* he wants to do it (through persistent prayer). We are called to ask, seek, and knock.

For years now, I have believed that I needed prayer to be a vital part of my preaching ministry. Only recently, however, a new thought came to my mind: why don't I treat prayer for my preaching with the same intentionality that I treat studying for my preaching? When it comes to studying for the sermons I preach, I try to start early in the week. I block out large chunks of time so that I can study hard, and I try to avoid letting anything but emergencies interfere with that time. Why don't I treat prayer that same way? Does God not call the preacher to be devoted to Word and prayer? If so, then shouldn't we give prayer the kind of focus we give to study? What would happen if we used the same intensity and focus in our praying that we do in our studying? I believe we might see more of the effective preaching we see in the book of Acts. Sadly, this kind of thinking is often unheard of among those who are preparing for ministry. "Rarely are seminarians taught to pray and fast and weep for the subjective and internal illumination of the Holy Spirit in correspondence with their diligent efforts in the sacred text."[4] Brothers, we study to know what the text means, but we must also pray for the Spirit's empowerment on our proclamation! We should be as familiar with petitions, fasting, and weeping as we are with commentaries, theologies, and the rigorous thinking that is required to rightly divide the Word.

With a Constant Reliance on the Prayers of Our People

Not only should we seek the Lord in prayer ourselves, but we should also ask our people to pray for us. The apostles modeled this practice. Notice what Paul does after he asks believers to pray for one another. He calls them to be "praying at all times in the Spirit, with all prayer and supplication. To that end keep alert with all perseverance, making supplication for all the saints, *and also for me*, that words may be given to me in opening my mouth boldly to proclaim the mystery of the gospel" (Eph 6:18–19, emphasis added). He makes the same request to the Romans when he writes, "I appeal to you, brothers, by our Lord Jesus Christ and by the love of the Spirit, to strive together with me in your prayers to God on my behalf" (Rom 15:30). He repeats this request again in 2 Corinthians 1:11, Philippians 1:19, Colossians 4:3, 1 Thessalonians 5:22, and Philemon 22. Paul asked for prayer for all aspects of his ministry, but especially for his preaching. We see this again in 2 Thessalonians 3:1, where he pleads, "Finally, brothers, pray for us, that the word of the Lord may speed ahead and be honored, as happened among you" (2 Thess 3:1). Paul was the guy in the prayer meeting who is always asking for prayer. Why did he do it? He believed prayer made a difference.

---

4. Azurdia, 39.

In church history, one of the men whose preaching was effective like that recorded in the book of Acts was Charles Spurgeon. When asked what the secret was to his success he answered, "My people pray for me."[5] If we would have the Spirit on our ministries we must not only make our requests known to God, we must make them known to our people as well.

Brothers, the Spirit is vital to our preaching. We must despair of doing anything in our preaching without him. We must understand how he works in and through preachers, and we must seek him in his Word. We must keep the focus of our preaching on Christ and his gospel, and we must seek his presence and power through our prayers and the prayers of our people.

---

5. Lewis A. Drummond, *Spurgeon: Prince of Preachers* (Grand Rapids, MI: Kregel, 1992), 211.

PART TWO

Preparing to Lead the People of God to Experience God: Early Preparation

CHAPTER
10

DELIVERY MATTERS

Preaching Is Primary

"How many of you were converted through a cold-turkey, one-on-one evangelistic encounter?" This is a question that I (Orrick) sometimes ask classes and congregations when I am about to make a point about the importance of preaching. In answer to my question maybe 1 percent raises their hands.

I ask again, "How many of you were converted through reading a gospel tract?" Occasionally someone will raise a hand.

"How many of you were converted through reading the Bible or a book about the Bible on your own?" Again, few hands are raised.

I may go on to ask about the effectiveness of other evangelistic endeavors, but my final question is, "How many of you were converted as a direct result of preaching?" Consistently, over 90 percent of hands go up. My informal surveys and my study of church history convince me that God uses the preaching of his Word to call sinners to himself, and he uses preaching more than all other means combined.

In asserting the primacy of preaching, I am in no way minimizing the importance of personal witnessing, tract distribution, and other means of evangelism. God gifts his people in various ways. Not everyone is called to preach, but every one of God's children has something he or she can do to help further the joyful news of salvation through Jesus Christ. For example, I know a man whose call to follow Christ commenced when, during a time of great grief, a Christian neighbor brought him a salad. He began seeking to know more about Christ because a concerned neighbor was using her gift of food preparation to reach out to him. So preaching is not the only means that God uses to sow the seeds of truth. In fact, I happily grant that preaching is usually most effective in the context of a church full of loving people who are seeking to be obedient to the Lord in using their various gifts to reach out to others. We all work together like the various parts of a body. Still, through the centuries, God has primarily used faithful preaching to communicate his truth to the world and to call his people to himself. And so it is reasonable that we should devote close attention to how we preach as well as what we preach, for God uses both content and delivery to communicate his truth.

Delivery Matters

Someone might take issue with that last sentence, and say, "Is it true that God uses *delivery* as well as content to communicate his truth? After all, the Spirit asserts that it pleased God through the folly of *what* we preach to save those who believe (1 Cor 1:21). Furthermore, on the surface it appears that Paul was minimizing the importance of delivery when he wrote that he deliberately avoided 'lofty speech and plausible words of wisdom' so that his ministry would be 'in demonstration of the Spirit and of power, that your faith might not rest in the wisdom of men but in the power of God' (1 Cor 2:1–5). So how can you maintain that delivery is a significant part of the message?" In the passages referenced, Paul is not asserting that delivery does not matter; on the contrary, he is asserting that delivery *does* matter because delivery has the potential to distract from the message or it has the potential to complement the message. While in Corinth, Paul deliberately chose a style of delivery that would enhance the message of salvation through faith alone in Christ alone. In determining his methodology, Paul considered the culture of Corinth and the characteristics of his hearers. Then, from a variety of rhetorical options, he chose the one that he believed was best suited for that particular setting and that particular group of people. This is a process that all effective preachers must go through. Virtually all effective preachers and teachers know the culture of their hearers and the unique characteristics of the particular congregation that will be in front of them when it comes time to preach. This enables the preacher accurately to predict how the congregation will receive or react to everything that is said. Good preachers and teachers know human nature, and they work hard to customize their delivery to their audience. Sometimes this customization means that the preacher leaves out certain oratorical or poetic flourishes of which he is capable, leaving them out because they would be a distraction. This is what Paul did at Corinth. Other times, a preacher must work hard to improve his grammar or his speaking skills because his poor delivery is a distraction for his audience. All the while, the preacher is thinking of his hearers because he wants them to understand and feel what is being preached.

I often hear preaching that causes me to suspect that the preacher is more concerned with getting through his notes than he is with getting through to his hearers.[1] Good teachers and preachers humble themselves and get out of the way so that the Word of God may be felt intensely and heard clearly by their audiences. The temptation to show off is a perpetual temptation to the preacher, but he fights the temptation because he knows that there is room at center stage for only one person; and that one person must be God, not the preacher. The preacher with integrity understands that he cannot at the same time say, "I am clever, so admire me," and "God is great, so worship him."[2] The effort to become a better preacher is an effort to become less visible so God will become more glorious. A good preacher is to the Word of God what a good accompanist

---

1. I heard Hershael York, professor of preaching at The Southern Baptist Theological Seminary—and my lifelong friend—say something like this.
2. This sentence is an expansion of an idea that I heard expressed by Reginald Barnard, professor at Mid-America Baptist Theological Seminary.

is to a great soloist; he uses his gifts to help the audience appreciate someone else.

Able to Teach

When the Holy Spirit insists that a pastor be able to teach (1 Tim 3:2), he is affirming the necessity of the pastor having good delivery skills. Note that Paul used the words "able to teach," not "able to learn," though that too is important. Yes, the pastor must learn, but then he must be able to deliver the learning that is in his head and his heart to the heads and hearts of others. We have all known men who were quite intelligent and who were highly educated who nevertheless were terrible teachers. Even a holy man who knows the Bible well may be disqualified from serving as a pastor because he cannot teach. The skills that help make a person a good teacher are so important that if a man does not have this set of skills, he is not qualified to be a pastor. Why is this so important? If a man cannot teach, it is a sure indication that something crucial to being a good pastor is missing. Certain qualities that are foundational to being a good teacher are also foundational to other roles that a pastor must fill. If a man cannot teach, he may be a good man who is well qualified to do many important jobs in the church, but he is disqualified from serving as a pastor.

One quality that all good teachers possess is the ability to anticipate how his words will sound in the ears of his hearers. He knows human nature. He knows how people think. Like a good chess player is able accurately to predict the moves that his opponent will make, a good teacher/preacher is able accurately to predict the reaction of his audience to what he says because he knows how people think. A man who can make such accurate predictions knows human nature, and a pastor must know human nature even if his primary responsibilities do not include regular preaching. A man who does not understand people will botch the task of ministering to people. Would you hire someone to take care of your sheep if he knew nothing about sheep? If an aspiring pastor does not know human nature, he will constantly be saying things that people are not interested in hearing; that is, he will be boring. A boring preacher is not a good preacher, and a boring preacher is not fully qualified to be a pastor. A consistently boring preacher either does not know the nature of his hearers or he does not care enough about them to do the hard work necessary to reach them. Either way, such a man has no business being a pastor—at least not yet.

As important as it is for a pastor to have the skills of delivery that lead to good teaching, being able to teach is not the only qualification for being a pastor. Sometimes bad men can be excellent teachers; and, of course, bad men must not be pastors. A friend of mine once told me about a pastor in his area who had a drinking problem. Sometimes on Sunday mornings the deacons would have to try to sober him up so he could preach that day. When my friend asked one of the deacons why the church tolerated such behavior from their pastor, the deacon responded, "You ought to hear him preach!" No matter how well the man could preach, his drunkenness disqualified him from being a pastor; almost everyone recognizes that. But thousands of churches are plagued with pastors who cannot preach, and these pastors are also unqualified.

Ultimately, it is God alone who can make a preacher. This may seem like a strange admission to appear in the pages of a book on how to preach an expository sermon, but none of us who have written this book believe that great preaching can be taught. Great preachers, like great sprinters or great baseball pitchers, are usually born with the natural abilities that make them great at what they do. But even gifted sprinters and pitchers must train their skills to be the best they can be. A man who has been called by God and genuinely desires to be a better preacher can usually improve. But it will take work, and willingness to work on delivery commences with the conviction that delivery is important. In fact, I want to convince you that the *delivery* of a message is an essential part of the message. How something is said is a critical part of what is said.

Delivery Is Part of the Message

The Bible itself, taken as a whole, is the best illustration that delivery is a crucial part of the message delivered. Contrast the way that the Bible is written with the way a book of systematic theology is written. I love systematic theology, and systematic theologians perform an indispensable service by summarizing what the Bible teaches on various subjects and arranging the truths in logical order. Some of my favorite books are systematic theologies. But the Bible plainly is not written like a systematic theology. Instead, the Bible is a collection of narratives, poems, letters, and various other kinds of literature. It is the basic task of the systematic theologian to objectively summarize the facts, but that is not the basic task of someone writing literature. A writer of literature wants to do much more than summarize the facts; he wants his readers to *feel* what he is writing, so he utilizes an array of literary devices to promote feeling in his readers. He uses word pictures that evoke emotion. He chooses words that have cultural connotations and emotional weight. He draws on his knowledge of human nature to set up scenarios that will produce predictable reactions in his readers. From an almost endless possibility of choices, he selects just the right facts to develop the characters in his story and emphasize the point of his story. A writer utilizes these various literary devices even when writing history. This was also true when a writer was writing Scripture under the inspiration of the Holy Spirit. Why did God inspire the holy men who wrote the Bible to write literature? Because not all truths are grasped through logic; some truth is simply recognized, and much truth is understood by means of faith. Skillful poets and other writers of literature are especially gifted at helping us to recognize truth by the *way* they write. In this the preacher is like the poet. How he delivers the message is a crucial part of the message.

There is an almost endless variety of ways to say something, but none of them communicate the exact same message. There is no such thing as an exact synonym. Even in a list of alleged synonyms, every word has a nuance of meaning. There is a difference between saying, "He is lean" and "He is skinny." As words carry nuance of meaning, so also do more protracted means of communication such as the genres or types of literature found in the Bible. The prophet Nathan could have simply told David, "I know that you had an affair with Bathsheba," but instead he told David the masterful story of the little pet lamb who was stolen and slaughtered by the rich neighbor. "Nathan's sword was within an inch of

David's conscience before David knew that Nathan had a sword. One sudden thrust, and the king was at Nathan's feet. What a rebuke of our slovenly, unskillful, blundering work!"[3] Isaiah might have predicted, "The Messiah will offer himself as a sacrifice of substitutionary atonement." Instead he wrote, "He was wounded for our transgressions, he was bruised for our iniquities: the chastisement of our peace was upon him; and with his stripes we are healed. All we like sheep have gone astray; we have turned everyone to his own way; and the LORD hath laid on him the iniquity of us all" (53:5, 6 KJV). Charles Wesley might have described his conversion by saying, "I recently believed the truth about Jesus Christ, and now I have become a Christian." Instead he wrote:

> Long my imprisoned spirit lay fast bound in sin and nature's
> night.
> Thine eye diffused a quick'ning ray; I woke, the dungeon
> flamed with light.
> My chains fell off, my heart was free!
> I rose, went forth, and followed thee.[4]

This verse has meaning beyond the unadorned statement. Wesley utilized words and metaphors that arouse appropriate emotion in the reader, and the appropriate emotional response is an essential part of understanding the message. Note the progression in the following illustration. First, imagine that you simply read the statement, "I recently believed the truth about Jesus Christ, and now I have become a Christian." Next imagine that you hear a good reader read Wesley's verse with passion. There is a big difference, right? Now imagine that you hear a soloist sing the verse set to Thomas Campbell's tune "Sagina." Finally, imagine that you hear a congregation of thousands singing the song. What if the congregation is located in a region of the world where the

3. Alexander Whyte, *Bible Characters*, vol. 2, *Gideon to Absalom* (Edinburgh and London: Oliphant Anderson and Ferrier, n.d.), 245. Available on Google Books at https://books.google.com/books?id=XTDku7qBvNwC&printsec=frontcover&dq=Bible+Characters,+Volume+2&hl=en&sa=X&ved=0ahUKEwi0yP7hmPvPAhUI6CYKHXngAbcQ6AEIHjAA#v=onepage&q&f=false.
4. From Charles Wesley's hymn, "And Can It Be?"

gospel has recently come with power, and the singers have all been recently converted? How something is delivered becomes a part of the message.

Hearing a preacher in person ought to be different than reading his sermons in a book, and it ought to be vastly better. Hearing him in person ought to be better than hearing him on a recording, watching him on television, or even hearing the sermon via live video feed. There is the potential for him to communicate so much more in person. This is one reason why a preacher's preaching is less effective when he has prepared his sermon with any audience in view other than the audience that will hear him at the moment it comes out of his mouth.[5]

I urge you to read some of the descriptive accounts of those who personally heard George Whitefield or C. H. Spurgeon preach. These gifted preachers astounded their hearers. They sometimes moved thousands to tears as they preached. Now read some of their sermons. Their printed sermons are excellent, but the printed sermons do not produce the same effects described by the eyewitnesses who heard them preach the sermons in person. Perhaps you have read "Sinners in the Hands of an Angry God," by Jonathan Edwards. Did it cause you to cry out in anguish or weep when you read it? Perhaps not, but many reacted this way when they heard Edwards preach it. Why the difference? The ultimate answer is "the Holy Spirit." But that ultimate answer demands that another question be asked: "Why did the Holy Spirit bless the personal delivery of a sermon in a way that he rarely blesses the personal reading of the same sermon?"

Delivery Is Customized

When a preacher preaches a sermon that he has prepared for the press, or for the Internet, or for any audience other than the one that will actually

---

5. "It is as easy to paint fire with heat, as with pen and ink to commit that to paper which occurs in preaching. There is as much difference between a sermon in the pulpit, and printed in a book, as between milk in the warm breast, and in a sucking bottle, yet what it loseth in the lively taste, is recompensed by the convenience of it" (William Gurnall, *The Christian in Complete Armour: A Treatise of the Saints' War against the Devil*, first published in three volumes between 1662 and 1665; reprinted in one volume by the Banner of Truth Trust [Carlisle, PA: 1964], 2).

hear him, he is like an amateur basketball player who tries to plan out ahead of a game the specific passes he will make and the specific shots he will take during the game. This is a recipe for defeat. On the other hand, great basketball players practice all the fundamentals ahead of time; but during the game they see the whole court, they know where everyone is on the court, they are aware of the skills of everyone on the court, and with all this in mind, they utilize their skill set to make the best possible play as it unfolds. Similarly, effective preachers put the required time into preparation, both long-term and immediate, but when it is "game time," they take a multitude of factors into consideration. They make decisions that demonstrate sensitivity to the text, to the audience, and to the Holy Spirit.

I have read that when C. H. Spurgeon was preaching, he continuously had seven distinguishable lines of thought coursing through his mind.[6] All seven were relevant to what he was saying at the moment; and from the seven, he chose the one he thought best expressed what needed to be said. At least he chose the one he thought was best for expressing the truth orally to the audience that was before him at the moment. As Spurgeon was preaching, stenographers created a verbatim manuscript of his sermon, and on Monday morning Spurgeon would review the manuscript and revise it for publication. His revisions were extensive, for he knew what I wish a great many more preachers knew—there is a vast difference between a sermon preached and a sermon printed. I say plainly what I previously intimated: if a preacher prepares and delivers his sermon with any audience in view other than the audience that is in front of him when he is preaching it, he is running the race wearing shackles, and he is quenching the Spirit.[7] That is a bold assertion, and I intend to come back to it in a later chapter, but for now, just consider how many times you have been disappointed with the preaching of a man whose writings have been a great blessing to you. The disparity between

---

6. Eric W. Hayden, "Charles H. Spurgeon: Did You Know?" *Christian History* 29 (1991), http://www.christianitytoday.com/history/issues/issue-29/charles-h-spurgeon-did-you-know.html.

7. If the sermon later becomes part of a book or is posted on the Internet, fine. But you are serving stale leftover bread crusts to company when you serve a chapter from a book to your congregation. Let your listeners have fresh, fragrant bread hot out of the oven.

a man's writing and his preaching can usually be traced to the fact that he has not made a sufficient distinction between the communication style appropriate for writing and the communication style necessary for preaching.

The average preacher will not have seven distinguishable lines of thought coursing through his mind as he preaches, but he will have more than one. As a preacher develops his gifts he will become more skilled at choosing just the right way to speak the truth of God's Word most effectively to those hearers the Lord has placed in front of him. It is a lifelong task that requires diligent attention and never-ending labor, but it is worth all the effort. Delivery matters.

READING THE SCRIPTURES WELL

Until I come, devote yourself to the public reading
of Scripture, to exhortation, to teaching.
—1 Timothy 4:13

Good Reading Is Good Teaching

Richard Owen Roberts was helping lead a tour group through Great Britain. The tour was focused on visiting various historic sites where God had sent revival or where he had otherwise blessed the ministry of the Word in a remarkable way. One of the sites they visited was Olney, where John Newton, the author of "Amazing Grace," had ministered for a number of years. When they visited the church building in Olney, there was no regularly scheduled meeting going on. No one outside the tour group was present. Mr. Roberts led the group to the front of the sanctuary, and he began reading a lengthy passage of Scripture aloud. While Mr. Roberts was reading to the tour group, the vicar of the Olney church came through the building for some mundane purpose—perhaps to pick up his mail. For some reason, he decided to sit down on the back row and listen to the reading, which was from the book of 2 Chronicles, and which included several chapters of the text. When Mr. Roberts concluded the reading, the vicar came to the front of the church, fell at Mr. Roberts' feet, and clasped him around his legs weeping. He said that since his ordination into the ministry, he had never been so moved by the Lord as he was in hearing Mr. Roberts read the Scriptures.[1] When God's Word is read well, it is a powerful thing. When a preacher reads God's Word well, his exposition of the text is more than half done. Good reading is good teaching, and it is a significant step toward good preaching.

A brief exercise will demonstrate to you that public reading, or oral interpretation of Scripture, also entails teaching. I want you to read Romans 1:16 aloud, or at least hearing it in your head. "For I am not ashamed of the gospel, for it is the power of God for salvation to everyone who believes, to the Jew first and also to the Greek." Now I want you to read it again with the following scenarios in mind. First, read it supposing that Paul was answering critics who said that the reason he had neglected to visit Rome was because he was ashamed to preach the simple gospel in such a prestigious academic environment. With this background information in mind, how ought the verse be read? Next, suppose that Paul is addressing those who claimed that the gospel was nothing more than a story about a noble teacher of morals—a great prophet, but not the Messiah. With this in mind, how ought the verse be read? Or what if Paul has in mind certain Jews who believed that Jesus was the Messiah, but he was the Messiah for Jews only? How ought the verse to be read? Or what if he has in mind certain religious men who argued that the way of salvation through Jesus entails faith, yes, but those who are saved are also required to keep the Law of Moses? How ought the verse to be read? If you take the time to read this one verse, keeping in mind the several scenarios that I have suggested, you will see that you will need to emphasize a different part of the verse with each reading. Which is the right way? Taking into account the context, all four scenarios are plausible. You must decide, and when you read it the way you believe it ought to be read you will inevitably be interpreting the verse. You will be teaching.

---

1. Dr. Tony Mattea, who was part of the tour group, recounted this story to me.

And yet, so few preachers take the time and effort to learn how to read the Scriptures well in public. At least, I hope that it is only lack of initiative that is the explanation for poor reading. I fear that there are often more serious causes. Sometimes when I hear a preacher read his text in a bland, passionless way, I think to myself, *He has never felt the power of that text. There is no way he could read that passage in such a bored monotone if he had felt the power of God in it.* Not only may poor reading sometimes reflect a lack of passionate engagement with the text, it may also indicate that the preacher has not thoroughly understood the text. Usually, a poor reading of the text is a gloomy prelude to a poor sermon. Good preaching begins with good reading because good reading is rooted in understanding the text and feeling the power of the text.

Along with being a preacher of God's Word, I also teach undergraduate students at Boyce College. One of the classes I teach is an introduction to English poetry. Most of my students have had very little exposure to poetry before arriving in my class, and consequently, some are not yet very proficient at interpreting poems. For the first several weeks of this class, much of my teaching consists of simply reading and explaining great poems. During those early weeks, for homework I assign the students to read the poems that I will explain the following week in class. Students have repeatedly testified that they had been puzzled by a poem until they heard me read it in class—not explain it—just read it aloud. Simply hearing someone who already understands the poem read the poem opens their minds to understand the poem. It is the same with the Bible. Simply hearing someone who understands the Bible read the Bible will open many minds to understanding the Bible.

Good Reading Promotes Love and Respect for the Bible

When you read the Bible well, not only will you help people to understand the Bible, you will also help them to love the Bible and regard it for what it is—the Word of God. A love for the Scriptures is *caught* more than *taught*, and the same may be said for the conviction that the Bible is the inerrant Word of God. The Holy Spirit testifies that the Bible is the Word of God, but it is not primarily through logical arguments that he accomplishes this. Augustine observed that believers throughout the world regarded the Scriptures to be God's Word, and this led to his believing the Bible to be the Word of God. "So, since we were too weak to discover truth by pure reason and therefore needed the authority of Holy Writ, I now began to believe that you could not possibly have given such supreme authority to these Scriptures all over the world, unless it had been your wish that by means of them men should both believe in you and seek after you."[2] The care and effort you put into reading well will say to your hearers, "This is God's holy Word, and it is a treasure." Some preachers will have the members of the congregation stand to their feet when the Bible is being read. Others conclude the reading of Scripture by saying, "This is the Word of the Lord," and the congregation responds with, "Praise be to God." I appreciate these gestures of reverence. But you will be far more successful at cultivating reverence for the Bible if you read the Bible as if God is speaking through the Bible and you are relishing every word of it. Conversely, even if you ask the congregation to stand, or assert "This is the Word of the Lord," and you read the Scriptures without expression and passion, you will not be as effective at cultivating reverence and love for the Bible as you might otherwise have been. If you had received a love letter from your girlfriend, and you were reading selections from the letter to a close friend, would you read it in a dull monotone? If you had received a note of appreciation from the president of your school, and you were reading it to your family, would you read it without emphasis? The excitement you would communicate in reading such letters would reveal much about how you valued what was written, and the same is true with the reading of the Bible.

Reading Well Is Worth the Effort

Most preachers simply do not pay enough attention to reading well. Some might protest, "I just do not have good reading skills." You can almost certainly improve your reading skills. I also teach public speaking classes, and in these classes I will sometimes spend a couple of weeks

---

2. Augustine, *Confessions*, 6.5.

teaching the oral interpretation of Scripture, and then each student will read an assigned passage for a grade. I have found that most students can significantly improve their public reading skills with a little effort and a little coaching. In fact, of all the skills involved in being an effective preacher, oral interpretation of Scripture is the skill that can be most improved with the least amount of effort in the least amount of time. I have seen more than one student progress from being a boring reader to become a pretty good reader in as little as two weeks. It is an investment that yields enormous dividends both for the reader and for the listener, so it is well worth the effort.

Others say, "I feel fake when I read with expression and emphasis; dramatic reading of Scripture sounds contrived." Sometimes it does! I am not trying to get you to read with a passion that you do not genuinely feel. Rather, I want to set you free from any inhibitions that are holding you back from reading as passionately as you do feel. Pretending to feel what you do not feel is off-putting to your hearers, and it may be compared to causing distortion in a sound system. If you try to put 100 decibels of volume through a sound system that is designed to handle only eighty decibels, you will distort the sound. So, I am not trying to get you to read in a way that is unnatural to your personality, but I do want to turn up your volume as much as possible without causing distortion. As you progress in your emotional sanctification, it will be like adding a power booster to your sound system. You will be able honestly to read with more passion when you honestly feel more passion.

In the Christian life, genuine passion grows out of understanding the truth. The most crucial factor in becoming a good reader of Scripture is to have a good understanding of what you are reading. In the short term, at the very least you ought to read beforehand any passage of Scripture that you are going to read in public. In the long term, we ought to become so familiar with the entire Bible that someone might randomly open the Bible to any passage of Scripture, and we will know the overall context of that passage, and we will be able to read it with understanding.

A Few Pointers

When reading aloud, do not read as if you are in a reading race. Slow down! I remember sitting in a circle in the first grade where each student in the circle would take a turn reading from our *Dick and Jane Reader*. Some students were eager to prove how well they could read by showing how fast they could read. I remember thinking that those speed readers sacrificed comprehension. (Though, in the first grade, I probably never thought those exact words. Apparently, even then God was preparing me to write this chapter!) The average listener cannot comprehend the Bible when it is read even at a normal walking pace, much less at a sprinting pace. Read about 10 percent slower than you would speak (unless you are Winnie the Pooh's friend Eeyore). No one will notice that you are reading slowly. From my experience in teaching public reading, I would say that the number one problem for oral readers is that they read too fast.

If you will just slow down, you will create space for several desirable reading skills to fall into place. A slower pace allows time for more deliberate pronunciation and enunciation. When you *pronounce* words well, you pronounce all the vowel sounds and consonant sounds that make a word unique and meaningful. Many English words are quite similar in pronunciation, but communicate different ideas: "When you *close* the doors on the stove, do not get so *close* that you catch your *clothes* on fire." In everyday speaking, we might get sloppy and leave the *th* sound out of the word *clothes*, but in public reading, be sure to deliberately pronounce words according to standard, educated usage.[3] Every preacher ought to own and use a good collegiate dictionary, and he ought to put in the effort to learn how to pronounce words correctly.[4] While you are in college, if not sooner, get in the habit of writing down every word you encounter that you do not thoroughly understand, and then learn what that word means and how to pronounce it.

---

3. Similarly, you ought to learn to speak with standard, educated grammar—not so that you will sound educated, but because your hearers will be able better to understand you.

4. If I were stranded on an island and could have only ten books with me, one of those books would be the latest unabridged edition of *The American Heritage Dictionary*. I would rather have the *Oxford English Dictionary*, but since it consists of twenty-two volumes, that might be cheating.

Good pronunciation will aid you in your enunciation. When you *enunciate*, you project your speech so that you can be heard by everyone who is trying to hear you. When you pronounce your words distinctly and enunciate them clearly, people can better understand what you are saying. I mean they can physically hear you. Older people who have experienced hearing loss will especially appreciate this. I cannot tell you how many times I have had older persons approach me after a church service and say with gratitude, "I could understand every word you spoke." But now, because of widespread abuse of ear buds, head phones, and other personal listening devices, it is not just older people who have difficulty hearing; most college freshmen have already experienced some hearing loss. Speaking with appropriate volume is crucial, but being understood physically is not simply a matter of speaking more loudly or turning up the volume of the building's sound system. When your pronunciation and enunciation are sloppy, increasing the volume only makes these deficiencies more obvious. Even without sound systems, preachers of the past could make themselves heard by thousands of hearers, and this was because of their enunciation. C. H. Spurgeon once

> told his students that it ought to be possible for a speaker so to whisper that his words could be heard all over [the Metropolitan Tabernacle, which seated 5,000]. They looked incredulous.
>
> "You do not think so?" he said. "Very well, gentlemen, adjourn to the Tabernacle and scatter over the building."
>
> The students trooped across the college yard to the great Tabernacle and scattered to the back of the top gallery and to the end seats in the area. Spurgeon came to the pulpit with a smile. Holding up his hand he whispered, Gentlemen, if you hear what I say, show your pocket handkerchiefs."
>
> From all over the building pocket handkerchiefs were exhibited by sixty or seventy men. Then in trumpet tones he called, "Gentlemen, put them away, they are not quite clean."[5]

5. J. C. Carlile, *C. H. Spurgeon: An Interpretive Biography* (London: The Religious Tract Society/Kingsgate Press, 1933), 209.

Another benefit of slowing down is that you are more likely to observe the rhetorical pauses that help make for good reading. Some of these pauses are indicated by the punctuation of the passage. A semicolon gets a longer pause than a comma. A period gets a longer pause than a semicolon. You probably already know that, but when you read too fast, these subtle nuances of good reading are often ignored. In well-written and well-read prose, the pauses are as important as are the rests in a musical score. For reading poetry—and remember that about one-third of the Bible is poetry—the importance of rhetorical pauses is exponentially increased. While many of the pauses are denoted by punctuation, many more are dictated by the meaning and arrangement of the text.

If you are reading a chapter that contains several movements or distinct ideas, such as a chapter in Proverbs or a chapter that contains several parables, pause between the movements so that someone who is only listening and not reading the text with you will know that something new is coming after the pause. Also, when reading the words that occur in a list, be sure to pause a bit after each word. Read the following verses at a normal speaking pace, and then read them again, pausing after each word in the list. "Now the fruit of the Spirit is love, joy, peace, longsuffering, gentleness, goodness, faith, meekness, temperance: against such there is no law" (Gal 5:22–23). When rain falls too hard and fast, it runs off and does not soak into the ground. The same is often true when you read without observing the pauses. Some ideas require a bit of time to percolate into the understanding.

As in preaching, when you read, use your natural voice and accent. Do not pretend to be someone else. It is distracting. After a long separation from one of my best preacher friends, I was surprised to hear him speaking to me in a fake accent that sounded suspiciously like the South Carolina accent of a preacher that he admired. We had been friends for many years, so I was slightly aggravated that he would try to impress me with a fake accent. I wanted to say to him, "You dope! Who do you think you are talking to? I know you, and I know that you are not from South Carolina." He dropped the ersatz accent after a few minutes without my saying anything. If you are from the southern United States, you will sound odd if you suddenly start reading as if you were from Scotland. Speak naturally, but articulately. Be yourself and forget yourself.

What applies to Scripture reading in general is doubly true for reading the text before your sermon. Do not read the text for your sermon in a perfunctory way, using a tone of voice similar to what you would use if you were answering roll call in class. The way some preachers read their text, it sounds as if they are getting through the unpleasant, albeit necessary, preliminaries to the really good stuff—namely, their sermon. They read the Scripture with the same degree of enthusiasm that goes into reading a disclaimer at the end of a medicine commercial or an advertisement for low interest rates on a used car. The attitude appears to be one that says, "We are required to do this, so let's get it over with as soon as possible."

By the way, if you go to pastor a church that does not have a Scripture reading as part of the worship services, you ought immediately to include it. I usually advise my students not to change anything during the first year of a new pastorate, but Scripture reading is an element of reform that can usually be implemented without causing trouble. Many churches that would call themselves liberal have more public reading of Scripture than do most churches that would call themselves conservative and who hold to the inerrancy of Scripture. Virtually no one will have the cheek to object to incorporating the reading of Scripture into public worship, and reading Scripture is one of the most effective ways of teaching large portions of the Bible. In only seven years I either preached through or read aloud nearly half of the Bible in one of the churches I pastored, and I never read more than one chapter per service. The Lord commands the public reading of Scripture (1 Tim 4:13), so let us do it, and let us do it well.

CHAPTER
12

HOW DOES IT FIT?
WHAT DOES IT SAY?

By now we hope we have convinced you that you will most effectively teach the whole counsel of God if you consistently preach expository sermons. In this chapter and the two that follow, we will teach you how to analyze a text for preaching by asking four simple questions:

1. How does this text fit into the overall context of the entire Bible?
2. What does this text say that furthers our understanding of the message of the entire Bible?
3. How is this text built?
4. Why does the truth of this text stay relevant through the centuries?

We will explain these four questions in this and the next two chapters, but first, here is an analogy to help you remember the questions.

I (Orrick) am a big fan of porches. I like how they look, and I like the philosophy of porches. That is, I think a good porch invites you to sit down, sip a cup of freshly brewed coffee, and enjoy quiet conversation with whomever you can get to sit down with you. One of the delightful features of the Orrick household is the morning porch-sit. Porch-sitting season starts in March and ends in November. We do not have a very big porch, but we use it a lot. I like porches.

Not long ago I was staying with some friends, and I had the house to myself in the morning. Naturally, I migrated out to their back porch. I had not been to their house for several years, and since my previous visit, they had added the porch. It was a great, spacious, beautiful thing. After a few minutes of enjoying the porch while sitting under it, I walked out in the dew-covered lawn to admire the porch from a distance. My friend had done it right. All the colors on the porch and its roof perfectly matched those on the rest of his house. The lines of the porch complemented the flow and architectural structure of his house. It fit the house. It also added to the house. It connected the indoors with the outdoors. That porch seemed to say, "Take time to slow down and enjoy God's good gifts." Back on the porch, I examined how my friend had built the porch. I noticed what he had used for columns, his bracing system, and the materials he had used to finish the underside of the roof. I took note of the flooring and the furnishings. I was thinking, "If I wanted to build this porch on the back of my house, how would I do it?" And that question led to another one: "How might I convince my wife that building a porch like this would be a worthwhile addition to our house?"

I find it interesting that in our frantically-paced culture, people continue to build porches on their houses, because the porches are seldom used. I rarely see people actually sitting on their porches. I suspect that they all intended to sit on them when they built their houses. The porch-builders fantasized about calm summer evenings sitting on the porch swing, sipping sweet tea, and reading a good book or casually chatting with a friend. But day after day the porches remain empty. The porches proclaim a need for quiet. The empty, dust covered rockers and porch swings proclaim that we intend to slow down and talk with someone one of these days. We'll get around to it one of these days.

You need to analyze a text like I analyzed that porch. I noticed how the porch fit with the rest of the house. You need to ask how your text fits with the rest of Scripture. I saw how the porch added to the appeal of the house. You need to see what your text adds to the message of Scripture.

I examined how the porch was built. You need to pay attention to how your text is built. And finally, I thought about how a porch—something that many would consider to be an outdated, unnecessary financial expenditure—actually speaks to the enduring need that we have for quiet and fellowship. You must see how the truth of your text is a truth that is relevant to today's world.

The four questions can be phrased in a tiny, easy-to-memorize poem:

> How does it fit?
> What does it say?
> How is it built?
> Why does it stay?

How Does It Fit?

The first question you ought to ask is, "How does my chosen text fit into its context?" As has been said, a text without a context is a pretext. From the outset, it is imperative that you ask how the text fits into the overall message of the Bible, and how it fits into the message of the particular book in which it appears. Some of what follows reemphasizes what Brian Payne wrote in his chapters on context.

First, how does the text fit into the whole Bible? All sixty-six books of the Bible present a coherent message from God. Each of the sixty-six books makes a unique contribution to the overall message. It is a grave error to read the Bible as if it were nothing more than a collection of religious sayings, so you must be careful not to encourage that error through the way that you preach. You ought to aim to preach the Bible the way you want your hearers to read the Bible. Every text has a context. It is not always necessary to remind your hearers of the context, but you must always preach the text in harmony with its context. To do otherwise is to mistrust the Holy Spirit who inspired the text in its context.

What is the coherent message of the Bible? The whole Bible is about Jesus Christ. It is correct to say that the whole Bible is about the Gospel of Jesus Christ as long as you do not make the erroneous assumption that the Gospel is nothing more than the basic historical facts about

Jesus's death, burial, and resurrection. Jesus Christ is a person—a living person who may be known and loved. God forgives sinners of their sins and accepts them as righteous in his sight when they receive a person, Jesus Christ, as their Lord. It is possible to believe right doctrine and not know the person. The aim of preaching is to make Christ known. Christ is revealed in the sixty-six books of the Bible. The most effective way to make Christ known is through explaining and applying the book that the Holy Spirit has written about him.

Yes, even the Old Testament books are about Christ. Think of the Old Testament as a basement that God built with the intention of later constructing a house over it. The New Testament is that house. For centuries, God's people had only the basement, and some of them mistakenly assumed that the basement was all that would ever be built. They thought the basement was the house, but the basement was just the foundation for the house that is being built by Christ under the new covenant. When we Christians talk about the basement, we no longer see it without the house. When we preach Christ from the Old Testament, we are not foisting our Christian bias into the text. Rather, we are seeing the basement from the perspective of someone who has seen the whole house.

What is the best way to gain familiarity with the message of the whole Bible? We have benefitted greatly from reading books of systematic theology, biblical theology, and confessions of faith. Memorizing the Baptist Catechism has been one of the most beneficial things I have ever done. But systematic theologies, confessions, and catechisms are useful only insofar as they summarize the message of the Bible. As useful as they are, there really is no substitute for the regular systematic reading of the Bible itself. Commentaries are useful, but young preachers commonly make two mistakes when it comes to commentaries. On the one hand, they arrogantly assume that they do not need the input of commentators, and they consequently sometimes make errors in interpretation. On the other hand, young preachers timidly assume that they can understand nothing without commentators, and they feel overwhelmed and paralyzed by their own ignorance. A humble, teachable reader of the Bible can understand the Bible. God will give you all the gifts you need to fulfill the ministry for which he is preparing you. Read the Bible thoughtfully and prayerfully and regularly, and through the years you will become not merely better acquainted with the Bible but better acquainted with Christ, and your preaching will be saturated with him.

Since the Bible is a coherent message from God about Jesus Christ, there will be no contradictions in the Bible. When you encounter a text that seems to be contradicted somewhere else in the Bible, you have misunderstood at least one of the texts. Let the Bible interpret the Bible.

Not only does your text fit into the overall message of the entire Bible, but it also is part of the message of the particular book in which the text appears. If you are going to thoroughly understand your text and preach it rightly, you must know thoroughly the book of which it is a part. When you first begin your preparation to be a preacher, try to take a Bible survey class or read a good Bible survey book. These survey classes and books will provide summaries of each book of the Bible. Also, Bible commentaries will usually have an introduction that gives an overview of the message of the book of the Bible that is explained in the commentary. But, once again, there is no substitute for plunging into personal study of the book itself.

If I were to ask you right now to summarize the book of Obadiah in one or two sentences, could you do it? How about the book of Hebrews? Will you be able to next year, or five years from now? Set your mind to be mighty in the Holy Scriptures. Give yourself to the task of knowing God. "Practice these things, immerse yourself in them, so that all may see your progress. Keep a close watch on yourself and on the teaching. Persist in this, for by so doing you will save both yourself and your hearers" (1 Tim 4:15–16).

Every passage in the Bible is rooted in a context. Jesus did not hand out little sayings like Chinese restaurants hand out little sayings in fortune cookies. His sayings came in sermons. The stories about him come in books. The verses we love to quote about him come to us in letters. It is vital that as we study individual passages we do not take the words we are reading out of context. If we commit this error, we will misinterpret

Scripture and distort biblical doctrines. However, if we keep verses in context we will discover gems of truth and beauty.

An example of how interpreters go astray when they take a verse out of context is afforded by a common misunderstanding of Matthew 7:1, which is part of Jesus's Sermon on the Mount. In this passage Jesus famously says, "Judge not, that you be not judged." This verse has been taken to mean that we should never judge anyone, and we should never call their actions evil or their hearts bad. The problem with that interpretation is that it not only contradicts the rest of the Bible, it also contradicts the rest of the Sermon on the Mount. Just five verses later Jesus tells us that we are to consider some people dogs, some people pigs, and we are to treat them accordingly (Matt 7:6). On top of this, Jesus tells us that we are to judge ourselves and then we are lovingly to judge others. That is clearly what he is calling for in Matthew 7:5 when he says, "You hypocrite, first take the log out of your own eye, and then you will see clearly to take the speck out of your brother's eye." Here the log and the speck refer to sins that we are to judge. We are not called to ignore specks and logs. Rather we are called to judge our own logs, and deal with them. And then we are to judge and deal with our brother's specks. Clearly Jesus is not trying to bring about a "judgment-free" existence (such an existence would have to smile at Hitler without judgment). Instead, it is clear that Jesus is trying to bring about a people who do not hypocritically judge others. That is Jesus's aim, and we will see it and preach it when we learn to pay attention to context.

Furthermore, if we learn to read Scripture in its context, we will avoid doctrinal imbalance. For example, in the book of Romans the Holy Spirit teaches that we are justified by faith. This is a glorious truth, and we should boldly proclaim that God justifies the ungodly (Rom 4:5). Some will hear this, however, and they will think that free grace is an excuse to sin. They will take the grace of God and they will excuse all manner of sin because they are already declared righteous. This kind of soul-destroying misinterpretation can be avoided if we simply continue reading in the book. In Romans 6, Paul, after explaining the free justification of God, asks, "What shall we say then? Are we to continue in sin that grace may abound? By no means! How can we who died to sin still live in it?" (Rom 6:1–2). He refutes the error that justification may lead to godlessness with the truth that we have died to sin, and therefore continuing in habitual sin is an impossibility.

If you are up to the challenge and you want to really learn the message of a book of the Bible, commit the entire book to memory. We are strong proponents of Bible memorization. When Orrick was a pastor, he required his pastoral interns to memorize the book of 1 Timothy. Fullerton has required his pastoral interns to memorize the book of Romans over a three-year period. We have been so blessed by memorizing lengthy passages of Scripture. Do not dismiss the possibility of your memorizing entire books of the Bible with the excuse that you have a bad memory. Anyone can memorize books of the Bible if he is willing to put in the work and the time, and it will require both. Is it worth the time and effort? Well, just ask anyone who has done it. But consider further, in addition to all the spiritual benefit that you gain from memorizing a book of the Bible, when you memorize a book, you will probably be ready to preach any text from that book with only a fraction of the preparation time that it would normally take. You already will have spent hundreds of hours meditating on the text in its context!

What Does It Say?

The second question you ought to ask is, "What does this text say that furthers our understanding of the message of the entire Bible?" There are a few texts in the Bible that are repeated verbatim elsewhere in Scripture, but in the vast majority of cases, the Holy Spirit will be saying something important in your chosen text that he does not say anywhere else in the Bible. Occasionally, your text will be the clearest statement of a foundational Christian doctrine. More often, your text will afford some fresh perspective or nuance on truth. The Holy Spirit has a good reason for including your text in the Bible. "All Scripture is breathed out by God and profitable for teaching, for reproof, for correction, and training in righteousness, that the man of God may be competent, equipped for every good work" (2 Tim 3:15, 16). You should prayerfully consider the likelihood that you ought to take advantage of the opportunity to point out what is unique about your text, but not always. As a preacher, you simply are unable to emphasize every idea that appears in every text. And even if you could, it probably would not be a good idea. There are certain passages in the Bible that may not be suitable texts for exposition in every public setting. For example, imagine how you might handle the Song of Solomon if you were leading a group of twelve-year-olds through a survey of all the books of the Bible. What you emphasized in that setting would be different from what you would probably emphasize if you were teaching the book to a class of married couples. Part of the gift package that makes an effective preacher and pastor is the ability to discern what needs to be emphasized. Your job is not to say everything that *might* be said from a particular text; your job is to say what *needs* to be said. You also need the blessing of the Spirit in deciding which texts to emphasize. Every text in the Bible is true, but not every text is equally important. You might take an entire year to work your way through Matthew 5, 6, and 7 (the three chapters that comprise the Sermon on the Mount). But you will probably empty the church if you take an entire year to preach through 1 Chronicles 5, 6, and 7 (which record genealogies).

CHAPTER
13

HOW
IS IT BUILT?

As we pointed out in a previous chapter, how something is said is an integral part of what is said. The message of a passage may be divorced from the form of a passage, but it will be impoverished by the divorce. There is an almost endless variety of ways that something may be said, but since we believe that the Holy Spirit is all wise, then it follows that the way that he said something in Scripture must be the best way it could be said. The form of your sermon ought to be influenced by the form of the text. This means that the ways you develop your exposition of a text will vary. Especially consider three issues of form: what *type of literature* the text is, the *method of development* in the text, and the *grammar* of the text.

Type of Literature

The Holy Spirit inspired the writers of the Bible to utilize many distinctive classes of literary composition. There are numerous sub-classifications of literary composition, but the two main classifications are poetry and prose.[1] The way you understand Psalm 23, which is a poem, is different than the way you understand Romans 8, which is

---

1. A good source for learning about the distinctive literary classifications in the Bible is *The Literary Study Bible*, Leland Ryken and Philip Ryken, eds. (Wheaton, IL: Crossway, 2007).

prose. In Psalm 23 you imagine scenes of green pastures, still waters, the valley of the shadow of death, and so on. These word pictures are meant to stimulate your imagination and stir your emotions. Since the Holy Spirit used poetry to communicate the message of Psalm 23, and since one of the primary functions of poetry is to stimulate emotional response, it follows that our understanding of the truths in Psalm 23 is enhanced by our emotional response to the text. The text was deliberately composed to elicit appropriate emotional response from the reader. If you have not felt the truth of the text, you have not understood the truth of the text. Your first task is to feel the truth of Psalm 23 yourself, and your next task is to expound it in such a way that your hearers feel it too. A skillful poet will use word pictures to lead from the familiar to the unfamiliar. Often the biblical poets utilized word pictures that are no longer familiar to modern readers. Our culture is sometimes vastly different from their culture. It is part of your task to bridge this cultural gap so that the word pictures are once again accessible. If you are preaching Psalm 23 to a congregation of shepherds, your sermon will be quite different from what it will be if you are preaching the same text to an urban congregation. In both cases, however, your sermon ought to be guided by the fact that Psalm 23 is a poem that uses word pictures and emotive language to communicate the truth.

In Romans 8, the prose is arranged similarly to the way this chapter is arranged: one idea is developed through several supporting ideas. That should influence the structure and presentation of your exposition of Romans 8. Even in Romans 8, however, there are word pictures that you will need to explain to our modern culture. For example, in Romans 8, what does "flesh" mean? If it does not refer to literal flesh (and it does not) why did the author choose to use this particular word to communicate the idea? Again, what does the word picture "Abba! Father!" communicate? What about "adoption as sons"? The overall structure of Romans 8 is logical, linear prose, but the competent interpreter must also grapple with literary features commonly associated with poetry.

Method of Development

Method of development has to do with patterns of organization that a writer or speaker uses to organize his ideas. For example, the book of Hebrews is one sustained *comparison/contrast* between the old covenant and the new covenant. In the book of Hebrews, the Holy Spirit shows that there are points of similarity (comparison) between the two covenants, but he also explains that there are significant points of difference (contrast). *Comparison/contrast* is a method of development. Another method of development is *narrative*. When a writer uses narrative, he gets his point across through telling one or more stories of how things happened. Much of the Bible is narrative, or stories. There are many sections of Scripture where the point is developed through *examples*, which is another method of development: "Now the works of the flesh are evident. . . . But the fruit of the Spirit is . . ." (Galatians 5). One book of the Bible, the Gospel of John, cites example after example of antagonism toward Jesus. These incidents show that the religious leaders were determined to kill Jesus. Other methods of development found in the Bible include *process* (how something came to be), *cause and effect* (not just *how* but *why* something is true), *persuasion or argumentation* (getting the reader to change his point of view) and *division* (dividing something into its component parts).[2] In most texts of Scripture, the Holy Spirit uses one or more of these methods of development.

In the preceding paragraph we defined methods of development as patterns of organization that a writer or speaker uses to organize his ideas. But it is not just writers and speakers who utilize methods of development. Listeners also utilize these patterns of organization when they try to make sense of what someone is communicating. Do not be afraid to identify for your listeners how the Holy Spirit organizes his ideas in the text, and furthermore, do not hesitate to identify how the organization of the text has influenced the organization of your sermon. Careful listeners will appreciate it.

---

2. For further explanation about methods of development, consult a basic college composition textbook, such as David Skwire and Harvey S. Weiner, *Student's Book of College English* (London: Pearson, 2015). You might also do an Internet search for "methods of development."

These various methods of development are not always consciously employed by writers, speakers, and listeners; but nearly everyone uses them, consciously or not. If you take the time to develop an acquaintance with the nine most commonly used methods of development, you will be better equipped to recognize when the Holy Spirit is utilizing one or more of them in your chosen text, and you will be better able to reflect his method in your sermon. Here are the nine, along with at least one example of where each is used in Scripture:

Narrative

Narrative includes the historical sections of the Bible as well as stories that Jesus and others told to make a point. Narrative is surely a very effective way to communicate truth, for most of the Bible is narrative. Your exposition of a narrative text will probably begin with asking, "What is the main point of this story?" In your sermon you will not merely retell the story, although that will surely be a part of your exposition. Rather, let the elements of the story influence the structure of your outline.[3]

Comparison and Contrast

As mentioned earlier, the book of Hebrews is one sustained comparison/contrast from beginning to end. Over and over the Holy Spirit reveals how the new covenant is similar to and different from the old covenant. For example, the old covenant had a high priest chosen from the family of Aaron. The new covenant has a high priest. He is not from the family of Aaron, but he is a high priest after the order of Melchizedek. In your sermon from such a text, point out these similarities and differences.

Example/Illustration

Virtually all of Paul's letters consist of two major sections. The first section of the letter establishes principles of thinking: "This is what is true." The second section gives examples of how these principles of thinking are expressed in action: "This is how you live in light of this truth." As

---

3. If I were to provide specific illustrations of how the various methods of development influence the exposition of a text, it would greatly expand the size of this book.

you preach through the section of the books that consists of examples, keep in mind that these practices are based on principles that undergird them. They are not rules without reason.

Process

Leviticus reveals the religious requirements of the old covenant: how God desired his people to worship him. When we ask why God required what he did, sometimes the answer is found in Leviticus, but often the reason is fully understood only in light of the information that we now have in the new covenant. Psalm 32 and Psalm 51 describe the process of repentance.

Cause and Effect

The life of David is one extended narrative illustrating the principle that we will reap what we sow. After his sin with Bathsheba (the cause), we read of the death of the baby, the rape of Tamar, the revolt led by Absalom, and other judicial effects of his sin. In the life of David, we see the cause first and the effects later. Sometimes the Holy Spirit begins with the effect and then leads us to explore the causes. In the Gospels we read of what Jesus said and did—the effects; in the Epistles we read of the causes—why Jesus had to do what he did.

Division

It is easier for us to understand a complex idea if someone divides that idea into more manageable divisions. So, for example, after he establishes the principle that we are to submit to one another out of reverence for Christ (Eph 5:21), the Holy Spirit informs us how that works out in our lives when he specifically addresses various groups, or divisions of Christians: wives and husbands, children and parents, slaves and masters (Eph 5:22–6:9). When the Holy Spirit addressed the issue of leadership in the churches, he divided the issue into three sections. First, he addressed the issue of women in positions of leadership. Second, he addressed the qualifications of those who aspire to the office of overseer. Third, he addressed the qualifications of deacons (1 Tim 2:11–3:13).

Classification

Classification is similar to division in that a topic is broken into subtopics, but there is this difference: the subtopics are rated according to a common standard. In the Bible this rating is not numerical as "first," "second," "third," etc. Usually it is a simpler classification system of good and bad. For example, in Jesus's parable of the sower, the various types of seed represent persons who hear the word. Hearing the word is the common standard according to which the seeds are then classified as bad or good. In Psalm 107 we read of how various groups respond to stressful situations (stressful situations being the common standard). The kings of Israel and Judah are classified according to whether or not they sought the Lord.

Description

When a skilled author develops his point through description, he never simply lists details; all the details are significant. In Psalm 22 we have one of the most detailed descriptions of the sufferings of Christ. The prophets are packed with detailed descriptions, as also are the Psalms and the book of Revelation. The descriptive details are there for a reason, but let me give a word of caution about dealing with descriptive passages: beware of dogmatically assigning doctrinal significance to details of description when all you have to rely on is your imagination.[4]

Persuasion or Argument

This category is composed of all the passages that aim to bring about a change of mind or action. Galatians is a good example. God has every right to command us without supplying reasons; and we are bound, in humility, to obey him even when we do not understand him. We insult him if we treat him like an unreliable witness and require reasonable evidence for everything he reveals. It is remarkable, therefore, that the

---

4. When interpreting descriptive details, or when interpreting any passage of Scripture, it is always wise to begin with what is plainly revealed and allow that plain meaning in the simple passages to inform how you interpret what is more difficult in more complex passages. Stated simply, proceed from the simple to the complex, not the other way around.

Holy Spirit so often graciously gives us reasons for what he commands. There is much truth that is beyond the reach of reason, and we access that truth by faith. Faith is a legitimate means of knowing. But when the Holy Spirit supports his position by reasonable arguments, we do well to explore and utilize those reasons in our preaching.

Grammar

Do not be intimidated by the word *grammar*. Grammar is just the way a language is put together, and everyone who can speak a language is an expert in the grammar of at least one language. You may not know what a nominative pronoun is, but you know that *me* should have used one in referring to myself in this sentence. Martin Luther had the right perspective when he observed that grammar is a means of grace.

If you have the opportunity, you ought to learn Hebrew and Greek, and there are several good reasons for doing so. You will understand the Bible better. There are nuances of meaning that simply cannot be translated from one language to another, and you will miss some of the meaning of the Bible if you do not know the original languages. Furthermore, the Holy Spirit inspired the Holy Scriptures to be written in Hebrew and Greek, and a preacher is supposed to be an expert in the Holy Scriptures. You would expect an expert in French literature to know French, wouldn't you?[5] Finally, learning another language is the best way to learn the grammar of your own language (through comparison and contrast). Even if you fail to keep up with your Hebrew and Greek, you will still benefit greatly from language study because you will have learned English grammar in the process, and your understanding of the English text will be greatly enhanced when you are able to recognize participles, prepositions, antecedents, and so on. It will help you to pay attention to details.

When studying any passage of Scripture, the Lord Jesus wants us to pay attention to the details. He wants us to notice everything that is

---

5. Hershael York, professor of preaching at The Southern Baptist Theological Seminary, made this very good point in a conversation with Orrick when they were discussing the urgency of learning Greek.

there in his gracious revelation of himself. He modeled this in his own life. In Mark 12, when the Sadducees came to test Jesus with a theological question, he rebuked them by saying that the reason they had a bad understanding of God was because they knew "neither the Scriptures nor the power of God" (Mark 12:24). The Sadducees did not believe in the resurrection (12:18). Jesus says that one of the primary reasons they did not believe in the resurrection was because they had not paid careful attention to the Scriptures they were reading. He traced their bad teaching back to their bad Bible reading and said to them, "As for the dead being raised, have you not read in the book of Moses, in the passage about the bush, How God spoke to him, saying, 'I am the God of Isaac, and the God of Jacob?' He is not the God of the dead but of the living. You are quite wrong."

Do you notice that Jesus corrects bad teaching by helping these men pay closer attention to the grammar of the Bible? He directs them to the tense of a verb. Years after Abraham, Isaac, and Jacob had stopped breathing, God said to Moses, "I *am* [present tense] their God." The Sadducees must have thought that God's use of the present tense was merely rhetorical flourish, but it was not. It was a literal statement of truth, and if they had paid more careful attention to the details of what was before them in the Scriptures they would have learned the truth.

The apostle Paul shows us that he carefully studied the Bible to notice every detail. In Galatians 3:16, Paul is explaining who will inherit the precious promises of God, and he makes a major theological argument based on the fact that God used a singular (not plural) noun in a very important promise to Abraham. Paul tells us that the promises that God made were made to offspring. "[The Lord] does not say, 'And to offsprings,' referring to many, but referring to one, 'And to your offspring,' who is Christ." Notice that Paul's whole point hinges on one letter in English: one *s*. If the promise was to *offsprings*, then many would have received God's promises without mediation. Since God said *offspring* it is clear that all of His promises would be fulfilled through the mediation of one man. By overlooking the fact that the word was a singular, the Galatians could have completely misunderstood who was going to receive the promises of God. By noticing that the noun was singular, Paul determined that all the promises of God were given to Jesus Christ. Paul was informed in his Christ-centered outlook by noticing the details.

We notice some of the most glorious doctrines of our faith by paying attention to the details of very basic texts. In Ephesians 2:8–10 Paul uses the little word "not" to show how we are saved: "For by grace you are saved through faith. And this is *not* your own doing; it is the gift of God; it is the gift of God, *not* a result of works." The most common error that men and women make is to believe that salvation is something you can earn (Rom 9:32). The clearest way you can refute that error and help people see the true path of salvation in your preaching is by pointing them to the details. Help them see the *not*.

You must never assume that you already know the details. Years ago I (Fullerton) attended a Sunday school class that was filled with seminary students. On my first Sunday, the class was going through the gospel of Mark. For the first half of the class the teacher forced the class to answer the most basic questions. Questions like, "Where was Jesus?" "Where was the boat?" and "Where were the disciples?" He asked extremely basic, almost insulting questions to this group of well-educated men and women. I didn't get it. That is, I didn't get it until I noticed what I had not noticed. I had not noticed the text. Once I began to humble myself and notice the words of the text—the inspired details of the story—then I began to understand the meaning of the text.

Now, if you are going really to glean from the Scriptures, you need to know how to notice all the details. We have already noticed the importance of the verbs, the nouns, and little words like *not*. Next, notice the big words. Our faith is full of rich, meaningful words that we need to understand. Words like *justification, propitiation, redemption,* and *regeneration* are all vital words for you to understand. When you are reading the Bible, it is important that you make note of the words you do not understand. When you see those words, you will need to figure out what they mean. There are many excellent Bible dictionaries that can help you with definitions. But before you grab a Bible dictionary off the shelf or consult the Internet, I would encourage you to try to find out what that word means by reading all the occurrences of that word in the Bible. Take the word *redemption*, for instance. By simply looking up that word in a concordance and then reading the passages where it occurs, you will find that the word often refers to something being delivered or freed by the payment of a price (Exod 21:30; Num 3:40–51). If we get even a little of this background, we will be helped when we read that "in Him [Jesus] we have redemption through his blood, the forgiveness of our sins" (Eph 1:7). We will begin to understand that we have been redeemed by the payment of Jesus's blood and that this frees us from our sins. Initially, you may not trust your ability to make these kinds of observations; but if you do the work and try to notice the details, you will be in a better position to discern if the Bible dictionaries or Bible commentaries you read are on the right track. And, as you continue this process of study, you will grow in your understanding of the big words of Scripture.

You must also learn to pay attention to prepositions. We have already seen that it is important to pay attention to verb tenses, and whether a noun is singular or plural. We have also noted that we need to understand the big words we find in the Scriptures. Finally, you need to understand all of the connecting words in the text. In a story, it matters if something happens before or after something else. So you need to notice when something is happening. Jesus was tempted by the devil's enticement to make bread out of stones because the devil came to Jesus at a particular time. It was "*after* fasting forty days and forty nights" (emphasis added), and "he was hungry." The prepositions tell us when things are happening, and that is vital to understanding a story.

Prepositions can also tell us why things happen. The apostle Paul says in Romans 5, "Therefore, since we have been justified *by* faith, we have peace with God *through* our Lord Jesus Christ" (emphasis added). In this passage the prepositions are gold. Why do I have peace with God? It is not because of me and my works. It is because I have been justified by faith. To be justified is to be declared righteous because of a free gift of righteousness (Rom 4:6; 5:17). My peace with God is an outworking, an implication, a *therefore since* of the fact that I have been justified. How did I get justified? Another preposition tells me: It is "through" our Lord Jesus Christ. It is through him that I am justified (Rom 3:24). So my peace with God is not because of my good works (praise the Lord) but because of God's work of justifying me, or declaring me righteous. And justification does not come through me either. It comes through Jesus. He is my source of justification, and therefore he is the foundation of my peace. Praise God for the details of Scripture.

Notice that when we apply what we have learned, we feed on this passage from Romans 5. First I figure out what the big word means (*justification* means "being declared righteous"). Then I notice a verb tense: I *have been* justified. It is in the past (not something I am still earning). Then I notice a plural "we," and I learn that this is the state of all Christians (Paul, the Romans, and me). Then I notice the prepositions, and I see that all this blessing is because of being justified through Jesus Christ. What a blessing to pay attention to the details of a text. Grammar, then, is an important part of the structure of the text.

WHY
DOES IT STAY?

When studying a text of Scripture, ask, "Why does this text have such stay-ing power? How does it address the enduring questions of humanity? With so little space in the Bible, why did God choose to put this text in?" When we ask, "How does it fit? What does it say? How is it built?" we are focusing on the task of interpreting the Scripture. Yet, if we become proficient at merely interpreting Scripture and not obeying the teaching of Scripture, we will miss the point of our existence: glorifying the Lord Jesus with our *lives*. That is, if our exegesis of a text is *spot on* but we do not tell our people how to apply the truths that have been set forth, we have not been as effec-tive as we might have been. This question—"Why does it stay?"—operates on the presupposition that Scripture is as relevant to our people as it was to the original audience. As the apostle Paul wrote to Timothy, "In the last days [the days ushered in through Jesus's resurrection from the grave] there will comes times of difficulty" (2 Tim 3:1). "But as for you, continue in what you have learned and have firmly believed . . . and how from child-hood you have been acquainted with the sacred writings, which are able to make you wise for salvation through faith in Jesus Christ" (2 Tim 3:14–15). Therefore, "preach the word" (2 Tim 4:2). Our responsibility as preachers is not to *make* the Scripture relevant, but to *show* its relevance. It is relevant to "reprove, rebuke, and exhort" (2 Tim 4:2).

Unfortunately, many preachers, though evangelical in their interpretation of Scripture, offer a moralistic application that is disconnected from the text. Haddon Robinson may not be exaggerating when he asserts that more heresy is spread in the preacher's attempt to apply Scripture than in his presentation of Scripture's meaning. Sometimes we apply the text in ways that might make the biblical writer say, "Wait a minute, that's a wrong use of what I said." This is the heresy of a good truth applied in a wrong way.[1] "Moralism assumes that we are not helpless sinners who need rescue but good, decent people who just need some good examples, exhortations, instructions."[2] Our exceeding sinfulness, however, reveals that we need more than mere moralism. Hence, it must always be remembered that although the Scriptures are permeated with moral instruction and ethical exhortation, the ground and motivation for new obedience is always found in the grace and mercy of God in Christ. Indeed, "The grace of God has appeared, bringing salvation for all people training us to renounce ungodliness and worldly passions, and to live self-controlled, upright, and godly lives in the present age" (Titus 2:11–12). That is what the apostle was getting at when he wrote, "Let your manner of life be worthy of the gospel of Christ" (Phil 1:27). The gospel must inform behavior, therefore we must preach with the intent of connecting the gospel with behavior. A crucial part of your job in preaching is to make the connections. If you fail to connect the truth of the text with the lives of your hearers, your preaching will probably be fruitless.

Before we address some general principles for gospel-centered application, it would be beneficial to first consider what has been labeled the Fallen Condition Focus of a passage (FCF).[3] Essentially, the Fallen Condition Focus stems from the reality that every passage of Scripture was breathed out by the Holy Spirit to address some aspect of our sinful condition—whether that sinful condition consists in sinful deeds, unbelief, or ignorance (for which we are still accountable).[4] As Bryan Chapell argues,

---

1. Haddon Robinson, "The Heresy of Application," *Leadership Journal* 18, no. 4 (Fall 1997): 21.
2. Michael Horton, *Christless Christianity* (Grand Rapids: Baker, 2012), 151.
3. See Bryan Chapell, *Christ Centered Preaching*, 48–52.
4. Consider Hebrews 9:7, which refers to the annual visit of the high priest into the Holy of Holies in order to offer sacrifice both for himself and "for the sins of the people committed in ignorance."

the fact that the Scriptures address our fallen condition reflects God's grace and mercy in addressing it so that we can be saved from this condition. In other words, every text provides the grace of our Lord Jesus Christ so that God's people can be set free from their sin.

An FCF will maintain fidelity to a text and will identify vital purposes of a text if the preacher uses three successive questions to develop the FCF: (1) What does the text say? (2) What spiritual concerns did the text address? (3) What spiritual concerns do the contemporary listeners share in common with the original audience? By identifying what the contemporary listener shares in common with the original audience, the preacher determines how the text is relevant for our time. Of course, the preacher does not identify the FCF simply to inform his audience of a problem. God expects the listener to repent of sin and conform his life to the teachings of God's Word.

The remainder of this chapter will be devoted to three considerations that will help you to identify and apply the enduring truths found in the text so that you can more effectively "bring about the obedience of faith" (Rom 1:5) with your listeners. We will discuss motivation for obedience, the necessity of considering the diversity of your audience, and the transferability of application from the original world of the Bible to our twenty-first-century world.

Motivation for Obedience

A first general principle that you need to consider before applying a text is that one's motivation for obedience matters before God. The Pharisees prove that one can do the right things for the wrong reasons. So the Holy Spirit gives three major motivations for obedience.[5] First, he appeals to God's past and future saving grace, which is sometimes called the history of redemption. In other words, saving grace is a primary motivation for obedience. For example, in Exodus 20:1, saving grace is presupposed to be the chief motivation for keeping the Ten Commandments: God has redeemed Israel from slavery in Egypt, therefore, his people should obey

---

5. John Frame, *The Doctrine of the Christian Life*, 29–32.

him. In the New Testament, the writers often urge us to do good works because of what Christ did to redeem us. The apostle Paul's pattern is to set forth what God has achieved in Jesus Christ for our redemption before he gives directions for Christian behavior. A classic case in point is Ephesians 4:1, where after three chapters of explaining the gospel, Paul writes, "I therefore . . . urge you to walk in a manner worthy of the calling to which you have been called." Our focus on the history of redemption is not limited to the past. We also anticipate what God will do for us in the future. God's promises of future blessing also motivate us to obedience. As Paul explains to Titus, we are called to live godly lives as we are "waiting for our blessed hope, the appearing of the glory of our great God and Savior Jesus Christ" (Titus 2:13).

In addition to God's saving grace, a second way the Holy Spirit motivates our obedience is by calling attention to God's authority to command. That is, because God is "Lord of heaven and earth" (Luke 10:21), we as his subjects have a duty to obey him. This is not duty born out of grudging necessity, but duty characterized by delight because of what God has graciously done for us in Jesus Christ (as seen in the history of redemption). For instance, the apostle Peter writes, "Set your hope fully on the grace that will be brought to you at the revelation of Jesus Christ. As obedient children do not be conformed to the passions of your former ignorance, but as he who is called you is holy, you also be holy in all your conduct, since it is written, 'You shall be holy, for I am holy'" (1 Pet 1:13–16).

Third, the very presence of the Holy Spirit is a motivation. Scripture calls us to a godly life, based on the activity of the Spirit within us. As the apostle Paul writes, "But I say, walk by the Spirit, and you will not gratify the desires of the flesh" (Gal 5:16).

Consider Your Audience

A second general principle for application is to consider your audience. It is too easy to think of your church audience as a monolithic group who are at similar places spiritually and who have related spiritual needs, but that is a highly naïve perspective. Although you cannot address the specific needs of every single congregant, there are strategic things you can consider to ensure you meet every single person at their point of need. To do this, it is helpful to think in terms of various categories: first, your people's spiritual *state*; second, the general *sin* that is common to all people; third, the *stance* of errant sheep; and finally, the various *stages* of life represented by your listeners.[6]

A first thing to consider with your audience is their individual spiritual *states*. Your listeners will either be *Christian or non-Christian:* we need to address both in every sermon. People in both groups will tend to either be *complacent* or *anxious*. The complacent need warnings more than promises, because God's promises do not mean much to them. The anxious need promises because they are already feeling what they lack, and they need hope. You will also have among your audience those who are *legalistic* and those who are *licentious*—not to mention all who fit between those extremes. The legalistic will listen intently for anything you say about law and rules, but may dismiss the gospel promises. The licentious will be eager to hear the gospel promises of grace, but may not appreciate teaching on repentance and lordship.

In addition to the spiritual state of your audience, a second consideration is to assume the following *sins* are true of everyone listening: *Idolatry*: Everyone is struggling with idolatry, which is inordinate love for the created order. Seek to identify specifically some of the idols the text speaks to, as they are expressed in our culture—power, pleasure, pride, etc. *Self-justification*: Ever since the fall, we have attempted to justify our idols, to excuse ourselves from our sin, and commend ourselves to God. We see it in our desire for praise from this world. But our desire for the praise of men is simply part of a larger conspiracy. Though we were made to give praise *to* God, in our hearts we long to receive praise *from* God based on our merits. *Love of the World*: Love of the world takes a multitude of forms: sex, money, power, possessions, entertainment,

---

6. For the ideas in what follows in this section we are indebted in large measure to Michael Lawrence, *Biblical Theology in the Life of the Church* (Wheaton, IL: Crossway, 2010). Lawrence revises a more complex version of this taxonomy that was developed by William Perkins, a sixteenth-century Puritan.

beauty, etc. The list is open-ended, but underneath the variation lies the constant theme of worshiping the creature rather than the Creator (1 John 2:15–17).

Correspondent to the spiritual *state* and the *sins* of your audience, a third thing to consider is the different *stances* of errant sheep that need the Word. As the apostle Paul contended: "We urge you, brothers, admonish the idle, encourage the fainthearted, help the weak, be patient with them all" (1 Thess 5:14): *The idle*: These are not lazy sheep so much as headstrong and impulsive; they reject discipleship. Paul says these worldly brothers and sisters need to be warned. This may well include addressing the congregation in the second person at times. *The timid*: These are sheep who are not obeying the Word, but not because they have rejected it outright. Rather, they are fearful of the consequences, and perhaps responsibilities, that come with faithful obedience. These sheep need to be encouraged with the promises of the gospel. *The weak*: In one sense all of us are weak, but here Paul seems to have in mind those whose lack of faith and obedience stems from spiritual weakness that is the result of poor teaching. These sheep need to be helped, says Paul, and we help them most through sound instruction.

Fourth, and finally, pay attention to the various *statuses* of your hearers. How does the text speak specifically to the following categories of people: men, women; singles, marrieds, the widowed; the elderly, the middle-aged, children; the employed, the unemployed, retirees; the wealthy, the poor; the educated, the under-educated; employers, employees?

Transfer of Application

Thus far we have considered our motivation for obedience and the importance of considering the diversity of spiritual needs in your audience. A third and final principle for application is that it is necessary for the preacher to consider the factors that limit the transfer of application from the original context to the contemporary context.[7]

---

7. These questions are from Michael Fabarez's *Preaching That Changes Lives* (Eugene, OR: Wipf and Stock, 2005), 44–54.

Does the Immediate Context Limit the Target of the Application? Certain passages in the Pastoral Epistles afford a good example. While many of the commands are universal and timeless, some of the application is directed specifically to pastors and ministerial leadership.

Does Any Part of the Bible Limit the Target of the Application? For instance, when we apply the teaching of Leviticus, our application will be shaped by the new covenant, which abolished the ceremonial codes of the old covenant (Heb 10:1–14; Matt 5:17).

Does a Cultural Condition Limit the Target of the Application? An example is Paul's instruction to Timothy to "use a little wine" for his stomach and frequent illnesses (1 Tim 5:23). Wine was used in the first century for medicinal purposes. In this case it is appropriate to modify the application in light of the first-century culture of medicine.

Does a Unique Historical Condition Limit the Target of the Application? When Jesus called the rich young ruler to follow Him, he told him, "Sell all that you have . . ." (Luke 18:22). The historical setting and its comparison with the rest of Scripture provide clues as to the reason for this specific summons. Jesus did not require others he called to sell everything they had. In this case Jesus demanded that the young man break from the hold that money had on him.

What Aspect of the Application Is Rooted in God's Character? For instance, when Jesus taught, "Love your enemies, bless those who curse you," he rooted his lesson in the nature of God's character: "that you may be sons of your Father in heaven . . ." (Matt 5:44–45). The application of this passage will be directly transferable because Scripture bases its practice on the nature of God.

What Aspect of the Application Is Reflecting God's Created Order? In Matthew 19:5 Jesus quotes Genesis 2:24 in his defense of monogamous marriage. This argument is rooted in God's created order and applies to every age.

What Aspect of the Application Is Delivered as Countercultural? Jesus pointed out to the crowd in the Sermon on the Mount, "You have heard that it was said," but he quickly raised the bar by adding, "But I say to you . . ." (Matt 5:21, 27, 33, 38, 43). The specific life change he was calling for in these passages ran against the grain of the culturally accepted mores of the day. This suggests that the application he was seeking was not bound to the specific context in which it was delivered. If the application was originally countercultural, then our modern application will almost certainly be countercultural.

What Specifically Does Your Audience Have in Common with the Original Audience? For instance, Colossians 2:16–17 states: "Therefore let no one judge you in food or in drink, or regarding a festival or a new moon or sabbaths, which are a shadow of the things to come, but the substance is of Christ." Both the original and the current audiences are professing Christians who are exposed to unbiblical religious regulations that are not founded in Scripture.

In What Specific Areas Does Your Audience Lack Commonality with the Original Audience? Unlike the original audience, your audience is not pressured to engage in Jewish or Old Testament customs.

How Is My Audience Practicing the Application? Spending too much time exhorting them to do what they already do, or to believe what they already believe, will waste valuable time.

Finally, *How is My Audience Currently Neglecting or Abusing the Application?* When Paul initially told the Corinthians to avoid associating with the sexually immoral (1 Cor 5:9–11), some believers apparently misunderstood his intent and withdrew from all sexually immoral people. The intended application had limitations that, when missed, led to abuse of the principle.

In this section, we have been seeking to answer the question "Why does it stay?" That is, why does a text have staying power? We know that it does. All Scripture is profitable for salvation. Sometimes, however, the preacher must shed blood, sweat, and tears to come to terms with *how* a text is profitable. When he comes to terms with that answer, the text's staying power becomes evident. In the end, all the toil will pay off because God's name will be hallowed and God's people will grow in the grace and knowledge of our Lord Jesus Christ as they cultivate their understanding of how the Scriptures apply to their lives.

Conclusion

"The gospel is the heart of the Bible. Everything in Scripture is either preparation for the gospel, presentation of the gospel, or participation in the gospel. . . . Accurately understanding and continually applying the gospel is the Christian life."[8] In other words, the preacher's task is by the gospel and for the gospel. To accomplish this enormous and glorious task, when considering a text of Scripture, the preacher ought to ask four questions:

- How does it fit?
- What does it say?
- How is it built?
- Why does it stay?

"Thus with Christ-crucified as the ground and goal and matter of every sermon (and all of life) the ultimate aim of God in creation is advanced: the praise of the glory of God's grace, through the joy of his people in him."[9] This is what people need from preachers.

---

8. Dave Harvey, *When Sinners Say "I Do": Discovering the Power of the Gospel for Marriage* (Wapwallopen, PA: Shepherd Press, 2007), 24.

9. John Piper, "The Ultimate Aim of All Christian Preaching" (unpublished).

PART THREE

"Come and Experience God with Me in This Text": Final Preparation

CHAPTER 15

READING
A FULL MANUSCRIPT

Final Preparation and Delivery

What should you take into the pulpit? A manuscript? An outline? Or nothing but your Bible?

I (Orrick) grew up playing in the woods, and camping has been a regular part of my life for many years. During my college years I took several hitchhiking treks, traveling all over the United States, and I would sometimes sleep outside for weeks at a time. How much equipment does one need for a trip of that duration? There is an almost endless list of camping paraphernalia that advertisers insist is necessary to enjoy a camping experience. I have sometimes succumbed to the mistake of believing the advertisers, and I have taken too much equipment. I found that all that unnecessary stuff actually interfered with my enjoyment of the outdoors. To paraphrase John Ruskin, in backpacking (and in life) every possession we acquire adds to the burden we must carry. On the other hand, I have sometimes made the mistake of taking too little equipment, and this was often because I wanted to camp like a pre-Columbian Native American. But I came to understand that a true outdoorsman is not necessarily the man who can survive on nothing, but the man who can be comfortable with little. It is fun to *rough it*; it is not fun to spend all night shivering in the cold, having nothing to eat.

Preparation for a long trek into the wilderness may entail the use of a lot of equipment that you will not put into your backpack. You may, for example, lift weights and exercise on a treadmill. But the time comes when you leave all that behind, load your pack with the essentials, and head out for your adventure. You ask, "What do I really need for this to be an enriching, enjoyable experience?"

In the chapters that follow, we help you to think about what you will take into the pulpit with you when you preach. This decision will affect your final hours of preparation. What has come in the chapters leading up to this one has had to do primarily with philosophy and theory of preaching: "This is why you ought to do it this way." Theory can be compared to the weight-lifting phase of preparation for a long wilderness trek. It gets you in shape for what you are about to do. You have studied your text in its context, you have considered the author's method of development, you have respected the grammar of the text, you have prayed and prayed, and perhaps you have consulted several commentaries and the original languages. While this has prepared you for preaching, like weight-lifting prepares you for hiking, you are not going to take all that stuff with you into the pulpit. What follows in these final chapters is like packing your backpack the day before you leave for your hike. Keep in mind that the great goal of preaching is to lead your hearers to experience God through understanding and feeling his Word. Remember, also, that this goal is most effectively accomplished when you, the preacher, are experiencing God while you are preaching. On a long wilderness hike, you will miss much of the beauty around you if you are constantly fussing with your pack, or if an ill-fitting pack is chafing your shoulders or hurting your back. It is ideal if you forget that the pack is there. Similarly, the final preparation you make to preach, including the notes you take with you into the pulpit, ought to become invisible in the glory of experiencing God. We will examine three options: full manuscript, brief outline, and no written notes. As you consider what notes you might take with you into the pulpit, let your thinking on the issue be guided by the question, "Will my notes help me to experience God and enhance my ability to lead my hearers to experience God, or will my notes interfere with these goals?" One of us (Brian Payne) writes a full manuscript of every sermon but does not take it into the pulpit, opting instead for an outline summary of the manuscript. Ryan Fullerton writes a full manuscript, and takes an outline that varies in length from a single page to several pages, but he preaches largely extemporaneously. I (Jim Orrick) am a strong advocate of preaching without notes. We devote a chapter to each practice, beginning with full manuscript.

Full Manuscript

A sermon manuscript is a word-for-word composition of what you will say when you preach. When you write a manuscript, you not only identify the ideas contained in your biblical text, you also choose the very words that you intend to use when you will talk about those ideas. While there are some advantages to having a full manuscript with you in the pulpit, it is our conviction that reading a manuscript usually interferes with preaching. So, in this chapter I will first explore the advantages of writing and using a full manuscript, but I will finally conclude that even if you write a full manuscript as part of your final preparation, you ought not to use it when you deliver your message.

ADVANTAGES

Especially while you are an inexperienced preacher, there may be significant advantages to composing a full manuscript of the sermon you intend to preach. These advantages are especially pronounced in an age when many young or beginning preachers have devoted very little time and effort to serious composition. It is easy to get through high school and even college without learning to write well. Many young people spend hours a day texting, but virtually no one puts serious effort into composing a text message with the style and grace requisite to skillful composition and articulate speech. If you are using this book as a text for a preaching class, and your professor requires you to write a manuscript of a sermon, the manuscript that you write for that assignment may be the first composition that some of you have ever written with care.

One great advantage of writing a full manuscript is that the process of composition is a very thought-provoking exercise. There is something about putting ideas down on paper or working on a keyboard-generated document that breeds ideas. When you do your best to write well about something you know to be important, and especially if you are writing in view of sharing what you are writing with an audience, composing a manuscript is like having an earnest conversation with a thoughtful, intelligent friend who is your equal in every way. When you write your thoughts, or even speak them, you have produced something that is an objective product of your mind. As long as your thoughts are inside your head, they are simply a subjective part of who you are. In order for us to critique our own thoughts, we must gain some objective perspective on them. Another person can give us an objective perspective, and it is usually profitable to discuss your ideas with an insightful and honest friend. But we often need to privately scrutinize some of our ideas ourselves, and writing can be an effective aid in this self-scrutiny. When we write with an audience in mind (and it may be an audience of one or of thousands), we imagine that audience reading or hearing what we are writing, and we think, "How will this sound to my audience?" As noted in an earlier chapter, one of the most crucial keys to writing or speaking well is that we are able to accurately predict what someone else will think when he reads what we have written or when she hears what we will say. The goal is to speak or to write so that our target audience will understand what we want to communicate. The act of intelligent composition requires us to look at our writing from the perspective of another person. This capacity to assume an objective perspective on our thoughts—or ourselves—is an element of our having been created in the image of God. No other animal has this level of self-awareness. When you cultivate this capacity and then modify yourself and your actions according to the Word of God, you are enhancing the image of God in yourself, and you are in a better position to enhance the image of God in others.

Not only can the process of writing a manuscript be a very thought-provoking exercise, it also can be a thought-correcting exercise. Since writing your thoughts gives you a measure of objectivity and perspective on what you are thinking, you are better able to detect errors or inadequacies in your thinking when you see your ideas on paper (or on screen) than you are when you are merely thinking without writing. This potential for self-correction applies not only to ideas, but also to organization, word choice, and even spelling. You probably have had the experience of writing down a word that just did not look right. When you were in the act of writing the word, you thought you were spelling it correctly; but once you saw it on paper, there was something in your brain that told you it was spelled incorrectly.

Sometimes you gain this objective perspective in the very process of writing a manuscript. But more often, this perspective of objectivity requires a couple of days to develop. When you first write something, it seems good and right—maybe even perfect. Leave the manuscript alone for a while—at least overnight, but two days is better—then read it again. You will be amazed at how much discernment you have gained during the waiting period. That phrase that sounded so "cutting edge" two days ago sounds crass on a fresh reading. That sentence that sounded so poetic two days ago sounds pompous today. Change it. Delete it. Two days earlier it was a darling part of you, and you could not bear to part with it; now you see it as a wart. Cut it off.[1] There is an old adage among teachers of composition: "There is no such thing as great writing, only great re-writing." So writing a full manuscript can not only promote original thinking, it can also promote the precise and critical thinking that comes from seeing your work from an objective perspective.

Another advantage to writing and preaching from a manuscript is that you are less likely to make mistakes in delivering your sermon. This applies to both verbal mistakes and doctrinal mistakes. Some speakers

---

1. You ought never to immediately send a harsh, rebuking letter or text message to someone, especially if you have written it in the heat of emotion. Let the message sit overnight. Let your passions cool, and then read the message again before you send it. This practice will save you much heartache that might otherwise spring from a hasty rashness.

have distracting habits of speech. They say "uh," or "um," or "you know," or "like" when they are gathering their thoughts and turning their thoughts into speech. These audible fillers are sometimes called *verbal bridges* because they fill the gaps between words. Since a bridge is generally a good thing, and these fillers are not, a more appropriate name might be "swampy, nonsense sounds that interrupt islands of coherent communication"; but we will stick with *verbal bridges* for now. Some preachers use more religious-sounding verbal bridges such as, "Amen?" "Glory to God," or "Brothers and sisters." Since these distracting verbal bridges are not written into the manuscript (one hopes), a preacher who uses a manuscript avoids them.

More significantly, a preacher who uses a manuscript should be able to articulate important ideas and doctrines in words that he has chosen carefully.[2] When a preacher says something that is inappropriately phrased, he may miscommunicate his ideas and mislead his hearers. Furthermore, in this day when nearly everything a preacher says is recorded and maybe even posted on the Internet, a spur-of-the-moment indiscretion can be highly embarrassing or even disastrous. It seems that nearly every month some public figure has his or her reputation ruined by some recording or video from the past that permanently documents an inappropriate, offhand comment. Adherence to a full manuscript ought to virtually eliminate these kinds of mistakes.

If you use a manuscript and read it from the pulpit, you will almost certainly stay on the topic of your text. Some preachers ramble and chase rabbits so far off the path that not only their hearers but the preachers themselves forget where they picked up the scent of that rabbit in the first place. At times, it is perfectly acceptable to pursue an unexpected and unrelated train of thought; but if you stray too much and too often from the main idea, you will come across as scatterbrained, incoherent, and ill prepared. And what is worse, you will give your audience the idea that the Bible is a scatterbrained, incoherent, and ill-written book.

---

2. If you memorize a good catechism, you should be able to articulate important doctrines extemporaneously.

I am astounded at how many audiences are consistently willing to tolerate incoherent preaching, but even these overly tolerant congregations have little patience with a preacher who preaches too long. A preacher who persistently preaches longer than his congregation can listen is being selfish. If these windy preachers who preach unnecessarily long sermons would use a manuscript, it would force them to exercise self-control. A preacher who uses a manuscript can read his sermon ahead of time and know almost exactly how long the sermon will be.

A manuscript is also a permanent record of your sermon. This record may be very valuable to you when you preach from the same text on another occasion. Ideally, you will have put much study and meditation into the sermon, and the manuscript will be the quintessence of your study and meditation. In a future sermon from the same text, you can build on the foundation you have already laid in preparing to preach this first sermon.

One final advantage: a manuscript may keep you from failing miserably in your sermon. A bright young man named Robert once climbed the stairs to the pulpit to preach his first sermon.

> After proceeding for some time with much facility, and to the delight of his audience, he suddenly stopped, covered his face with both his hands, and exclaimed, "Oh, I have lost all my ideas!" He sat down, his hands still covering his face. His failure, however, by no means diminished the persuasion which his tutors and his hearers entertained of the promise which he gave of future power, could he but acquire self-possession; so he was appointed to speak again on the same subject in the same place on the ensuing week. And a second time he failed, and the failure seems to have been still more grievous to witness, and still more painful to bear; he hurried into the vestry exclaiming, "If this does not humble me, the devil must have me!"[3]

---

3. Reverend E. Paxton Hood, *Robert Hall* (New York: A. C. Armstrong and Son, 1881), 17.

What a disastrous beginning! If Robert had utilized a full manuscript, this disaster might have been averted because there is a limit to just how badly you can fail with a manuscript. A most disastrous beginning for Robert, yes, and for many it would have been the end as well. But the Word of God was like a fire shut up in his bones, and he could not hold back. When he preached again—still without a manuscript—he did quite well. He continued to do quite well until Robert Hall went on to become the most celebrated preacher of his day. Some students of pulpit rhetoric regard Robert Hall to be the greatest orator that the Baptists have ever produced. He never did use a manuscript.

Let us review the advantages of writing and then using a manuscript in the pulpit. First, when you apply yourself diligently to the task of composing a manuscript, you cultivate precise thinking. Second, you are able to say exactly what you want to say while avoiding verbal bridges. Third, you are able to stick to your subject and not preach too long. Fourth, you create a permanent record of the quintessence of the preparation that went into the sermon. And, fifth, you will likely avoid a total disaster in delivery.

DISADVANTAGES

So, what's not to like about a manuscript? "Sign me up," right? Not so fast. Here are some disadvantages to taking a manuscript into the pulpit and reading it. First, with very few exceptions, sermons read from a manuscript are boring. I have been a student of public speaking for many years, and I have taught public speaking off and on for more than twenty years. Furthermore, having spent most of my life in the world of Christian academia as well as the world of pastoral ministry, I have heard a lot of speeches, lectures, sermons, and reading of academic papers. Some speakers depend heavily on a manuscript but do not outright read it. Others just read it word for word, barely ever looking up from the manuscript to make eye contact with the audience. Here is what I have observed: among those speakers who depend heavily on a manuscript but do not read it, there are a few—but very few—who can maintain the interest of a motivated audience. But among those who depend entirely on a manuscript and read it, there are virtually no speakers who can maintain the interest of an audience for any length of time. Not all are equally boring; but when a speaker reads a manuscript, it is almost guaranteed that he will lose the audience. It does not matter how profound your insights might be or how precisely you have written out those insights; if you are so boring that your audience cannot listen to you, you might as well be speaking a foreign language.

Second, when you use a manuscript, you run the risk of crowding God out of your sermon. You leave no room for sudden flashes of insight and inspiration that come from the Holy Spirit when a man of God opens the Word of God to the people of God and they are experiencing God together. Of course, God can give you those sudden, unexpected insights while you are composing your manuscript; but if you are reading a manuscript, then about the best you can do is to try to recapture the excitement that you felt when you experienced (past tense) God during your preparation. A manuscript generally quenches the free movement of the Holy Spirit on a preacher while preaching.

Several years ago I read an interview with the late pop star Michael Jackson. He explained to the interviewer that when he and his fellow musicians went into the studio to record a song, they all had a basic idea of the song and what each person would contribute to the recording, but they never had everything planned out. Jackson explained, "Leave room for God to walk in the room."[4] He was exactly right, and this is certainly truer in preaching than in the recording of "pop music." It will not do to appeal to the sovereignty of God and say that he can interrupt your boring reading if he pleases. There is such a thing as quenching the Spirit, and we are told not to do it (1 Thess 5:19).

Francis Wayland, president of Brown University and one of the leading Baptists of the nineteenth century, wrote concerning Baptist preachers of the eighteenth and nineteenth centuries,

---

4. "Michael Jackson in His Own Words" *Ebony* (December 2007): 80ff: "The key to being a wonderful writer is not to write. You just get out of the way. Leave room for God to walk in the room." Though Jackson was associated with the Jehovah's Witnesses (whose views about Jesus and the Bible are erroneous), and though I certainly do not endorse his lifestyle, he was exactly right about the importance of leaving room for God to walk in the room—and this is particularly true of preaching.

"They almost universally preached without notes. It was not uncommon to distinguish extempore from written discourse by different appellations. Delivery without notes was alone called *preaching*, but when a manuscript was used, it was called merely *reading*. Baptists generally considered the latter a very different thing from preaching, and they disliked it extremely. They rarely attended the ministry of other denominations, even occasionally, where it was practiced. As ministers from the East, however, came westward with their written discourses, the people gradually became accustomed to them, but it cost a severe struggle before they would tolerate the change. It was no uncommon thing to see several of the oldest and best members of our churches rise and leave the house when a minister opened his book and began to read from his manuscript. If I do not misremember, I have several times seen this myself."[5]

Probably every reader is now able to think of some prominent, Spirit-anointed preacher from the past or present who utilized or utilizes a manuscript in the pulpit. As for those from the past (Jonathan Edwards is erroneously cited as an example[6]), it may be that audiences in the past were better able to pay attention than audiences are today. You, however, will not be preaching to an eighteenth-century congregation. As for those preachers from our own generation who utilize a manuscript in the pulpit, the only preachers I have ever observed capable of maintaining audience interest while even consulting a manuscript are those who had absolutely no need to have a manuscript with them. They knew the text and what they wanted to say about the text. They maintained eye contact with the audience. The only evidences that they

---

5. Francis Wayland, *Notes on the Principles and Practices of Baptist Churches* (New York: Sheldon, Blakeman, 1857), 23–24. This quote is taken from the chapter, "Baptist preaching formerly extempore, that is without written preparation. Advantages of this mode of preaching for the cultivation of pulpit eloquence." It is well worth reading. On a similar note, see C. H. Spurgeon's chapter, "The Faculty of Impromptu Speech" in his *Lectures to My Students* (Peabody, MA: Hendrickson, 2010).

6. Ian Murray, in his biography of Jonathan Edwards, devotes three pages to the question of whether Edwards read a manuscript in the pulpit. He determines that it is highly improbable that Edwards ever read his sermons, and it is almost certain that he did not in later life. See Ian Murray, *Jonathan Edwards: A New Biography* (Edinburgh: Banner of Truth, 1987), 188–91.

were using a manuscript were a certain stiffness of expression and the inevitable distance that is created between a manuscript reader and his audience. As evidence of this stiffness and distance, simply contrast their sermons with their everyday conversation or with their extemporaneous responses when participating in a panel discussion.

Third, a persistent reliance on a manuscript retards the development of the kind of speaking skills that would eventually render a manuscript unnecessary. A preacher needs to learn to "think on his feet" and speak confidently. He needs to interact with the faces and the thoughts of those who are looking to him for spiritual food. Hungry listeners care very little if he can turn a fine phrase and quote all the experts; they want to be fed.

If you will prayerfully practice real, live communication, you will improve in your thinking and speaking skills. But if you never take the training wheels off your bicycle, you will never know the joyful freedom of flying down a hill and leaning around a curve with the wind whistling past your ears. Sure, you will wreck sometimes. Get up, get back on, and ride. God has given us a spirit not of fear but of power and love and self-control. You do not have to have a piece of paper to force you to stop rambling in your sermon and preach a focused message in a reasonable amount of time; you have the Holy Spirit. One of the fruits of the Spirit is self-control. It is self-love that enables you to ramble and preach too long when your hearers cannot follow you or endure you. You love to hear yourself even if no one else does. Repent of excessive self-love. Learn how people think. Learn their interests and their limits. A manuscript can retard this process.

Fourth, while a manuscript can be a valuable summary of the study that went into the preparation of a particular sermon, it becomes a disadvantage if it discourages you from freshly encountering God when you preach from the same text in the future. Anyone who preaches for any length of time will preach from the same text more than once.[7] Do not

---

7. George Whitefield preached thousands of times from the text, "Ye must be born again." Those who travelled with Whitefield heard the sermon over and over, yet they testified that it was always fresh and powerful when they heard it.

succumb to a laziness that says, "I already have a sermon on this text; I'll just preach that again." Are you the same man as you were when you preached that sermon the first time? Have you no fresh insights on the truth that the Lord has taught you since you last preached this text? When I begin a new sermon on a text from which I have previously preached, I confess that I often wish I had a full manuscript, or at least fuller notes, of my previous sermon. That may be my lazy wish at the beginning of my preparation, but I rarely feel that way at the end. Why? Because I have been forced to meditate again on the text, and in my meditations I have encountered God afresh. I have gleaned new insights that bring me to life and make me feel the joy of the Lord. I feel the fire of God's Word burning hot in my bones.

How often have you reread a text of Scripture and been blessed by something you have never seen before? Or perhaps, because of new experiences you have had in life, you feel the truth of a text more deeply than ever before. That new insight, that new emotion ought to enter into your understanding and preaching of that text. Do not let a record of God's previous blessings keep you from experiencing fresh blessings and allowing those fresh blessings to flow through you to others who hear you preach.

Finally, a manuscript may apparently deliver you from experiencing a total disaster, but I think that the possibility of disaster in delivery is a good thing. We are preaching the Word of the living God, and that is a fearful responsibility. We do not need to get cozy with our task. "Who is sufficient for these things? For we are not, like so many, peddlers of God's word, but as men of sincerity, as commissioned by God, in the sight of God we speak in Christ" (2 Cor 2:16–17). We need God, and it is dangerous for us to engage in any practice that makes it possible for us to carry on with "business as usual" in the event that God does not bless. We do not want this book to be a textbook on "How to Pretend You Are Preaching When God Is Not in the House," and we do not want to encourage any practice that might promote this deplorable mentality. I have heard some men talk about how to conduct a so-called revival meeting, and I have thought that their talk might have been entitled, "Advice on

How to Pretend That You Are Having Revival When the Holy Spirit Is Nowhere to be Found." Superficial religion is nauseous to God and to thinking men. If you are called to preach, God has given you the gifts to preach, and you are responsible to fan those gifts into flame. A disastrous preaching experience ought to make you examine yourself and correct any problems that might have caused the disaster. Pain makes you go to the doctor so you can find out what is causing the pain. You might be able to avoid the pain with a pain-killer, but the health problem remains. Treat the sickness, and the pain will go away.

In the first half of this chapter I cited a number of significant advantages to using a manuscript. What about those? The greatest advantages are that the process of careful composition promotes thorough thinking and precise expression of ideas. A preacher may enjoy these advantages if he writes a full manuscript of his sermon and then leaves the manuscript home when he preaches the sermon. He also may reap most of the other benefits we have mentioned simply through the exercise of writing the manuscript but not preaching from it.

Because writing a manuscript is so beneficial, our recommendation is that a beginning preacher go through the discipline of preparing a full manuscript of his first fifteen sermons. Do not take the manuscript with you into the pulpit, and do not try to memorize it. Writing the manuscript is a conditioning, training exercise, like those days in the weight room that prepare you for a long, arduous trek in the wilderness. If you find that producing a full manuscript is the most effective way for you to prepare to experience God and to lead others to experience God through your preaching, then continue the practice for as long as it is the most effective means of preparation. It is time consuming, so be dead certain that you are not misusing the practice by allowing it to crowd out rather than to enhance prayer and meditation.

PREACHING
FROM AN OUTLINE

We advocate that preachers use an outline to help them experience God and lead others to experience God through the preaching of the Word. I will later discuss whether or not a preacher ought to take a copy of the outline into the pulpit when he preaches. But an outline is a useful tool for helping the preacher accomplish four crucial goals. First, it helps him understand the text. Second, it helps him experience God in the text. Third, it helps him organize the text. And, fourth, an outline helps him remember the message of the text. But before we get into these four points, here is some good news: the outline is in the text.

The Outline Is in the Text

Your responsibility is not to figure out a clever way to outline your text. You task is to discover the outline of ideas that the Holy Spirit put in the mind of the author when he was inspired to write the text. Not that the author started with a formal outline, but there is usually at least a loosely organized progression of ideas in the text.[1] To discover this inspired "outline," you must begin by prayerfully analyzing the text using the

---

1. Note that I say "usually." Sometimes the text does not readily demonstrate a steady progression of thought in which this idea leads to that idea that is supported by these ideas. We need to be careful not to impose structure upon the text.

ideas and guidelines we presented in the earlier chapters. In brief, at this stage, you are primarily using tools of analysis that anyone might use to analyze any text in view of discovering the author's process of thought. So, for example, it would be pretty easy to figure out how I intend to handle the subject of outlining in this chapter. The basic outline would look something like this:

> *Main point of the chapter:* There are four advantages to using an outline.
>> *Introduction:* The outline is in the text.
> I.   An outline will help you understand the text.
> II. An outline will help you experience God in the text.
> III. An outline will help you organize the ideas in the text.
> IV. An outline will help you remember the ideas in the text.

Now, let us suppose that you have been assigned the task of explaining to a group why I believe that outlining a text of Scripture is an effective aid to preaching. Your job is not to improve on what I write in this chapter. Your explanation ought to have the same four main points as my four main points. If you are faithful to your assignment, you will not add a couple of additional points of your own. Perhaps you think that I ought to have devoted some time to reasons other than those I cite. If your assignment had been to analyze and criticize and improve the case I am making for outlining a text, you might well have critiqued what I have written. But if your assignment is to summarize what I have written, then you must limit yourself to what is in this text. Your task as a preacher is similar, and in preaching, you ought to be able to assert what our Lord asserted on several occasions, "I have not spoken on my own authority but the Father who sent me has himself given me a commandment—what to say and what to speak" (John 12:49). When a preacher addresses a controversial subject, the expositor of Scripture ought to be able to point to the Bible and to say to his hearers, "We may not like what the Bible says here, but you can plainly see that this is obviously what the

Bible says. I did not write this. I agree with it because I believe the Bible is the Word of God, but there is no sense in your getting angry with me about it. I did not write it. If you reject it, you are not rejecting my word; you are rejecting the Word of God."

When exploring a text that the Holy Spirit inspired, you need not waste your time in imagining that you might discover a more clever and effective way to communicate the truths of the passage. When it comes to the idea being considered in the text, rest assured that the author is the leading expert in his field, and your attempted improvements to his handling of the idea will not be improvements.

Imagine that you are standing in the National Gallery of Art admiring a Rembrandt painting when a man approaches with a bucket of white paint held in one hand and a dripping paintbrush held aloft in the other. With a glazed stare, he stumbles toward the Rembrandt muttering, "It's too dark." Someone ought to stop the maniac before he defaces a masterpiece. His alleged improvements will only mar perfection. Similarly, a preacher's task is not to attempt to improve the Holy Spirit's masterpiece of revelation; the preacher's task is to discover and display the skill and artistry of the Master. The preacher's task is more like the docent at the art gallery who, with a practiced eye and fluent enthusiasm, explains to the circle of listeners the artist's use of color, light, texture, and subject to create the awe and delight that a viewer of a masterpiece ought to feel.

The Outline as a Means of Understanding the Text

The most effective way of understanding a text is to note how the Holy Spirit communicates the main idea of the text, and then note the ideas that he marshals in support and development of this main idea. The main idea of the text ought to be the main idea, or thesis, of your sermon, and the supporting ideas in the text ought to be your main points. Later in this chapter I will illustrate how to do this.

If we ignore the Holy Spirit's method of developing his message, or if we lift a phrase from the Bible and use it to mean something other than what the phrase means in its context, we demonstrate an arrogant disregard for the Holy Spirit's work. I once attended a Bible conference in which a speaker had been assigned the topic, "When a Pastor Ought to Retire." He took as his text, 1 Corinthians 16:13, which in the King James Version reads, "Quit you like men." In 1611, that sentence meant "Act like men," and it did not mean "Retire like men." To make matters still more convoluted, in opposition to his misreading of the text, the preacher's point was that pastors ought never to quit! On another occasion, I heard a preacher say that he had once cancelled his plans to travel by airplane because on the morning that he was scheduled to fly, he read in his devotions, "For ye shall not go out with haste, nor go by flight" (Isa 52:12 KJV). This sort of subterfuge is not "rightly handling the word of truth" (2 Tim 2:15). We are all offended when our words are taken out of context and used to mean something we never intended. Is the Holy Spirit pleased when we do this with his words? When we engage in such shenanigans, we are only confirming the suspicions of critics who allege that there is no certain message from God and that Christians, to suit their own agenda, make the Bible say whatever they want to make it say. Every sermon we preach ought to be evidence that we long to submit not only to the Holy Spirit's teaching, but also to the Holy Spirit's method of teaching, using his ideas to support his ideas. In the Bible, the Lord not only teaches us *what* to think—he teaches us *how* to think. As noted earlier, our preaching of the Bible ought to model for our hearers how they ought to be reading the Bible. This is the way to understanding, and understanding God's Word is the means that God uses to reveal himself to us.

The Outline as a Means of Experiencing God

When we observe the Holy Spirit's outline of truth in a text, this ought also to be a means of experiencing God. As important as it is for us to understand the text, simply understanding the text is not the ultimate goal for ourselves or for our hearers. Knowing God is the goal. Participating in the divine nature is the goal (2 Pet 1:3–4).

It is possible to see the structure of the text and not experience God. There are some who are "always learning and never able to arrive at a knowledge of the truth" (2 Tim 3:7). I used to lead a Bible study that was attended by several lost persons. The most skilled exegete in the group was a young lady who made no claim to being a Christian and who was openly pursuing a sinful lifestyle. She understood the content and structure of the text better than some of the Christians present! It is possible to accurately analyze a text and still not know God. The Pharisees diligently studied the Scriptures, but their study did not lead them to Christ (John 5:39).

There is a supernatural step in this process that God himself must accomplish in us and in our hearers. Those who come to Christ must be drawn by the Father, and they must be taught and enabled by God (John 6:44–45, 65). Apart from his supernatural work, exegetical excellence is nothing more than dry bones. God must breathe life into the bones. When he was a young man, C. H. Spurgeon compiled a notebook of his sermon outlines, which he called skeletons, and on the cover page of the notebook he wrote "Skeletons—I to LXXVII and only skeletons without the Holy Ghost."[2]

From the perspective of God's action, this supernatural work is called *drawing* or *teaching* or *enabling*; from the perspective of human response, this supernatural work is called *hearing*. Hearing the Word of God comes before faith and always results in faith. Note the progression in Romans 10:17 "Faith comes from hearing, and hearing through the word of Christ." With this in mind, consider the significance of Jesus's oft repeated phrase, "Let him who has ears to hear, hear." Again, ponder this prophecy about the Lord Jesus: "Morning by morning he awakens; he awakens my ear to hear as those who are taught. The Lord GOD has opened my ear, and I was not rebellious; I turned not backward. I gave my back to those who strike, and my cheeks to those who pull out the beard; I hid not my face from disgrace and spitting" (Isa 50:4–6). According to this prophecy, God opened the ears of Jesus, and this hearing led to his faithful obedience. Jesus did not need to be converted—he had no sin, but even the sinless Savior needed daily, "morning by morning," to

---

2. C. H. Spurgeon, *C. H. Spurgeon's Autobiography*, vol. 1 (London: Passmore and Alabaster, 1897), 215. The old four-volume autobiography has a facsimile of the cover page drawn in Spurgeon's hand. If you get the opportunity, take a look at it. Spurgeon was quite an artist!

experience God through hearing him. No wonder Jesus said, "The one who is hearing my word and believing him who sent me has eternal life" (John 5:24, author's translation).

As already stated, this supernatural step is one that can be accomplished by God alone. Unless God acts, we will never experience God ourselves, and our preaching will be meaningless. Spiritual life is commenced (John 3:3) and sustained by God's life-giving power.

Since we cannot accomplish this process even in ourselves, much less in our hearers, are we then consigned to fold our hands and wait idly for God to move? Not at all! God uses means to accomplish this supernatural work, and the means that he uses is his written Word. Remember the progression, "Faith comes from hearing, and hearing *from the word of Christ*." God has recorded the Word of Christ in the Bible. If you want to experience God yourself—to hear him—then interact with his written Word. Jesus said, "The one who is hearing my word . . . has eternal life." Do you want to hear Jesus? Interact with his Word. It is true that you must be born from above or you will never see any of this, but how does God bring about this supernatural birth? "You have been born again, not of perishable seed but of imperishable, through the living and abiding word of God" (1 Pet 1:23). Do you desire to go through life like Jesus did, with your ears open every day hearing God's voice? He calls you to this very kind of glorious and excellent life: "His divine power has granted to us all things that pertain to life and godliness through the knowledge of him who called us to his own glory and excellence, by which he has granted to us his precious and very great promises, so that through them you may become partakers of the divine nature, having escaped from the corruption that is in the world because of sinful desire" (2 Pet 1:3–4).

An outline is a map of an author's thinking or reason. When we read the Bible, the ultimate goal is not merely to identify the map of God's thoughts; it is to follow the map and think God's thoughts after him: to think and feel like God thinks and feels. If we would interact with God—if we would experience and know him, we must interact with the *logos*, the Word or reason. God the Father is the God of reason. God the son is the *logos*, or reason. God the Holy Spirit inspired a book in which he not only reveals the commands of God, he also explains the reasonable basis for nearly every command he gives. The fact that God is a God of reason is really the only good basis for our confidence that reason itself is a reliable means of discovering truth. If God has not authorized and empowered reason, then our reasoning process is ultimately just the result of the random movement of mindless atoms.[3]

Some readers mistakenly approach the Bible as if it were a magic talisman or a good luck charm. It is only slightly better that some approach the Bible as if it were nothing more than a collection of wise, religious sayings and stories. You, man of God, must teach them better. You must teach them to see the Bible as a coherent, reasonable message from God meant to reprogram our way of thinking and transform our way of living. It seems almost laughable to write it, but it is true: the lowly outline is a valuable means of achieving this great end. The outline is a means of grace!

The Outline as a Means of Organizing the Text

The Bible, as a whole, has a main idea that is supported by sub-points. It can be outlined. Each book of the Bible has a main idea that is supported by sub points. The books can be outlined. Most books of the Bible can be subdivided into smaller sections, each having a main point supported by sub-points. The sections can be outlined. And it is not uncommon for even a single verse of the Bible to have a main point supported by sub-points. These individual verses can be outlined. Which of these outlines ought you to use when you are organizing your text to preach? The answer to that question depends on a couple of considerations.

First Consideration: Purpose—What Kind of Tour Are You Leading?

One consideration that will help determine your focus is how thoroughly you intend to explore the passage. I (Orrick) wrote the rough draft for

---

3. Among others, C. S. Lewis explores this idea in his classic book *Miracles* (New York: HarperOne, 2015).

this chapter while enjoying a summer of ministry on the island of Maui in the Hawaiian Islands. Maui is surely one of the most beautiful places on earth, and there are several ways to see the island. You might hire a helicopter and fly over the entire island. You might drive around the island in an automobile. You could ride a bicycle, or you could hike. Each of these modes of transportation has its advantages, and in what follows, I use them to represent four approaches to the exposition of Scripture.

From the air, you can get the big picture and see how Maui is situated in relation to the other islands. You can see the overall shape of the island and note its outstanding features, like the mountains and the bays. There is real advantage to seeing a book of the Bible as if from a helicopter. This "fly-over" tour represents the depth of exposition you might employ as part of a year-long survey of the Bible. Your goal is to help your congregation see the big picture of the Bible. In the chapter on topical preaching, Ryan Fullerton recounted how he preached over the entire Bible in a single Sunday morning sermon. That was more like a space shuttle tour of the earth!

A driving tour is a bit more detailed. On a driving tour of Maui you can experience various climates and ecosystems, from the balmy breezes along the coast to the cold, windswept summit of the dormant volcano, Haleakala. You can drive through rain forest on one side of the island, and within an hour you can be in desert on the other side. When he was pastor of the Storms Creek Missionary Baptist Church in Ironton, Ohio, my father, Jim B. Orrick, took seventeen years to preach through the entire Bible on Wednesday nights. He would commonly cover three or four chapters per night. That is a lot of Scripture to cover in a thirty-minute sermon, but he was guiding a driving tour.[4]

A bicycle tour would be still more intimate. On a bicycle, it is easy to stop at a waterfall or to admire the flowers and the trees more closely. I once preached through the book of Hebrews, which has thirteen chapters,

---

4. When he told me that he had finished his survey of the Bible and how long it had taken, I asked him what he was going to do next on Wednesday nights. He answered that he was going to start through the Bible again, only he intended to go slower. He was pastor there for more than forty-one years.

in fourteen sermons. You cannot explore all the details, but you can see a lot more detail from a bicycle than you can from a plane or a car.

Finally, there is a hiking tour. If you have the time, energy, and resources, this is a wonderful way to explore. You can swim in the mountain pools, smell the flowers, and nibble the wild fruits. Puritan Joseph Caryl took twenty-four years to preach through Job, and his 424 sermons on Job make up twelve volumes. D. M. Lloyd-Jones's sermons on Romans fill fourteen volumes. One of Lloyd-Jones's most famous sermons is an exposition of only two words from Ephesians 2:4: "but God." That is the sort of thing that a preacher can do when he is leading a hiking tour.

The Four Approaches Illustrated

On a helicopter tour of the gospel of Matthew, I might cover in a single sermon two of the three chapters of the Sermon on the Mount. I would probably identify 5:20 as the thesis of the passage: "Unless your righteousness exceeds that of the scribes and Pharisees, you will never enter the kingdom of Heaven." In the introduction, I would explain that although we may not have scribes and Pharisees any more, the characteristics of their teaching remain alive in every generation. Since Jesus contrasts the righteousness of his true followers to that of the scribes and Pharisees, I would cast every point as a contrast:

I. Your character must be transformed and not merely your behavior (The beatitudes, 5:1–12)
II. You must benefit the world rather than withdraw from it (The similitudes, 5:13–16)
III. Your attitudes must be righteous and not merely your actions (5:21–48)
IV. Unlike the hypocrites, you must not use religion to show off (6:1–18)
V. Seek God's kingdom before all else (6:19–34)

Even on a helicopter tour that would be a lot to cover, but it might be done.

182 of Encountering God through Expository Preaching

On a driving tour, I might try to cover only chapter 5, use the same thesis as above, but I would look more carefully at points I, II, and III.

On a bicycle tour, I might focus on only one section of the chapter, for example, the section dealing with anger, and I could outline it like this:

I.   Jesus asserts the true character of anger (5:21–22)
II. Jesus teaches that peace with our brother is a prerequisite to worship (5:23–24)
III. Jesus illustrates the importance of quickly solving interpersonal conflicts (5:25–26)

On a hiking tour, I would spend an entire sermon on each of the beatitudes, and my sermon outline would be the same for each of the beatitudes:

I.   What does it mean to be _____?
II. Why are they blessed?
III. How can we become more like this?[5]

For each of these points in the hiking tour approach, I am obviously going to have to look outside the text to see what the rest of the Bible says about my text, but I would still be focused on explaining the text.

A Second Consideration: Needs of Your Hearers

When deciding which outline to utilize, you must also consider the capacities and needs of your hearers. If you know your congregation, you will have a better idea of what you need to emphasize and illustrate in the text. One of the fundamental components of good public speaking in any context is *know your audience*. It is doubly imperative for the preacher to know his audience, for while always remaining faithful to the Holy Spirit's message in the text, a sensitive pastor/preacher will customize

---

5. I would develop this third point topically in the way Ryan Fullerton describes in the chapter on topical preaching.

each sermon to suit the needs and capacities of his hearers. This customization will usually be reflected in the outline for the sermon.

Let us suppose that God has moved you deeply while meditating on a passage of Scripture. Your heart is full of God's truth, and the thought goes through your mind, *The next time I get an opportunity to preach, I am going to preach from this passage.* Just then the phone rings, and your pastor asks, "Are you available to preach next week?"

"Yes!" you answer.

He continues, "Good, because I need you to preach for me at _____." Now consider various possibilities for filling in the blank, and think of how each possibility will affect the way you handle the text when you preach it. Suppose the blank is filled with "the prison ministry," or "the youth campfire," or "the senior citizens' dinner," or "the children's Sunday school banquet." Or imagine that he asks you to preach at all of these venues! If you were to preach from the same text to each of these audiences, the message of the text remains the same; but your approach to explaining the text will be customized: your outline will be affected and each of your sermons will be noticeably different—or at least it ought to be. A challenging aspect to preaching to a local church is that persons from all these various groups may be present in one congregation, and you are responsible to feed all of them from the Word of God!

In a healthy church, on any given Sunday morning fully one-third of the congregation will consist of children who are under the age of twelve. Many of them are unconverted. It is unacceptable that the preacher should preach even one sermon that contains nothing that the children understand. In every sermon, the preacher who preaches to a congregation containing children ought to say something that will arrest the attention of the children and help them understand the truth. No child—no person of any age who is willing to listen—ought to walk away from one of your sermons saying, "I did not understand a single thing that he said." Complex, incomprehensible preaching is not a sign of intelligence; it is a sign of arrogant carelessness.

Besides considering the age of your hearers, you ought also to consider their level of spiritual maturity, doctrinal understanding, capacity to concentrate, level of education, vocation, and various fluctuating cultural concerns. A preacher must be able to step outside himself and objectively consider how his words will sound in the ears of various groups in his congregation. If he cannot do this, he will not be a good teacher. And if a potential pastor is not able to teach, he must do one of two things: he must either work hard to become a good teacher, or he must face the fact that he is not called to be a pastor since being able to teach is a qualification for being a pastor (1 Tim 3:2). Since you are reading this book, we hope you are working hard to become a good teacher.

When you consider your audience, you not only help them to understand the text, you yourself will often gain fresh insights into the text. When you preach through books of the Bible, there will be times when you will be stumped as to how you are going to handle a particular passage of Scripture and present it to your congregation. You may not even understand the passage yourself! Despair begins to set in. I have heard that John Knox once rose before a congregation of thousands who expected him to preach, and he said, "Brethren, the Lord hath not spoken to me this week." Then he sat down. In your perplexity over the meaning of the text, you begin to wonder if you can get away with saying what John Knox said and did. Probably not. What to do? You remember a hospital visit that you need to make. "I might as well do it now," you think, and off you go to minister to one of your flock. Or perhaps your sermon preparation is interrupted by some urgent, unexpected situation that calls for your attention, and you go to take care of it. You might even be frustrated at the interruption. But when you return to the text that was causing you such anguish, much to your amazement the clouds of confusion have dissipated; and in a flash of inspiration you not only understand the text, you also know exactly how you will preach it. Your outline is completed in a matter of minutes. What happened? Interaction with people has opened a fresh perspective on God's truth. Sometimes pastoring is the best hermeneutic. It is no wonder, then, that a pastor's best preaching is almost always done at his own church where he knows the people best.

If you do not know the congregation where you will be preaching, you may still make some accurate general predictions that will influence your handling of the text. Every good speaker, and especially every good preacher is a careful observer of human nature and of his own culture.

Remember, no matter the age or socioeconomic status or educational level of the congregation, every person in your audience needs to hear the Word of God preached by a man of God who is experiencing God. If you start trying to impress the doctors and lawyers and college professors with your knowledge of their respective fields of expertise, you are doomed. They need the Word of God. Be an expert on the Word of God. Love people enough to preach it in a way that they can understand it and feel it, and you will do well. You do not have to be the most intelligent person in the room to feed the people of God with the Word of God.

Brian Payne and I teach at Boyce College, which is the undergraduate college at The Southern Baptist Theological Seminary in Louisville, Kentucky. We have chapel twice a week at Southern. All three authors of this book have preached in chapel numerous times, and we can testify that chapel at Southern Seminary is one of the most potentially intimidating preaching venues we have faced. Many of the world's leading conservative evangelical scholars are sitting in that chapel. When you stand to preach, there may be men sitting before you who have written commentaries on the book of the Bible from which you take your text. Many of the professors and students will be reading your text in the original languages. Occasionally, a chapel speaker will make the dreadful mistake of trying to come across as deeply learned. He nearly always makes a mess of things. On the other hand, most chapel speakers approach the task with fear and trembling, seeking to honor God with the simple, heartfelt exposition of the Word. Here is what we have observed again and again through the years: the great scholars sitting in the chapel want to hear the Word of God, and they are deeply moved and deeply appreciative when they do hear it. Regardless of a person's income or education, if that person is a healthy child of God, he wants to hear the Word of God. Someone in your congregation may have spent the week performing heart surgeries. Someone else may have spent the week working as a janitor. Another may have spent the week learning the alphabet. Preach the Word, and all will be fed.

In 1740, George Whitefield visited Northampton, Massachusetts, where Jonathan Edwards was pastor. Edwards asked Whitefield to preach. Think of it: a twenty-five-year-old man standing before one of the keenest theological and philosophical minds in the history of Christianity. Whitefield preached the Word. Jonathan Edwards sat in the pew a few feet away and wept through the sermon.[6] Oh, the power of the preached Word!

The Outline as a Means of Remembering the Text

When we seek to memorize something, we look for patterns and/or a manageable grouping of the information. We break up phone numbers into a three-digit area code, a three digit prefix, and a four digit number. Most of us memorize our Social Security numbers in the same way: we break the nine-digit number into three manageable units. We look for the same sort of patterns and units when memorizing Scripture. If you were to memorize 2 Timothy 1:1–7, you would do well to observe that there are four verbs that have to do with remembering or reminding. If you were to memorize 2 Timothy 2:3–7, it would help you to see that there are three illustrations: a soldier, an athlete, and a farmer. These sorts of patterns are present in virtually every text of the Bible, and they often suggest a structure that makes for a very memorable outline of the text. A good outline is a brief summary of the text, and it ought to help us and our hearers to remember the truth of the text.

Seek to make the outline memorable, but beware of striving after cleverness or cuteness that will potentially distract from the meaning of the text. Some preachers put obvious effort into making all the points of their sermons begin with the same letter of the alphabet. The practice is overdone, and it is usually ill done. Occasionally, you might find that three out of your four points in your outline begin with the same letter,

---

6. See George Whitefield, *George Whitefield's Journals*, repr. (Carlisle, PA: Banner of Truth, 1960), 476–77.

and you might see if the fourth point will allow itself to begin with the same letter as the other three. If it does not cooperate, do not fret with it. Slavish alliteration is a burden that neither we nor our fathers have been able to bear.

Since you have gone to the effort to construct an outline that reflects the structure of the text, and since a well-constructed outline is a means of experiencing God in the text, make your outline obvious to your listeners. Use transitions to progress from one point to the next. Say, "The first point is. . . ." When you have finished with the first point, say something like, "So we have seen first . . . Now let us go on to see second . . ." Speakers sometimes feel like they are being overly simple when they proceed with such plainness, but remember that while you are very familiar with your text and the way that you are handling it, your hearers are not that familiar. Use transitions to make your outline plain. If you use transitions that summarize your previous points, you will give your listeners more than one opportunity to hear what you have said. Nearly every listener will have lapses in attention. If you use transitions that review, motivated listeners can catch up on what they have missed during their lapse. Another benefit of using good transitions is that it gives your listeners a sense that your sermon has a goal, and you are making progress toward that goal.

Whether you preach using a manuscript, an outline, or no written notes at all, take the time to compose a good introduction and a good conclusion to the text. When a diligent hostess prepares a holiday feast, she presents the meal on her finest china, and the table may have a lovely centerpiece. She cares about the food, yes, but she also obviously cares about how the food is presented. Whether served on paper plates or on fancy plates, the food will keep you from starving, but it is more appealing when it is tastefully presented. The fact that God inspired his Word to be written in beautiful language is indisputable evidence that he cares about presentation. So when you give attention to details of presentation, you are following the divine example. In a good introduction you will do three things: first, you will arrest the attention of the people. Second, you will summarize what the text is about. And, third, you will make them want to listen to the message of the text. In a good conclusion you bring a sense of finish to the sermon. I usually review the main points, and often use an illustration to tie them all together. It is well known that listeners have a tendency to remember best whatever comes first and last in a presentation, so take the time to make your introduction and conclusion worth remembering.

CHAPTER

17

PREACHING
WITHOUT NOTES

For the modern archer, there are some amazing bows available today. These bows are made from space-age materials, and they are equipped with a seemingly endless variety of gadgets to help an archer shoot an arrow with incredible speed and accuracy. There are cams, releases, range finders, and sights. A competent instructor can have a capable student shooting arrows in five-inch groups at thirty yards within half an hour of picking up the bow for the first time. Using one of these high-tech bows, a good archer is capable of consistently hitting his target at fifty yards or more. Those bows are great for some hunters, but I do not use a high-tech, modern bow because it would interfere with my hunting experience.

I (Orrick) am a bow-hunter who uses primitive archery tackle. I make the bows I hunt with using staves from trees that I have cut down myself. My bow is essentially a stick and a string. I shoot wooden arrows fletched with wing feathers from wild turkeys that I have harvested. I can shoot confidently to a distance of only about twenty yards. I shoot instinctively. I do not estimate the distance to my target; I just pull back the arrow and let it fly. I have done this so many times that I usually hit my target.

When you throw a baseball or a Frisbee, or shoot a basketball, do you consciously estimate distance in feet and adjust your throw or your shot mathematically? No, of course not. You have thrown that baseball so many times, or you have shot that basketball so many times that you just know instinctively how to do it with accuracy. Consulting a range-finder would only interfere with your throwing or shooting.

There may come a time in your preaching ministry when you no longer need to take all the gadgets with you into the pulpit. After thorough preparation, if you have the Word of God and the Spirit of God, you have what you need to preach.

Instinctively shooting a primitive bow requires practice. Throwing a baseball or shooting a basketball instinctively requires practice. But with practice it can be done, and it is the best way to do it. To switch the metaphor, I am not throwing you into the deep end of the pool and telling you to swim or drown, but I am going to try and convince you that preaching without notes is the best option when your goal is to open the Word of God and say to the people of God, "Come and experience God with me in this text." In this chapter, I note what is required to preach without notes and the advantages of doing so. I will not throw you into the deep end, but there comes a time when you have to take off the water-wings, let go of the side of the pool, kick off, and swim.

What Is Required to Preach Without Notes

Personal Holiness

First and foremost, you must be walking with God in your everyday life and in your everyday personality. Of course, this is required of any man of God, whether he preaches without notes or with a full manuscript. It is, however, doubly important for the preacher who preaches without notes since quality extemporaneous speech is drawn from a storehouse of ideas that are accumulated through a lifestyle of meditation and from experiencing God in everyday, natural living. Then when you preach in your everyday, natural personality, you will be overflowing with ideas, illustrations, and applications that you have been learning from your everyday walk with God.

I have often observed preachers who adopt a different persona when they preach. They sometimes speak in an unnatural way. I have heard men pretend to have a European accent, or a Southern accent. They might try to imitate the speaking patterns of an admired preacher. Some lower the natural tone of their voice. Whatever the affected idiosyncrasy, they pretend to be someone else when they are preaching. They adopt a role just as if a stage director had said to them, "Now, you play the part of the preacher." I want to be as generous as I can, and so I grant that sometimes this play-acting is the result of a particular Christian sub-culture or denomination that just expects their preachers to sound like that. Or the preacher may be nervous or attempting to "fake it till he feels it." But I fear that one of the main reasons that these play-acting preachers adopt an unnatural persona when they preach is because these men are not experiencing God in their everyday selves; so when they stand to preach, they must pretend to be someone who is experiencing God. This is a charade that is sad beyond words, and one of the unintended messages such behavior communicates is that God is a Sunday-morning-only God.

The sermon must be an outgrowth of a holy life lived in continuous interaction with the thoughts of God. To state it negatively, the sermon cannot be an episodic interruption to a secular life. The sermon must be a natural eruption of the passion and fire that are always bubbling beneath the surface of the preacher's everyday existence.

Sometimes Calvin and Luther would preach nearly every day, and they were not preaching reruns. They were working their way through books of the Bible. You can read those sermons, and you will see that they are not shallow fluff. How could they generate such an impressive volume of high-quality material? They walked with God in their everyday lives. When he first came to London, C. H. Spurgeon would sometimes preach thirteen times during the week. George Whitefield often preached two or three times a day for weeks on end. How did they do it? They walked with God, and their hearts were full of God. All these men might have used notes, but I guarantee you that most of what they said was unscripted.

I sometimes sit through sermons that are unnecessarily dry because the speaker is reading when he ought to be preaching. Often the material he is reading is uncomplicated—maybe even an account of a personal experience. I am filled with sadness (on my good days), and I think to myself, *Really? You need a manuscript to tell us how God has been sufficient for your family during your wife's ordeal with cancer? Put down your paper, look us in the eye, and let your spirit rise. Speak with a tear trickling down your cheek and with a lump in your throat, and just see if we can sleep through that!*

The first prerequisite for preaching without notes is that you are walking with God day-by-day. If you are, then his Word will be "a fire shut up in your bones"; and when you stand to preach, the fire will burn through you to warm and enlighten others.

As I write this, I have been preaching for nearly forty years. I was seventeen when I preached my first sermon to a group of about twenty-five people in the congregation of Faith Baptist Church in Lee County, Kentucky. That evening, I used an ill-constructed outline that fit on one side of a piece of paper torn from a small spiral bound notepad. I continued to use such brief, mostly one-page outlines for close to twenty years. All those twenty years I repeatedly noticed something about my preaching: the most powerful and Spirit-filled parts of my sermons were consistently those parts for which I did not need my notes at all. During those parts, I was most earnestly engaged, and I could see that the congregation was more attentive to what I was saying. Sometimes it was almost as if we were all under a spell. But inevitably, the spell would be broken when I came to the end of that "without notes" section and had to look down at my notes to see what I was supposed to say next. Persons would shift in their seats, papers would rustle, people would clear their throats, look at their watches, or indicate in some way that their attention had strayed. It was a letdown for me as well. It was as if we all fidgeted when I left off preaching and went back to lecturing. There is nothing wrong with a lecture in its proper place, but the pulpit is not that place.

I finally realized that notes were interfering with my hearers' and my own experiencing God, and I took the frightening step of preaching without notes. That has been my practice ever since.

The Main Divisions of the Sermon Must Reflect the Structure of the Text

Second, while it is important that every expository preacher base the structure of his sermon on the Holy Spirit–inspired structure of the text, it is indispensably crucial for the preacher attempting to preach without notes. If he should forget what his next point is, it is no problem: the next point of his sermon is right there in the text, and he will probably remember it by merely glancing at the text.

During his preparation, the "without notes" preacher does make a careful outline of the text. He will usually write it down, but he does not take the written outline with him into the pulpit. After all, the purpose of an outline is to remind you what to say. If, however, your outline is obviously taken from the text, then why do you need the outline anymore? You have the text to remind you. When I say that the sermon outline must be obviously based on the text, I mean obviously. The preacher ought to be able to say, "My first point is . . . and you can see the basis for this point if you look at verse __." When he then reads the specified verse, everyone ought to be able to see why that verse is the basis for his first point. If the first point has two subheadings, the preacher ought to be able to direct his hearers to the text so they can see that the basis of his two subheadings is right there in the text.

The Outline Must Be Memorable

Third, if you are to preach successfully without notes, not only must you base your outline on the text, you must also make the outline memorable. You must be able to remember the outline having no reminder other than the text. But is that so hard? It may be a challenge if you have grown accustomed to preaching complicated sermons that neither you nor anyone else can remember without notes. Do you want people to be able to remember what you preach? How do you expect them to remember it if you cannot?[1] If they should forget, they ought to be able to go home and remember the main points of your sermon the same way that you remember them: by reading the text.

If the outline is to be memorable, it must be simple. As a general rule, the average person has difficulty managing more than three to five main ideas in a sermon. Choose the length of your text with these realistic limitations in mind. The text will supply supporting ideas for these three to five main ideas, and the supporting ideas may be further developed in the text. If your situation requires that you examine the text in a more thorough and detailed manner, you might consider handling the text in more than one sermon so as to keep the outline simple. As a general rule, if your outline requires symbols beyond Roman and Arabic numerals and upper and lower case letters, your outline is too complicated, and you probably cannot preach it without notes. So simplify it! It is too complicated to follow and to remember. What good is it to preach a sermon that is so complex that even the person doing the preaching cannot remember it? Make it simple; make it memorable.

I suspect that some people are under the impression that a preacher who preaches without notes need not prepare as thoroughly as one who uses a manuscript, but this is not necessarily true. It is very likely that the preacher who preaches without notes spends much less time writing than does the preacher who writes out a full manuscript of his sermon, but the "without notes" preacher probably spends more time on other aspects of preparation. Preaching without notes requires a different sort of preparation because the preacher must have such a thorough understanding of the text that he can readily recall it without any prompting other than the text. He must not only see how the Holy Spirit unfolds the truth in the text; he must see it and remember it under pressure.

Those last two sentences in the preceding paragraph will cause some readers to grimace and say, "That is just the problem: I do not dare even to consider preaching without notes because I have a terrible memory!" To speak frankly, most people do not have a good memory because they

---

1. I heard B. Gray Allison, a very fine "without notes" preacher, ask this question. The question influenced me profoundly.

never try to memorize anything. You might think of your memory as if it were a muscle.[2] If you do not use it, it will be weak. If you do use it, it will get stronger. Get your memory into shape. Devote a few minutes every day to memorizing something meaningful, such as Scripture, poetry, or the names of people. Do this consistently for six weeks, and then tell me you cannot memorize anything. If you are bright enough to read and understand most of this book, you almost certainly have the mental capacity to remember an outline that is based on the Scripture and to preach without notes. On the other hand, if you are not willing to make the effort to improve your memory, then preaching without notes is probably not for you.

It is not strictly accurate to say that I advocate preaching without notes. What I advocate is being so thoroughly engaged with the thoughts of God expressed in the text that written notes become a distraction. For this level of engagement to occur consistently, the preacher will have mental notes but not written ones.

You Need the Holy Spirit

If you have the gift of gab, you may be able to deliver a clever and engaging speech without notes. But to preach without notes—and do it with power and authority—you need much more than a loquacious bent: you need the Holy Spirit. Again, this is true for any preacher, no matter whether he preaches using no written notes or if he preaches using a full manuscript. Without the Holy Spirit, you are a man pretending to preach. I know that I have been far more conscious of my dependence on the Holy Spirit during the years that I have been preaching without notes.

In one of Ryan Fullerton's chapters on the necessity of the Holy Spirit in preaching, he led us to consider that, in light of our desperate need for the Spirit's empowering, it is incongruous that we pray so little about our preaching compared with the amount of time we put into other aspects of pulpit preparation. After reading that, you might have wondered, "What could I possibly pray about for that length of time?" Answer: pray

---

2. Even if this is not accurate neurologically, it is true practically.

through the text. Ask the Lord for insight into the overall meaning. Ask him to show you how this ancient text has modern applications. Ask him to remove your preconceived notions that cloud your understanding. Ask him to illumine any difficult ideas. Talk to him about the message he has sent, and the way you can most effectively present it to the people that both of you love.

In certain poems that I love, there occur lines that I do not understand. In my quest to understand the confusing section, I might consult literary criticism that has been written on the poem, but often there is disagreement among the scholars. What if I could ask the author of the poem? Well, when you face puzzling sections of the Bible, you can ask the author! In Isaiah 22:8–11, the Lord rebukes the people of Jerusalem because in all their preparations for war, they did not look to him. God does not discourage the use of means, but he is displeased when we behave as if means can be effective without him. Similarly, when King Asa of Judah was diseased in his feet, the Holy Spirit says to Asa's discredit, "Yet even in his disease he did not seek the Lord, but sought help from the physicians" (2 Chron 16:12). Might not the Lord bring a similar accusation against many a preacher? "In his perplexity with the text, he did not seek the LORD, but sought help from the commentators." While the Lord gives us astoundingly gracious promises regarding the prosperity of his Word, nonetheless, "Thus saith the Lord GOD; I will yet for this be enquired of by the house of Israel, to do it for them" (Ezek 36:37 KJV).

After the study is done and the text is organized; after you have thought through the text until you could paraphrase it, if not quote it verbatim; after the outline is made; when you are so ready that you could preach this sermon right now if you had to; leave time to take a quiet walk and enjoy the truth of God's Word in God's presence. Walk with God like Enoch did.

This interaction—this prayerful meditation with the Lord and his Word—is an essential part of preparing to preach without notes. And it is the ultimate joy of life. It is the wind of eternity blowing through your human soul. Really, when you preach in the Spirit, you are sharing with others the painful joy and the joyful pain that has been cultivated in your soul by interacting with God in your prayerful meditations on his Word. You share it in such a way that you and your hearers join together in experiencing him again, and you really live.

Advantages to Preaching Without Notes

It Motivates You to Do What You Ought to Be Doing Anyway

Nearly all my life I have attempted to eat right and stay in good physical condition. Through the years I occasionally have had persons say to me, "You spend all this time exercising and eating good food, but in spite of all your efforts, you know that you are going to die one day." I do know that, and it is good to remember that physical fitness is of limited value. There seems, however, to be a mistaken assumption in the reminder from this well-intentioned, overweight person munching on a donut. He seems to think that the only reason I exercise and eat right is to live longer, when, in fact, a healthy life is a reward every day, and I am glad to have pursued a healthy lifestyle even if I should die tomorrow. While that is true, I confess that I do not naturally relish the everyday routine of vigorous exercise. It hurts. But most days, I do it anyway. Often, motivation to "do it anyway" comes from my resolve to reach a goal that I have set for myself. Maybe I set a goal to bench press a certain amount before a determined date. Maybe I want to get in better-than-average condition because of a scheduled hunt that will be in the mountains. The goal helps motivate me to do what I ought to be doing anyway. When I know that I will fail to reach my goal without proper preparation, it motivates me to prepare.

I have cited four necessary qualities for preaching without notes: personal holiness, the sermon outline must be obviously based on the structure of the text, the outline must be memorable, and the presence of the Holy Spirit. I have presented these four qualities almost as if they are prerequisites, but you can surely see that all of them are not merely prerequisites to preaching without notes; they all ought to be characteristic of any God-called preacher. So, for example, it is a bit skewed to say, "I am going to pursue personal holiness so that I can preach without notes," or "I am going to pray to be filled with the Holy Spirit so that I can preach without notes." A more healthy perspective will have you saying, "I want to preach in such a way that I will be constantly forced to walk with God. I want to encourage such habits in my life that I continually and acutely feel my dependence on the Holy Spirit." I fear that one reason so many of us experience so little of the Holy Spirit's power is because we rarely attempt anything that will be a dismal failure without his power. In much of our public worship, everything is so neatly planned and orchestrated by human endeavor that most people simply will not notice if the Holy Spirit is not present. If, on the other hand, you are attempting something that will fail without the Holy Spirit, you are motivated to pray for the Holy Spirit. You ought to be praying for the Holy Spirit anyway, but think about it: would you pray more earnestly for the Holy Spirit's blessing if you were going to preach without notes? When we know that we will fail without proper preparation, we are motivated to prepare. I propose that preaching without notes is a worthy goal that will motivate you to do what you ought to be doing anyway.

It Makes It Easier to Practice Excellent Communication Skills

EYE CONTACT

Preaching without notes makes it easy to maintain appropriate eye contact with your listeners, and this is a critical component of effective communication. The preacher who has good eye contact comes across as trustworthy. People are more prone to like you and listen to you when you have good eye contact. When you preach in the United States of America, you need to look into the eyes of the persons in your congregation. Do not look at the floor. Do not look over their heads and sweep your gaze from one corner of the room to the other. And do not fix your eyes on your notes or manuscript. Look into the eyes of the people; it communicates love. Do not stare at anyone, but look at everyone for just a couple of seconds. There are differing protocols regarding eye contact for various cultures around the world, but in the United

States it is bad manners not to look steadily at the person speaking, and a speaker communicates insecurity if he will not look his listeners in the eye. In conversation, while the listener is to maintain constant eye contact with the speaker, the polite speaker looks away every few seconds. The same rules apply to eye contact while preaching. Some people never get this right, and it is a serious impediment to effective communication. If you are reading this book in a preaching class, your professor will be able to critique your eye contact. If you do not have a preaching professor, ask someone who hears you preach if you maintain appropriate eye contact.

Gestures, Facial Expressions, and Movement

Preaching without notes makes it easier for you to make appropriate gestures and facial expressions. Not being tied to his notes, a preacher is more likely to move around, not always standing behind the pulpit. Gestures and movement communicate earnestness, and they help attract and hold interest. Ancient orators emphasized the importance of movement for the public speaker to the point that some insisted that action was the most essential component of effective public speaking. If you do not naturally gesture with your hands, or if you are not very expressive with your facial expressions, try to improve in these areas. Do not become a fake and pretend to be what you are not, but see this as a way that you can serve the Lord by becoming a better speaker so that his children will not keep falling asleep when you preach.

Vocal Variety

All that goes into preaching without notes will increase your vocal variety because you are more likely to feel the emotions prompted by the text. Also, since you are able to watch the congregation instead of your notes, you will feel an energy that comes from the people who are excited that someone is finally looking them in the eye and talking to them like a man. When you are looking out on a congregation that is hungrily taking in the Word of God, you cannot speak in a monotone. You and they are experiencing God together.

It Encourages Masculinity

Every semester, I teach several seminars on the great books of Western Civilization. In Great Books I, we read and discuss *The Odyssey* by Homer. One of the main themes in *The Odyssey* is the maturing of Odysseus's son, Telemachus. When we first encounter Telemachus, he is a tentative, hesitating boy; by the end of the book, he is a mighty warrior fighting by his father's side. I ask the class, "Why do you think there is such protracted immaturity among males in our society? What is it that helps a boy to mature into a man?" It always leads to a fascinating and enlightening discussion. There are several answers that surface: "A boy becomes a man when he is around men." "A boy becomes a man when he is assigned meaningful work." "A boy becomes a man when he is given significant responsibility." Our culture is not very good at helping boys to become men; and sadly, our churches are no better at it. But for a culture to be strong, we must have men who are truly masculine. For preaching to be effective, the preacher must be a masculine man. An effeminate man cannot be an effective preacher. Our culture has foggy notions about what constitutes masculinity; and if you recoil at what I am writing, allow me to clarify what true masculinity is, and why it is essential for the preacher.

When people find out that I am working on a preaching book, they often ask me, "What is the title of the book?" I have sometimes jokingly responded, "Stand Up and Preach Like a Man, You Sissy." You might be amazed at how many people have thought that such a book needs to be written. God is not being sexist when he restricts the privilege of preaching to men. Masculinity is essential to the task. The masculinity that is essential to preaching is not the blustery, chest-thumping masculinity that consists in using women, delighting in violence, and bullying everything in sight. That brand of masculinity is more animal than human. The essential characteristic of true masculinity is initiation of good. A godly, masculine man wants to conquer things, but he wants to conquer things so that he can make them better. A truly masculine man is looking for ways that he can better the people and the situations around him. A man is not a real man who takes pleasure from a person and leaves that person worse off. A real man gives pleasure and leaves persons and situations better off. I believe that most men and women are glad to submit to leadership when they are convinced that the leader loves them and that he has their good at heart. And most people are eager to listen to a preacher who preaches with a godly masculinity. Masculinity is cultivated by doing difficult things—things that challenge you and force you to grow. Preaching without notes may be one of those things. Even if you never get to the point that you can preach without notes, if you consistently pursue the kind of masculine communication that I am advocating, you will grow in your ability to engage the confidence of your listeners.

It Helps You Relate to the People

Not long ago I preached at a men's retreat that lasted for three days. There were only three items on the schedule: eating, shooting, and preaching. We had a great time. After the retreat was over, I received a very thoughtful note of appreciation from a construction worker who was at the retreat. He wrote, "You are the only educated man that I have ever been able to understand." I was flattered, but what a sad note. It is not uncommon for me to hear similar sad comments regarding the incomprehensibility of preaching done by educated men. Since I have a PhD, I cannot be accused of sour grapes when I say that having a PhD communicates only one thing with certainty: you are capable of sitting still for long periods of time and voluntarily submitting yourself to torture. It does not mean that you are educated. And may God deliver us from the sort of education that makes a preacher feel justified in being incomprehensible and boring. People appreciate it when you have gone to the effort to make the message clear and to present it in an interesting way.

Other Advantages

You Forget Stuff

I know some of you are wondering if I have accidentally listed *forgetting* as an advantage rather than a disadvantage. It is not an accident. When

I preach, I nearly always forget something that I planned on saying, but that is probably a good thing because it leaves room for something better to be said. See, along with forgetting stuff that I planned to say, I nearly always think of something that I never planned on saying, and not uncommonly, that unplanned segment is the most powerful part of the sermon! Several years ago, I was preaching at a conference, and near the beginning of the sermon, I had already said that my first point had three subheadings. I got through the first two subheadings, but I drew a blank on the third. I could read the word that was supposed to prompt my memory, but my memory was not cooperating. I paused briefly and then told the congregation that I could not think of the third subheading. Then I said, "Let's pray." I asked the Lord to help me remember what I had forgotten, but if I could not remember, then would he please help me to carry on. When I said amen, I still could not remember the third subheading, admitted as much, and carried on. In the following days of the conference, I had person after person come up to me and say, "Your message was a blessing to me, but the part that blessed me most was when you forgot, prayed, and then went on." I have heard that a manuscript preacher who was present at that conference has used my experience as an illustration to urge his protégés to use a manuscript! I did take one lesson away from that experience: since then I usually will not be as specific about how many subheadings I have!

You Are Able To Readily Customize Your Sermon

As I was working on this chapter, I participated in a forum in the association of churches to which my church belongs. The topic of the forum was church discipline, and I was scheduled to speak second. The man who spoke first did a wonderful job. In fact, he covered about two-thirds of what I had prepared to say. Now what would a manuscript preacher do in such a situation? I fear that most would read their dreary manuscript, going over the same material that the first speaker had already gone over. Since I was not tied to notes, I saw it as a golden opportunity to present some ideas that the first speaker had not covered, and I immediately scuttled most of what I had planned to say. I have thought a lot about church discipline through the years. I have had a lot of experiences with church discipline. I got to say a lot of things that I originally never thought I would get to say, and the Lord blessed.

I occasionally preach at churches that have more than one preaching service on Sunday mornings. Of course, I preach from the same text at both the services, but the sermon is probably around 30 percent different the second time. Only an hour or so has elapsed since I preached the first sermon, so obviously I have not gained many new insights on the text. What has happened? I am not different, but the congregation is different! Since I am not tied to the particular insights that appear on a manuscript, I am able to customize the sermon for the new congregation that is in front of me. We pray that God will use our words and meditations to communicate his truth and meet the needs of the various persons who make up our congregations; but when we have every idea or even every word of the sermon planned out, we become pretty inflexible.

Preaching Without Notes Is a Joyful Way to Preach

I have never preached from a manuscript, but I preached with notes for about twenty years and now have preached without notes for about twenty years. I can tell you that preaching without notes is more difficult, and it is more exhausting, but it is also more exhilarating. There is real joy in it.

I know a man who goes elk hunting every year. He has a friend in Colorado who has elk in his yard, and the man I know shoots an elk out of his friend's yard nearly every year. He could shoot them from the porch if he wanted to. He gets an elk, but I want to ask him, "Don't you miss the mountain?" I was able to go elk hunting in Colorado recently, and for nearly two weeks I was by myself in the Rocky Mountains. I never killed an elk, but I felt the snow in my face. I saw the first rays of the rising sun strike snow-capped mountain peaks. I felt my heart beat and my legs ache with the strain of trudging up and down mountains day after day. I came across bear tracks in freshly fallen snow. One day a big bull elk bugled about fifty yards from where I was set up. I briefly caught a glimpse of his massive antlers as he quietly passed through brush that no bullet could penetrate. I never shot an elk, but I experienced the mountain.

At the conclusion of this last chapter of this book on preaching, I want to urge you: Do not miss the mountain. Some of you reading this are just starting out in your ministry. You may not have even preached your first sermon yet. Do not cut yourself ruts in ministry that will have you bored in ten years, and will probably have the people in your congregation bored before that. Do not succumb to the easy ways of getting sermons, always borrowing from someone else, or worse, subscribing to a sermon service. Walk with God. Meditate in God's Word. Be a man of prayer. Be a holy man of God. And when you preach, open the Word of God and say to those who have come to hear you, "Come, experience God with me in this text."

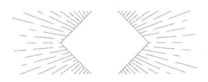

Conclusion

It is not what you expected. It is better.

When I (Orrick) was about twenty-three years old, I read Arnold Dallimore's two-volume biography of George Whitefield,[1] as well as Whitefield's *Journals*.[2] I was deeply moved. One of the most impressive features of Whitefield's amazing ministry was his preaching in the open air. He had been denied access to many indoor pulpits, and anyway, there was no church building that could hold the crowds that flocked to hear him, so he took the novel and controversial step of preaching outdoors. Tens of thousands crowded around to listen to Whitefield preach the Word of God.

I was taking some classes at the University of Kentucky at the same time that I was reading about Whitefield. I began to feel strongly that the Lord might be leading me to preach in the open air on campus. It was an agonizing decision for me. I knew that I would be branded as a fool, but I hoped that God might use me to stir up a great awakening in our day.

---

1. Arnold A. Dallimore, *George Whitefield: The Life and Times of the Great Evangelist of the Eighteenth-Century Revival*, two vols. (Westchester, IL: Cornerstone Books, 1970). Now published by Banner of Truth.

2. *George Whitefield's Journals* (Carlisle, PA: Banner of Truth Trust, 1960).

206 Encountering God through Expository Preaching

I imagined myself standing on a concrete wall, preaching, while the Holy Spirit arrested students who could not resist stopping, until, like George Whitefield, I was surrounded by thousands of eager listeners.

On a crisp October day, I rode my bicycle to UK and parked it near a busy concourse on campus. The cafeteria was nearby. I waited until 11:50 a.m., when the students were crowding the sidewalks, making their way toward the cafeteria for lunch. I stood on a concrete bench, I lifted up my voice, and I preached a brief sermon from John 14:6. The multitudes never came. In fact, as far as I could see, not one person stopped to listen to me. Not one! I came back a few days later and preached again. No one listened. I returned again and again until I felt that I was released from the impulse that I had taken to be God telling me to preach on that college campus. I was relieved when it was over. No one ever listened to me. It was not what I expected.

When I was pastor in the hills of West Virginia, I would sometimes sit on the front steps of the church at 6:55 p.m. on Wednesday evenings, wondering if anyone was going to show up for prayer meeting. Someone always did, but it might be only a handful of people. One night, when only about six people had made their way to church, one old farmer said with a twinkle in his eye, "Now, Preacher, when I go to feed my cows and only six of them show up, I don't give them the whole load!"

I had sort of figured that once I was pastor of a church, word would spread in the community about what a good preacher I was, and the building would soon be crowded. I was wrong. It was not what I expected.

In most books, when you read stories like the two I just related, there is a follow-up story about how the experience that seemed to be next to useless was, in fact, secretly used by God, and the discouraged preacher did not learn about it until years later. I do not have that follow-up story. I trust that my character bears the lasting imprint of these and many more humbling experiences, and that is much. God will use me if it pleases him. "It is the LORD; let him do what seems good to him" (1 Sam 3:18). We are servants. "Whoever would be great among you must be your servant, and whoever would be first among you must be your slave, even as the Son of Man came not to be served but to serve, and to give his life as a ransom for many" (Matt 20:26–28). "They also serve who only stand and wait."[3] It is a good day when you learn to say, "O LORD, my heart is not lifted up; my eyes are not raised too high; I do not occupy myself with things too great and too marvelous for me. But I have calmed and quieted my soul, like a weaned child with its mother, like a weaned child is my soul within me" (Ps 131:1–2). I can now see that many of my youthful aspirations in the ministry were little different from the longings that many unconverted people have. What a mess I would be in today if God had always given me what I prayed for! Still, it can be disappointing to realize the implications of the fact that "you have died, and your life is hidden with Christ in God" (Col 3:3). I had hoped that I might not be quite so hidden.

The disciples had to go through similar humbling, attitude-correcting experiences. One of them took place at Caesarea Philippi. As is often the case, the humbling experience followed a moment of exhilaration. It had become clear to the disciples that Jesus was the Messiah. Peter spoke for them all when he triumphantly declared, "You are the Christ, the Son of the living God!" (Matt 16:16). Their expectations were high. The kingdom was about to come, and they were part of the King's inner circle. Things were about to get good. Some of them were already secretly jostling for the best seats on the right and left hands of Jesus. Just then, "Jesus began to show his disciples that he must go to Jerusalem and suffer many things from the elders and chief priests and scribes, and be killed, and on the third day be raised. And Peter took him aside and began to rebuke him, saying, 'Far be it from you, Lord! This shall never happen to you.'" (Matt 16:21–22). It was as if Peter were saying, "Now, wait a minute, Lord; you do not understand how this kingdom thing works. Let me explain it to you. The King will be on a throne! The King will be in a chariot, leading armies to conquest! The King will not be on a cross!"

After sharply rebuking Peter, Jesus went on to explain that in his kingdom, not only would the King go to a cross, but all his followers

---

3. The last line from John Milton's sonnet that begins, "When I consider how my light is spent" (public domain). It is a wonderful poem to help disappointed preachers think right about their place in God's kingdom.

would also have a cross to bear: "If anyone would come after me, let him deny himself and take up his cross and follow me" (v. 24). Jesus did not allow his disciples to continue in their fleshly misunderstanding about him, his kingdom, and their role in it. He informed them, "It is not what you expected."

Not only in Matthew, but also in Mark and Luke, the Holy Spirit recorded the events of this disappointing, deflating day in Caesarea Philippi. Just when the disciples were pumped full of enthusiastic optimism, Jesus punctured their expectations with one nail from his cross. In the uncomfortable silence that must have followed, you could almost hear the discordant hiss of their joy escaping. It was not what they expected.

In all three gospels, the Holy Spirit followed the account of this deflating experience with the account of the transfiguration, when Jesus's "face shone like the sun, and his clothes became white as light. And behold, there appeared to them Moses and Elijah, talking with him" (Matt 17:2–3). And Moses and Elijah "spoke of his departure [Greek, *exodus*] which he was about to accomplish at Jerusalem" (Luke 9:30–31). Jesus's pending death, which the disciples had found so perplexing and so deflating, was not going to be a triumphing by evil; it would be the King triumphing *over* evil (Col 2:15). His departure from this world would not result in the disintegration of his followers; it would signal the "new Exodus," by which he would lead the scattered children of God out of the slavery of sin to become the Israel of God! Moses, representing the Law, spoke to Jesus about his exodus. Elijah, representing the prophets, spoke to Jesus about his exodus. Jesus himself was resplendent in light. Something gloriously supernatural was going on. Then, as august as the company was already, the glory became nearly unbearable when "a bright cloud overshadowed them, and a voice from the cloud said, 'This is my beloved Son, with whom I am well pleased; listen to him'" (Matt 17:5). No wonder "the disciples fell on their faces and were terrified" (v. 6).

This time Peter did not impudently attempt to set Jesus straight about the kingdom agenda. Moses had spoken; Elijah had spoken; Jesus had spoken; God had spoken! In placing the account of the transfiguration immediately after the confusion of Caesarea Philippi, the Lord is saying, "No, it is not what you expected. It is better."

Some of you reading this book are like the disciples on the morning of the day at Caesarea Philippi. You have lofty aspirations for the kingdom. You are already imagining how it will be to occupy a position of influence at Jesus's right hand. Some of you have real talent, and a talented man nearly always knows his talent. Some of you have already felt the thrill of having a congregation look at you with sincere admiration and hungry expectation. People recognize your wisdom and listen to your ideas.

I applaud you in the dew of your youth. God be praised that you have dedicated your morning years to God. But I assure you, as God is a merciful Father, before evening falls, you will feel a pricking, deflating nail from the cross. And with your perplexed head hung low, you will think, *This is not what I expected.*

Indeed, it is not what you or I expected. Thank God, it is not. It is immeasurably, inconceivably better than we expected. We are disciples of the Son of God, and he summons us to his own glory and excellence and to be a partaker of the divine nature (2 Pet 1:3–4). We are ambassadors for Christ (2 Cor 5:20). You are a preacher of God's holy Word. It would be a step down for you to become president of the United States. Do not set your heart on a big salary, which may ruin you even if you get it; set your sights on the Pearl of Great Price, which will enrich you in time and in eternity. Sell all you have to get it (see Matt 13:45–46). Do not strive to win the fickle smiles of the masses; set your heart on being one of the godly whom God has set apart for himself (Ps 4:3). The treasures of heaven are open to those who will ask for them, seek them, and knock for them. Do not settle for the paltry pleasures of earth; take the kingdom of heaven by violence and storm the gates of eternity for the pleasures that are at God's right hand forevermore (Ps 16:11).

Do not settle for less. I fear for you preachers who are never separated from your cell phones, and who spend more time reading the blogs than you spend reading your Bibles. You are settling for less. Do not continue to dawdle away your fleeting life by pecking out an endless stream of mindless text messages. I know all your peers are doing it, "but thou are a thing preferred to honour: thou are thyself a fragment torn from God:—thou hast a portion of Him within thyself. How is it then that thou dost not know thy high descent—dost thou not know whence thou comest?"[4] You may walk with God! Do not settle for less.

My fear is not so much that you will end your ministry by plunging headlong into a sea of scandalous sin. You may. But it is far more likely that you will waste your life slowly dissolving in puddles of mediocrity when you might have been great in God's kingdom. I fear that you will continue to fritter away precious, irretrievable hours watching inane videos on the Internet and playing video games. I fear that you will spend your lives creating and maintaining a pseudo-self on social media, and on your deathbed, you will realize that you have lived only a pseudo-life. I fear that your marriages will be plagued and your views of women are being irreparably perverted because your mind is full of images that degrade women, and degrade intimacy, and degrade you—images that can continue to enthrall you only because you continue to think of your-self and of women as if you were no better than animals, and not sons and daughters of God. I fear that you will realize too late that the thing you settle for will crowd out the thing you might have done, and that the trivial movies you watch and the trivial music that you listen to will seep into the well of your soul until you become a trivial man. I fear that you will live your life in the fleshly, man-centered morning of Caesarea Philippi, and you will never see the Mount of Transfiguration and hear the voice of God. But it does not have to be that way.

Now hear the word of the Lord. You are summoned to an assembly, and this assembly is every bit as august and awe-inspiring as the assembly on the Mount of Transfiguration. God is in this assembly. Christ Jesus is in this assembly. You, man of God, are in this assembly. The Holy Spirit speaks to you and says, "I charge you in the presence of God and of Christ Jesus, who is to judge the living and the dead, and by his appearing and his kingdom: preach the word; be ready in season and

---

4. *The Golden Sayings of Epictetus*, LX., vol. 2, The Harvard Classics (n.p.: P. F. Collier and Son, 1937), 137.

out of season; reprove, rebuke, and exhort, with complete patience and teaching" (2 Tim 4:1–2).

> Rise up, O men of God;
> Have done with lesser things;
> Give heart, and soul, and mind, and strength
> To serve the King of Kings![5]

Be a holy man of God. Ask him to fill you with his Holy Spirit. Spend your days walking with God. Every time you have the opportunity, stand up like a man, open the Word of God, look your hearers in the eye, lift up your voice like a trumpet, and say with every fiber of your being, "Come! Encounter God with me in this text."

---

5. From the hymn "Rise Up, O Men of God," by William P. Merrill, 1911; first published in the Presbyterian newspaper the *Continent*.

SCRIPTURE INDEX

5:1–2 *181*
5:1–12 *77*
5:13–16 *77, 181*
5:17 *156*
5:17–20 *77*
5:20 *181*
5:21–22 *182*
5:21, 27, 33, 38, 43
   156
5:21–48 *181*
5:23–24 *182*
5:25–26 *182*
5:44–45 *156*
6 *138*
6:1–18 *181*
6:19–34 *181*
7 *138*
7:1 *136*
7:5 *136*
7:6 *136*
11:28 *53*
12:8 *53*
13:45–46 *209*
16:16 *207*
16:21–22 *207*
16:24 *208*
17:2–3 *208*
17:5 *208*
17:6 *208*
19:5 *156*
20:26–28 *206–7*

Mark
1:15 *55, 56, 80*
10:21 *100*
10:37 *2*
12 *146*
12:18 *146*
12:24 *146*

Luke
1:37 *26*
1:46–55 *93*
2:40 *93*
5:27–32 *67*
7:7–9 *24*
9:30–31 *208*
10:21 *153*
11:9–13 *108*
18:22 *156*
22:20 *45*
24 *86*
24:27 *107*
24:32 *90*
24:49 *94*

John
1:1, 14 *25*
3:3 *178*
5:24 *178*
5:28–29 *84*
5:39 *177*
6:31–35 *53*
6:39 *56*
6:44–45, 65 *177*
6:63 *26*
7:16 *13*
8:47 *25*
8:51 *84*
8:56 *54*
9 *79*
11:24 *56*
11:32–37 *84*
12:41 *55*
12:47–50 *25*
12:48 *56*
12:49 *174*
13:27 *41*
14:6 *206*
14:23–26 *25*
15:5 *93*

15:26 *25*
16:7–11 *92*
16:13 *25, 26*
17:17 *26*

Acts
1:7 *42*
1:8 *95, 107*
1:11 *56*
2 *76, 104–5*
2:1–4 *26*
2:8 *76*
2:11 *76*
2:12 *76*
2:13 *76*
2:17 *56*
2:17ff *52*
2:37 *88, 94*
2:42 *88*
2:47 *88*
4:4 *88*
4:13 *96*
4:29–30 *96*
4:30–31 *105*
4:31 *96*
5:14 *88*
9:27–28 *95*
10:38 *94*
11:24 *88–89*
12:24 *75, 89*
13 *102*
13:46 *95*
14:3 *95*
16:5 *89*
16:30 *93*
17 *102*
18:26 *95*
19 *86*
19:8 *95*
19:20 *89*
20 *86*

NAME INDEX